THE SHORTER POEMS
of the EIGHTEENTH CENTURY

A

THE SHORTER POEMS
of the EIGHTEENTH CENTURY

AN ANTHOLOGY

SELECTED & EDITED
WITH AN INTRODUCTION *BY*
IOLO A. WILLIAMS
AUTHOR OF BYWAYS ROUND HELICON, ETC.

PUBLISHED BY WILLIAM
HEINEMANN, LTD., 21 BEDFORD
STREET, LONDON MCMXXIII

Printed in England at
The Westminster Press, Harrow Road,
London, W 9

To
EDMUND GOSSE

Introduction

THE first duty that any anthologist has, in his introduction, to perform, is to state the rules that he has set himself, their reasons, and the occasions on which he has broken those rules.

In making this book I have tried to represent those English poets the main body of whose work was produced between the years 1700 and 1800. To that end I have excluded poets born before 1660, on the grounds that a writer's style is, normally, pretty firmly fixed by the time that he is forty, and that to put my first birth-date back any further would be to let in a flood of poets of the Restoration period —a period which I believe to have been already fairly thoroughly anthologised. The only exception that I have made to this rule is the inclusion of Lord Peterborough's charming poem, than which I know of none more fitted for the opening of this anthology, and which was, in fact, written long after the beginning of the eighteenth century. For similar reasons I have included no writer born in 1770 or later, and have cut rather short the selection from those born in the sixties, and even in the fifties, of the century ; for in its last few years the tradition and spirit to which my book is devoted had worn rather thin, and what was finest in the poetry that was being written belonged to a new school which has not suffered, in recent years, from any lack of publicity. Unfortunately, however, periods in English literature are not cut off, the one from the other, by sharp divisions ; and, if my book has rather blurred edges, I must just admit that it is so, and beg to be excused.

The next thing to be explained is that this is a book of *shorter* poems, and that, as a purely arbitrary distinction, I have decreed that a " shorter " poem is one of a hundred lines or less. This rule, however, I have broken in, I think, four instances—by the inclusion of Dyer's *Grongar Hill*, Prior's *Jinny the Just*, Tickell's *Lines on the Death of Addison*, and Gray's *Elegy*. These poems I felt it impossible to avoid, both for their intrinsic merits and for the historical importance of at least two of them. But with these exceptions a hundred lines has been my limit, a limit which (since

I have allowed myself no extracts) has led to the very scanty representation, in this volume, of some poets—Garth, Somerville, Green, Thomson and Smart for example— and to the total exclusion of Armstrong, Blair, Churchill, Young, and other writers of importance. Among my minor regrets, in this connection, is that for the absence of Mrs. Piozzi's *Three Wishes* ; this poem was just over my limit, and, much as I liked it, I felt that it was not really important enough to allow an exception to be made in its favour.

I remarked a few lines back that I had allowed myself no extracts in this book. To this rule I have made, I think, no exception, though, when a poem exists in two or more versions, I have not necessarily chosen the longer, and I have, of course, not hesitated to print poems taken from plays or from sequences. But if any poem in this anthology is incomplete, the incompleteness is due to my error and not to my intention. Every poem that I have considered I have considered on its merits as a whole, and have tried to decide whether it was, as written, good enough, in spite often of defects, for inclusion, or whether the faults outweighed the merits. It has always seemed to me unfair to print in a collection (as so many editors have done) a stanza or a few lines from a poem as if it, or they, were an independent and complete lyric. The result of my decision in this matter has been that many pleasant poems have been rejected, and that some bad stanzas or lines will certainly be found in this book. I believe, however, that the advantages of the system I have chosen outbalance its disadvantages, and I also hope that there is no poem in this collection that will not reveal easily, to any reader who will take the trouble to attune his ear to the music and vocabulary of the century, the merits which have led me to include it here. Occasionally what is no more than a pleasant copy of verses has been printed, and once or twice, perhaps, my tongue has slipped its tip just a very little way into my cheek as I made my selection. May I mention, as instances wherein this must surely have happened, Mrs. Rowe's *Laplander's Song* and the affecting verses of Mr. Henry Jones, the bricklayer poet and *protégé* (until his drunkenness and idleness proved his undoing) of Lord Chesterfield ?

INTRODUCTION

Naturally the same standard cannot be applied throughout the whole of an anthology of this sort : poems by great writers are necessarily excluded which are better than some of the included verses of the minors ; if this were not done the book would resolve itself merely into a reprint of the works of a dozen or so writers whose works are already in every poetical library. But on the whole I feel that I may claim for this book that it contains nothing (save the exceptions hinted at above) that has not some share of poetical beauty, taking that to include, as it was then held to do, not only the deeper emotions, but also " true wit " that is " like the brilliant stone," and even the broadly comic. For in the eighteenth century the scope of poetry was definitely widened, with the result that it had a greater public then than at any other period, perhaps, in English history.

But before I go on to discuss further the qualities of the poetry of the period, let me indicate briefly two more limitations that I have set myself. Of these the first is that I have included in my selection no poem that offends against the standards of decency which we, to-day, generally expect in literature. This might be thought, by one only casually acquainted with eighteenth-century verse, to have handicapped me severely ; but, in truth, I can remember very few things which it has caused me any pang to reject upon this score, save Lords Bath and Chesterfield's lines to Molly Lepell :

> Had I Hanover, Bremen, and Verden,
> And likewise the Duchy of Zell ;
> I'd part with them all for a farthing,
> To have my dear Molly Lepell !—

and Lord Chesterfield's " Whenever, Chloe, I begin," which is so exquisitely neat and witty that I dare not, for fear of corrupting public morals, reprint it here ! Apart from these things, as I say, I can think of little that I regret, for the poets of the eighteenth century were surprisingly decent, even verbally. Yet perhaps this is not surprising after all, for decency is merely one form of restraint, and restraint and good manners were among the tenets of the poetic faith of the English Augustans. The second of my two final limitations is that, this being a collection of *English* poems, I have excluded poems written in the Scottish dialect (and also, incidentally, those in English dialects), with the results that Burns is represented by only three poems, and that many other well-known poets are absent altogether. My reasons for this have been two : first, that the Scottish dialect poets were trying to do something entirely different from the work of their English contemporaries ; and second, that it seems in the highest degree improbable, from the admirable national characteristics of the Scottish race, that there can be any Scotch writer who is rated below his true merit or stands in any need of the anthologist's offices to bring his work once more to the public notice.

There can be no doubt that the poetry of the eighteenth century was much out of favour during the eighty years or so that followed the highest point of the romantic revival ; and even now, though it is certainly winning itself a more honourable place in the general estimation, it cannot be said to be widely read or known. Probably we are only now arriving at a point sufficiently distant from the eighteenth century to enable us to see it in something like perspective. After all, it is only a little more than a hundred years since the merit of the Elizabethan poets began to be recognised. And, as the eighteenth century neglected the seventeenth (such part of it, at least, as came before Waller), so did the nineteenth despise the eighteenth ; and as 1820 began to see the beauty of 1620, so also, I venture to think, may 1920 begin to estimate—with some hope of reaching a true judgment—the beauties of the poetry of two centuries ago. Indeed, it almost seems as if the poetical eye of mankind had a blind spot in it, which regularly obscured the merit of almost all verse about a century old. It will be interesting, to us who are young enough, to notice whether this blind spot will soon blot out—temporarily—the period of Keats, of Shelley and of Wordsworth ; to a certain extent, even, this has already happened, for Byron is surely the most neglected of all great poets, and I doubt whether many people read anything of Coleridge's save *Khubla Khan* and *The Ancient Mariner*. And as for the minors of the first half

INTRODUCTION

of the nineteenth century—does any one (save the inevitable gentleman who will write to protest that he does so)
read them in this age, in which even such a giant as Landor
is all but unregarded ? Yet they had merit, and they too will,
in the cycle of time, be rediscovered and have their beauties
extolled. But I digress—though to make a point which is,
I hope, pertinent—and I must return more nearly to my
subject.

The poets whom the reader will find in this anthology
are handicapped by many things. Some of them are even
handicapped by quite irrelevant and silly things, such, for
example, as their names : can a poet called Tickell be said
to start his race even from Scratch ? But there are more
serious and more ordinary obstacles : a hundred years of
romanticism have so biased our minds that most of us can
only recognise, as poetry, verse that is dished up with one
particular kind of sauce, with the result that many people
cannot tell a good poem of the eighteenth century from a
bad one. Or perhaps it would be more true to say that they
think they cannot, because they have never tried. And the
change in diction which the romantics originated—quite
rightly, for the diction of the eighteenth century was wearing
into holes at the end of its time—has made the preceding
verbal fashion seem to unaccustomed ears sometimes
ridiculous, and sometimes quaint, whereas it was neither,
in the hands of a capable writer, but a sensitive and gracious
instrument, admirably adapted to express the thoughts and
emotions of the age. Naturally the poetasters used *clichés*—
did poetasters in any age ever avoid them ? But the eighteenth
century did not produce only poetasters ; it produced great
poets, and good poets, and men who wrote happily upon
occasion, and men who never wrote well at all, exactly as
every other century has done in England. The English are
probably the supreme race in poetry, and had they, for a
hundred years when they were in many other things at the
height of their greatness, ceased to write poetry, it would
have been a wonder the like of which has never happened in
the history of mankind. But they did not cease to be poets,
as I trust will be admitted by anyone who will do me the
honour—and, I venture to believe, give himself the

pleasure—of glancing more than cursorily at this anthology. This then is my aim, to produce a volume which will give a proper view of the shorter poems of the eighteenth century, and which will vindicate that century from the too often, and too thoughtlessly, levelled accusation of poetic sterility.

And now, quite briefly, let me give some indication of what the poets, who were writing from about the year 1700, were, as I conceive, attempting to do. Primarily they were trying to save English poetry from the chaos in which it found itself in the middle and end of the seventeenth century—a chaos of which anyone, who will read through the three enthrallingly interesting volumes of Mr. Saintsbury's *Minor Caroline Poets*, may make himself cognisant. The process of redemption had begun with Waller (and even before that, in a few writers), Dryden continued it, and Pope brought the reform to completion. Much, of course, was lost in the change ; much good is always lost in every change. But very much, also, was gained. The older tradition of English poetry was, in the year 1650, or thereabouts, heading straight for madness. The younger writers of the Restoration period, following Waller and Dryden, did much to restore order, though they still had, as it were, one foot in the older camp. Transitions are never abrupt, and the transitional poets shared some of the peculiar excellences of the Elizabethans and Carolines, and have caught some part of the praise that has been showered so lavishly upon their predecessors. At any rate, the Restoration poets have been often and well anthologised, and though, logically, I might have begun my collection with the poets who *wrote* from 1660 onwards, I felt that nothing was to be gained by printing once more the hundreds of more or less famous poems of the Restoration. But from the year 1700, or so, the position is quite different, and all but a few poets are unknown to-day to most of those who are potentially their admirers. These poets were the logical outcome of the work of Waller and of Dryden, and it is a mere commonplace to add that the chief of their school was that great genius, Alexander Pope. Their object was to create for England a great classical school of poetry, a school in which the masters should be Horace and Virgil and the poets of the Greek Anthology. The aim became restraint, exact expression, thought rather than a fancy which had often been merely fantastic, wit rather than mere high spirits. They aimed, in the phrase of the time, at " correctness." Some of the writers, of course, overdid the thing ; instead of regulating their minds they stifled them. But others did not, and they added to English poetry a grave and solemn majesty of utterance, and—in other moods—a clear and sparkling wit, that were new to our poetic literature. It is perhaps for these qualities that their poetry is the best fitted of all for reading aloud. These poets restored to us a sense of form, they explored also the formal delights of eloquence and of antithesis, and the best of them moved gracefully and easily in their new restraints. At the same time they widened the subject matter of poetry ; the familiar Horatian poem, the epistle, the essay in verse, the georgic, and the didactic poem all began to flourish. They produced many of the greatest English hymns, those of Watts, Cowper and the Wesleys, for instance, hymns which are still sung every Sunday in our churches, and which still voice the deepest religious emotions even of many who do not adhere to the doctrines that the writers themselves held.   The epigram, which had but rarely been written successfully in the seventeenth century, suddenly appeared as a poetic form of great vigour and flexibility, capable of any effect from the most deeply moving pathos to the broadest farce. The heroic couplet rose to its full power, and the octosyllabic couplet jumped, from being the vehicle of the delightful but rough humour of *Hudibras*, to being that of the urbane and exquisite fables of Gay. Later in the century new delights were added in the sombre, yet many-coloured, and magnificent stanza in which Gray wrote the *Elegy*—probably, when all is said, the greatest poem in our language— and in the pretty Dresden-china pastoral school of Shenstone, Cunningham and such writers. Truly the first sixty or seventy years of the eighteenth century gave a very large bulk of magnificent poetry to us, did we but know it. And the poets who wrote during those years were those who saved our verse from unthinkable chaos, who gave us back thought, the appeal to the normal reasoning powers of man, and a poetry which was capable of being appreciated by, and of leading on to a love of poetry, the numbers (steadily increasing throughout the eighteenth century) of the literate public. It was the eighteenth century which created the instrument that the romantic revival was, with much silly abuse of its benefactor, to adapt and use for its own purposes, and which also, by rescuing our verse from the nightmare which had seemed to threaten it, confirmed the educated Englishman in his habit of verse-reading, and created for the romantics—those ungrateful dogs—their audience.

The worst part of the century from which I have selected the poems in this volume is the final thirty years or so. How bad most of the verse of that patch is, I trust that few, save myself, have had the painful necessity of discovering. I have drawn very lightly from it; especially have I gone easy with what the poet Hayley called, in all seriousness and flattery,

The mild Effusions of a Female Mind,—

the dreary poetisings of Anna Seward and her like. From Lady Miller's famous Batheaston Vase I have drawn nothing at all, and the Della Cruscans—Robert Merry, Hannah Cowley, Bertie Greathead and the rest of them—are also absent from my pages. Most of these persons were, so to speak, half-baked romantics, and, great as the flower of the romantic movement was to be, there are no writers in the world, I suppose and trust, so dull as these abortive buds of the seventeen-seventies and -eighties. A little man, if he is neatly dressed and cheerful, may be an excellent companion ; but when he struts in a cloak too large for him, and weeps copious tears, we are apt, like Dr. Johnson on a famous, if hypothetical, occasion, to think very ill of our company. These last years of the century will therefore appear in my book as very lean and poor ones.

I believe that the present anthology is the first modern attempt to represent, in one volume, the poetry of the eighteenth century. The only two recent scholars who have, to my knowledge, tried to cover the period, are Mr. W. S. Braithwaite and the late Professor Edward Arber. Of these

INTRODUCTION

Mr. Braithwaite divided the period between the end of his *Book of Restoration Verse* and the beginning of his *Book of Georgian Verse* ; and Professor Arber split the century into three volumes, his *Pope Anthology, Goldsmith Anthology,* and *Cowper Anthology.* Both these scholars, and more particularly Professor Arber, have done work for which I am profoundly grateful, and which I have not hesitated to build upon, though I think I may truthfully say that the number of poems which I have taken direct from their collections does not exceed, if it reaches, a dozen. The work of these gentlemen I should be the last person to belittle. But it was because their books did not satisfy me ; because, the more I got to know about my favourite period, the less did I agree with other people's judgments and selections, and the more writers of merit, totally unrepresented in any anthology, did I discover ; and because I felt that a selection in one volume was a thing much to be desired by students, that I set about compiling the present book. Naturally I have chosen many poems that have been chosen by my predecessors—the making of anthologies would be far more glorious work than it is, did one's predecessors invariably print the worst poems ! But I think that I have really broken a great deal of fresh ground, and that there are many poems in my book that have never been reprinted for at least a hundred years, and many also that have never been reprinted at all, even in such contemporary collections as those of Dodsley and of Pearch. In a good many instances, also, I have been able to correct previous misattributions, though I realise that my book is certainly not perfect in this respect, and that very much research and textual criticism yet remains to be done. I should also like to point out that I have hardly attempted to touch the vast field of songs embedded in the works of the dramatists, and that I have not searched at all for good poems in the sheet music, and the primarily musical collections, of the period. It is work that I hope may be done soon either by myself or by someone else, and it would no doubt add materially to the value of this collection. But for the few songs, taken from music sheets, which are to be found in the pages that follow, I frankly admit that I am indebted to the work of others. In ten or twenty years' time I should, I presume, be able to do this book better than it is now done ; but in the meantime I venture to present it to the public, done as well as I at present know how, to mark, as it were, a milestone upon the way yet to be travelled.

One other previous collector I must mention, Frederick Locker Lampson, whose *Lyra Elegantiarum* contains much good eighteenth-century poetry of the lighter kind ; and one scholar, the late W. P. Courtney, whose research into the lives of the minor poets of the period, especially his book (privately printed, alas !) on the contributors to Dodsley's Miscellany, is of inestimable value to students.

To the writings, also, of the late Austin Dobson, of Mr. Saintsbury, of Mr. Courthope, and of Mr. Gosse—whose History of Eighteenth Century Literature is the best short view of the subject which I know—I must express my gratitude. And to Mr. Gosse, and to Mr. J. C. Squire, personally, I owe my very best thanks for many most valuable suggestions, for much encouragement in my task, and for going through my manuscript, at various stages in its career, for me. Mr. Edmund Blunden I must also thank for several suggestions.

To Mr. F. L. Clarke, late bursar's clerk of King's College, Cambridge, and to various contributors to *Notes and Queries*, particularly Mr. Russell Markland, my thanks are also due for supplying me with information.

The only copyright poem in this book is Prior's *Jinny the Just*, which is included by kind permission of the Marquess of Bath and of the Cambridge University Press.

A paragraph must be added about punctuation and spelling. As to the former I have pleased myself, and put whatever punctuation seemed to me to be best, and in the matter of inverted commas I have not adopted any uniform system, but have used them, or omitted them, as appeared to suit each individual poem. The spelling I have modernised, but I have used the apostrophe in past participles, except when the final -ed is to be sounded ; in verbs ending in -ie or -y, however, I have preferred to write died, cried, fancied and married, rather than dy'd, cry'd, fancy'd and marry'd.

With that I leave to the critics and to the public what

INTRODUCTION

I dare to hope that they will find a readable book, and a collection of fine poetry. This anthology will, if only part of its compiler's hopes are realised, lead to a reassessment of the value of the poetry of the eighteenth century, not so much as it was written by the greatest poets (for with many people's estimate of Gray, for instance, I should not be inclined to quarrel), but by the minor writers. This, however, is not now for me to decide, it rests with my readers, who may, I trust, find the poems that are here offered to them as beautiful as they seem, after much study, to myself.

Index of Authors

INDEX OF AUTHORS

INDEX OF AUTHORS

INDEX OF AUTHORS

INDEX OF AUTHORS

INDEX OF AUTHORS

INDEX OF AUTHORS

xxvi

INDEX OF AUTHORS

INDEX OF AUTHORS

INDEX OF AUTHORS

INDEX OF AUTHORS

INDEX OF AUTHORS

INDEX OF AUTHORS

INDEX OF AUTHORS

INDEX OF AUTHORS

INDEX OF AUTHORS

INDEX OF AUTHORS

xxxviii

INDEX OF AUTHORS

INDEX OF AUTHORS

CHARLES MORDAUNT, Earl of PETERBOROUGH
(1658-1735)

I said to my Heart

I said to my heart, between sleeping and waking,
" Thou wild thing ! that always art leaping or aching,
What Black, Brown, or Fair, in what clime, in what nation,
By turns has not taught thee a pit-a-pat-ation ? "

Thus accus'd, the wild thing gave this sober reply :
" See the heart without motion, though Cœlia pass by.
Not the beauty she has, nor the wit that she borrows,
Gives the eye any joys, or the heart any sorrows.

" When our Sappho appears, she whose wit so refin'd
I am forc'd to applaud with the rest of mankind,
Whatever she says is with spirit and fire ;
Every word I attend ; but I only admire.

" Prudentia as vainly would put in her claim ;
Ever gazing on Heaven, though Man is her aim.
'Tis Love, not Devotion, that turns up her eyes !
Those stars of this world are too good for the skies !

" But Cloe so lively, so easy, so fair !
Her wit so genteel, without art, without care !
When she comes in my way, the motion, the pain,
The leapings, the achings, return all again."

O wonderful creature ! a woman of reason !
Never grave out of pride ; never gay out of season !
When so easy to guess who this angel should be,
Would one think Mrs. Howard ne'er dreamt it was she ?

Sir SAMUEL GARTH, M.D. (1661-1718)

An Anacreontic Epistle to Mr. Gay on his Poems

When Fame did o'er the spacious plain
  The lays she once had learn'd repeat ;
All listen'd to the tuneful strain,
  And wonder'd who could sing so sweet.
'Twas thus. The Graces held the lyre,
  Th' harmonious frame the Muses strung,
The Loves and Smiles compos'd the choir,
  And Gay transcrib'd what Phoebus sung.

An Imitation of a French Author

Can you count the silver lights
That deck the skies, and cheer the nights ;
Or the leaves that strow the vales,
When groves are stript by winter gales ;
Or the drops that in the morn
Hang with transparent pearl the thorn ;
Or bridegroom's joys, or miser's cares,
Or gamester's oaths, or hermit's prayers ;
Or envy's pangs, or love's alarms,
Or Marlborough's acts, or [Wharto]n's charms ?

? The Rt. Rev. FRANCIS ATTERBURY, D.D., Bishop of Rochester (1662-1732)

Song*

Fair Sylvia, cease to blame my youth
  For having lov'd before ;
So men, till they have learn'd the truth,
  Strange deities adore.

My heart, 'tis true, hath often rang'd
  Like bees on gaudy flowers,
And many a thousand loves hath chang'd,
  Till it was fix'd on yours.

*This poem has also been attributed to Prior.

2

But, Sylvia, when I saw those eyes,
'Twas soon determin'd there ;
Stars might as well forsake the skies,
And vanish into air.

When I from this great rule do err,
New beauties to adore ;
May I again turn wanderer,
And never settle more !

The Rev. RICHARD BENTLEY, D.D.* (1662-1742)

Verses in Reply to Mr. Titley's Imitation of Horace, Book III, Ode II

Who strives to mount Parnassus hill,
And thence poetic laurels bring,
Must first acquire due force and skill,
Must fly with swan's or eagle's wing.

Who Nature's treasures would explore,
Her mysteries and arcana know,
Must high as lofty Newton soar,
Must stoop as searching Woodward low.

Who studies ancient laws and rites,
Tongues, arts, and arms, all history,
Must drudge like Selden, days and nights,
And in the endless labour die.

Who travels in religious jars,
(Truth mixt with errors, shade with rays,)
Like Whiston, wanting Pyx and stars
In ocean wide or sinks, or strays.

* The famous Master of Trinity College, Cambridge.

3

But grant our hero's hopes long toil
   And comprehensive genius crown ;
All sciences, all arts, his spoil,
   Yet what reward, or what renown ?

Envy, innate in vulgar souls,
   Envy steps in and stops his rise ;
Envy with poison'd tarnish fouls
   His lustre, and his worth decries.

Inglorious, or by wants enthrall'd,
   To College, and old books, confin'd,
A pedant for his learning call'd,
   Dunces advanc'd, he's left behind ;
Yet left content, a genuine Stoic he,
Great without patron, rich without South-Sea.

WILLIAM KING, D.C.L. (1663-1712)

Song

You say you love ; repeat again,
   Repeat th' amazing sound,
Repeat the ease of all my pain,
   The cure of every wound.

What you to thousands have denied,
   To me you freely give ;
Whilst I in humble silence died
   Your mercy bids me live.

So upon Latmos top each night
   Endymion sighing lay,
Gaz'd on the moon's transcendent light,
   Despair'd, and durst not pray.

But divine Cynthia saw his grief,
   Th' effect of conquering charms,
Unask'd the goddess brings relief,
   And falls into his arms.

GEORGE STEPNEY (1663-1707)

Verses

imitated from the French of Monsieur Maynard to Cardinal Richelieu

When money and my blood ran high,
  My Muse was reckon'd wondrous pretty ;
The Sports and Smiles did round her fly,
  Enamour'd with her smart *concetti*.

Now, who'd have thought it once ? with pain
  She strings her harp, whilst freezing age
But feebly runs through every vein,
  And chills my brisk poetic rage.

I properly have ceas'd to live,
  To wine and women, dead in law ;
And soon from fate I shall receive
  A summons to the shades to go.

The warrior ghosts will round me come
  To hear of fam'd Ramillia's fight,
Whilst the vex'd Bourbons through the gloom
  Retire to th' utmost realms of night.

Then I, my lord, will tell how you
  With pensions every Muse inspire,
Who Marlborough's conquests did pursue,
  And to his trumpets tun'd the lyre.

But should some drolling sprite demand,
  " Well, sir, what place had you, I pray ? "
How like a coxcomb should I stand !
  What would your lordship have me say ?

5

WILLIAM WALSH (1663-1708)

To His Book

Go, little book, and to the world impart
The faithful image of an am'rous heart ;
Those who love's dear, deluding pains have known,
May in my fatal stories read their own.
Those who have liv'd from all its torments free,
May find the thing they never felt, by me ;
Perhaps, advis'd, avoid the gilded bait,
And warn'd by my example, shun my fate.
While with calm joy, safe landed on the coast,
I view the waves on which I once was toss'd.
Love is a medley of endearments, jars,
Suspicions, quarrels, reconcilements, wars ;
Then peace again.   Oh ! would it not be best
To chase the fatal poison from our breast ?
But since so few can live from passion free,
Happy the man, and only happy he,
Who with such lucky stars begins his love,
That his cool judgment does his choice approve.
Ill-grounded passions quickly wear away ;
What's built upon esteem can ne'er decay.

The Unrewarded Lover

Let the dull merchant curse his angry fate,
And from the wind and waves his fortune wait :
Let the loud lawyer break his brains, and be
A slave to wrangling coxcombs for a fee :
Let the rough soldier fight his prince's foes,
And for a livelihood his life expose :
I wage no war, I plead no cause but love's,
I fear no storms, but what Celinda moves.
And what grave censor can my choice despise ?
But here, fair charmer, here the difference lies ;
The merchant, after all his hazards past,
Enjoys the fruit of his long toils at last ;
The soldier high in his king's favour stands,
And after having long obey'd, commands ;

6

The lawyer, to reward his tedious care,
Roars on the bench, that babbled at the bar ;
While I take pains to meet a fate more hard,
And reap no fruit, no favour, no reward.

To His False Mistress

Thou saidst that I alone thy heart could move,
And that for me thou wouldst abandon Jove.
I lov'd thee then, nor with a love defil'd,
But as a father loves his only child.
I know thee now, and though I fiercelier burn,
Thou art become the object of my scorn.
See what thy falsehood gets ; I must confess
I love thee more, but I esteem thee less.

Sonnet on Death

What has this bugbear Death that's worth our care ?
After a life in pain and sorrow past,
After deluding hope and dire despair,
Death only gives us quiet at the last.

How strangely are our love and hate misplac'd !
Freedom we seek, and yet from freedom flee ;
Courting those tyrant-sins that chain us fast,
And shunning Death that only sets us free.

'Tis not a foolish fear of future pains,—
Why should they fear who keep their souls from stains ?—
That makes me dread thy terrors, Death, to see :
'Tis not the loss of riches, or of fame,
Or the vain toys the vulgar pleasures name ;
'Tis nothing, Celia, but the losing thee.

Song

Of all the torments, all the cares,
With which our lives are curs'd :
Of all the plagues a lover bears,
Sure rivals are the worst !

By partners, in each other kind,
    Afflictions easier grow ;
In love alone we hate to find
    Companions of our woe.

Sylvia, for all the pangs you see
    Are labouring in my breast ;
I beg not you would favour me,
    Would you but slight the rest !
How great soe'er your rigours are,
    With them alone I'll cope ;
I can endure my own despair,
    But not another's hope.

The Despairing Lover

Distracted with care
For Phyllis the fair,
Since nothing could move her,
Poor Damon her lover
Resolves in despair
No longer to languish,
Nor bear so much anguish :
But, mad with his love,
To a precipice goes ;
Where a leap from above
Would soon finish his woes.

When in rage he came there,
Beholding how steep
The sides did appear,
And the bottom how deep ;
His torments projecting,
And sadly reflecting,
That a lover forsaken
A new love may get ;
But a neck, when once broken,
Can never be set :
And that he could die

8

Whenever he would ;
But that he could live
But as long as he could :
How grievous soever
The torment might grow,
He scorn'd to endeavour
To finish it so.
But bold, unconcern'd
At the thoughts of the pain,
He calmly return'd
To his cottage again.

JOHN GLANVILL (1664 ?-1735)

Song

Can nothing, nothing move her
  To save a hapless swain ?
Nor kindness for the lover ?
  Nor pity of the pain ?
See, how she flies denying
  To hear me but complain,
Leaves me all faint and dying,
Helpless, and vainly trying
  To bring her back again.

Let nothing, nothing move her
  To save a hapless swain,
Nor kindness for the lover,
  Nor pity of the pain.
Yet seeking no restoring,
  No change his faith shall stain ;
Nor will he cease adoring,
Nor sighing, nor imploring,
  Though all shall be in vain.

But hopeless thus to languish
  When he no more shall bear,
But, pin'd with ceaseless anguish,
  Shall sink beneath his care ;

9

Then she, that did bereave him
   Of life, shall mourn his fate ;
Then wish she could retrieve him,
Then willing to relieve him,
   But then 'twill be too late.

Iphis and Ianthe

Ianthe the lovely, the joy of her swain,
By Iphis was lov'd, and lov'd Iphis again ;
She liv'd in the youth, and the youth in the fair,
Their pleasure was equal, and equal their care ;
No time, no enjoyment the dotage withdrew ;
But the longer they lov'd, still the fonder they grew.

A passion so happy alarm'd all the plain,
Some envied the nymph, but more envied the swain ;
Some swore 'twould be pity their loves to invade,
That the lovers alone for each other were made ;
But all, all consented that none ever knew
A nymph yet so kind, or a shepherd so true.

Love saw them with pleasure, and vow'd to take care
Of the faithful, the tender, the innocent pair ;
What either did want, he bid either to move,
But they wanted nothing but ever to love ;
Said 'twas all that to bless them his Godhead could do,
If they still might be kind, and they still might be true.

To Phyllis

Phyllis, how long thus wildly gay
   Shall we false joys approve ?
We idly laugh our time away,
   And do but fool with love.
For trifles we great leisure find,
   Those warmly are pursu'd ;
Should we not too a little mind
   Neglected flesh and blood ?

JOHN GLANVILL

Trust me, howe'er the vain may jest,
 Or the severe advise,
'Tis passion only makes us blest,
 And only shows us wise.
Take human life in all its shapes,
 Free from Love's gentle rules
We're all but pert light giddy apes,
 Or dull grave solemn fools.

Think then how we've the past misspent,
 And what's to come improve ;
Betimes grow wisely penitent ;
 Take up, and turn to Love.
So good a work needs no debate,
 'Tis high time 'twere begun ;
When pleasure on repentance waits,
 Who can repent too soon ?

MATTHEW PRIOR (1664-1721)

An Ode

The merchant, to secure his treasure,
 Conveys it in a borrow'd name :
Euphelia serves to grace my measure ;
 But Cloe is my real flame.

My softest verse, my darling lyre
 Upon Euphelia's toilet lay ;
When Cloe noted her desire,
 That I should sing, that I should play.

My lyre I tune, my voice I raise ;
 But with my numbers mix my sighs :
And whilst I sing Euphelia's praise,
 I fix my soul on Cloe's eyes.

Fair Cloe blush'd : Euphelia frown'd :
 I sung and gaz'd ; I play'd and trembled :
And Venus to the Loves around
 Remark'd, how ill we all dissembled.

11

MATTHEW PRIOR

To Cloe Weeping

See, whilst thou weep'st, fair Cloe, see
The world in sympathy with thee.
The cheerful birds no longer sing,
Each drops his head, and hangs his wing.
The clouds have bent their bosom lower,
And shed their sorrows in a shower.
The brooks beyond their limits flow ;
And louder murmurs speak their woe.
The nymphs and swains adopt thy cares :
They heave thy sighs, and weep thy tears.
Fantastic nymph ! that grief should move
Thy heart, obdurate against love.
Strange tears ! whose power can soften all,
But that dear breast on which they fall.

Song

Farewell, Amynta, we must part ;
   The charm has lost its power,
Which held so fast my captiv'd heart
   Until this fatal hour.

Hadst thou not thus my love abus'd,
   And us'd me ne'er so ill,
Thy cruelty I had excus'd,
   And I had lov'd thee still.

But know, my soul disdains thy sway,
   And scorns thy charms and thee,
To which each fluttering coxcomb may
   As welcome be as me.

Think in what perfect bliss you reign'd,
   How lov'd before thy fall ;
And now, alas ! how much disdain'd
   By me, and scorn'd by all.

Yet thinking of each happy hour,
Which I with thee have spent,
So robs my rage of all its power,
That I almost relent.

But pride will never let me bow,
No more thy charms can move :
Yet thou art worth my pity now,
Because thou hadst my love.

The Lady who offers her looking-glass to Venus

Venus, take my votive glass,
Since I am not what I was ;
What from this day I shall be,
Venus, let me never see.

Epigram

To John I ow'd great obligation ;
But John, unhappily, thought fit
To publish it to all the nation :
Sure John and I are more than quit.

Epigram

Yes, every poet is a fool :
By demonstration Ned can show it :
Happy, could Ned's inverted rule
Prove every fool to be a poet.

Cupid Mistaken

As after noon, one summer's day,
Venus stood bathing in a river ;
Cupid a-shooting went that way,
New strung his bow, new fill'd his quiver.

With skill he chose his sharpest dart :
With all his might his bow he drew :
Swift to his beauteous parent's heart
The too well-guided arrow flew.

" I faint ! I die ! " the Goddess cried :
  " O cruel ! couldst thou find none other
To wreck thy spleen on ? Parricide !
  Like Nero, thou hast slain thy mother."

Poor Cupid sobbing scarce could speak :
  " Indeed, Mamma, I did not know ye ;
Alas ! how easy my mistake !
  I took you for your likeness, Cloe."

Song

In vain you tell your parting lover,
You wish fair winds may waft him over.
Alas ! what winds can happy prove,
That bear me far from what I love ?
Alas ! what dangers on the main
Can equal those that I sustain,
From slighted vows, and cold disdain ?

Be gentle, and in pity choose
To wish the wildest tempests loose :
That thrown again upon the coast,
Where first my shipwreck'd heart was lost,
I may once more repeat my pain ;
Once more in dying notes complain
Of slighted vows, and cold disdain.

The Garland

The pride of every grove I chose,
  The violet sweet, and lily fair,
The dappled pink, and blushing rose,
  To deck my charming Cloe's hair.

At morn the nymph vouchsaf'd to place
  Upon her brow the various wreath ;
The flowers less blooming than her face,
  The scent less fragrant than her breath.

The flowers she wore along the day,
  And every nymph and shepherd said
That in her hair they look'd more gay,
  Than glowing in their native bed.

Undress'd at evening, when she found
  Their odours lost, their colours past ;
She chang'd her look, and on the ground
  Her garland and her eye she cast.

That eye dropp'd sense distinct and clear,
  As any Muse's tongue could speak ;
When from its lid a pearly tear
  Ran trickling down her beauteous cheek.

Dissembling what I knew too well,
  " My love, my life," said I, " explain
This change of humour : prithee tell :
  That falling tear—what does it mean ? "

She sigh'd ; she smil'd : and to the flowers
  Pointing, the lovely moralist said :
" See ! friend, in some few fleeting hours,
  See yonder what a change is made.

" Ah me ! the blooming pride of May,
  And that of beauty are but one :
At morn both flourish bright and gay,
  Both fade at evening, pale, and gone.

" At dawn poor Stella danc'd and sung ;
  The am'rous youth around her bow'd :
At night her fatal knell was rung ;
  I saw, and kiss'd her in her shroud.

" Such as she is, who died to-day ;
  Such I, alas ! may be to-morrow :
Go, Damon, bid thy Muse display
  The justice of thy Cloe's sorrow."

MATTHEW PRIOR

To a Lady :

*She refusing to continue a Dispute with me, and leaving me
in the Argument*

An Ode

Spare, gen'rous victor, spare the slave,
  Who did unequal war pursue ;
That more than triumph he might have,
  In being overcome by you.

In the dispute whate'er I said,
  My heart was by my tongue belied ;
And in my looks you might have read,
  How much I argu'd on your side.

You, far from danger as from fear,
  Might have sustain'd an open fight :
For seldom your opinions err :
  Your eyes are always in the right.

Why, fair one, would you not rely
  On reason's force with beauty's join'd ?
Could I their prevalence deny,
  I must at once be deaf and blind.

Alas ! not hoping to subdue,
  I only to the fight aspir'd :
To keep the beauteous foe in view
  Was all the glory I desir'd.

But she, howe'er of vict'ry sure,
  Contemns the wreath too long delay'd ;
And, arm'd with more immediate power,
  Calls cruel silence to her aid.

Deeper to wound, she shuns the fight :
  She drops her arms, to gain the field :
Secures her conquest by her flight ;
  And triumphs, when she seems to yield.

16

So when the Parthian turn'd his steed,
    And from the hostile camp withdrew ;
With cruel skill the backward reed
    He sent ; and as he fled, he slew.

The Lady's Looking-glass

Celia and I the other day
Walk'd o'er the sand-hills to the sea :
The setting sun adorn'd the coast,
His beams entire, his fierceness lost :
And, on the surface of the deep,
The wind lay only not asleep :
The nymph did like the scene appear,
Serenely pleasant, calmly fair :
Soft fell her words, as flew the air.
With secret joy I heard her say,
That she would never miss one day
A walk so fine, a sight so gay.

But, oh the change ! the winds grow high :
Impending tempests charge the sky :
The lightning flies : the thunder roars :
The big waves lash the frighten'd shores.
Struck with the horror of the sight,
She turns her head, and wings her flight ;
And trembling vows, she'll ne'er again
Approach the shore, or view the main.

 Once more at least look back, said I ;
 Thy-self in that large glass descry :
When thou art in good humour dress'd ;
When gentle reason rules thy breast ;
The sun upon the calmest sea
Appears not half so bright as thee :
'Tis then, that with delight I rove
Upon the boundless depth of love :
I bless my chain : I hand my oar ;
Nor think on all I left on shore.

17   C

" But when vain doubt, and groundless fear
Do that dear foolish bosom tear ;
When the big lip, and watery eye
Tell me the rising storm is nigh :
'Tis then, thou art the angry main,
Deform'd by winds, and dash'd by rain ;
And the poor sailor, that must try
Its fury, labours less than I.

" Shipwreck'd, in vain to land I make ;
While Love and Fate still drive me back :
Forc'd to doat on thee thy own way,
I chide thee first, and then obey :
Wretched when from thee, vex'd when nigh,
I with thee, or without thee, die."

A Better Answer to Cloe Jealous

Dear Cloe, how blubber'd is that pretty face,
    Thy cheek all on fire, and thy hair all uncurl'd :
Prithee quit this caprice ; and (as old Falstaff says)
    Let us e'en talk a little like folks of this world.

How canst thou presume, thou hast leave to destroy
    The beauties, which Venus but lent to thy keeping ?
Those looks were design'd to inspire love and joy :
    More ord'nary eyes may serve people for weeping.

To be vex'd with a trifle or two that I writ,
    Your judgment, at once, and my passion you wrong :
You take that for fact, which will scarce be found wit :
    Od's life ! must one swear to the truth of a song ?

What I speak, my fair Cloe, and what I write, shows
    The diff'rence there is betwixt Nature and Art :
I court others in verse ; but I love thee in prose :
    And they have my whimsies ; but thou hast my heart.

18

The God of us verse-men (you know, child) the sun,
    How after his journeys he sets up his rest :
If at morning o'er earth 'tis his fancy to run ;
    At night he reclines on his Thetis's breast.

So when I am wearied with wandering all day,
    To thee my delight in the evening I come :
No matter what beauties I saw in my way,
    They were but my visits ; but thou art my home.

Then finish, dear Cloe, this pastoral war ;
    And let us like Horace and Lydia agree :
For thou art a girl as much brighter than her,
    As he was a poet sublimer than me.

A Letter

to the Honourable Lady
Miss Margaret Cavendish-Holles-Harley

My noble, lovely, little Peggy,
Let this, my first epistle, beg ye,
At dawn of morn, and close of even,
To lift your heart and hands to Heaven :
In double duty say your prayer,
Our Father first, then *Notre Père ;*
And, dearest child, along the day,
In everything you do and say,
Obey and please my Lord and Lady,
So God shall love, and Angels aid, ye.

If to these precepts you attend,
No second letter need I send,
And so I rest your constant friend,

                                M. P.

MATTHEW PRIOR

To a Child of Quality

five years old, the Author then forty.
Written in 1704

Lords, knights, and squires, the numerous band,
    That wear the fair Miss Mary's fetters,
Were summon'd by her high command,
    To show their passions by their letters.

My pen amongst the rest I took,
    Lest those bright eyes that cannot read
Should dart their kindling fires, and look
    The power they have to be obey'd.

Nor quality, nor reputation,
    Forbid me yet my flame to tell,
Dear five years old befriends my passion,
    And I may write till she can spell.

For while she makes her silk-worms beds,
    With all the tender things I swear,
Whilst all the house my passion reads,
    In papers round her baby's hair,

She may receive and own my flame,
    For though the strictest prudes should know it,
She'll pass for a most virtuous dame,
    And I for an unhappy poet.

Then too, alas ! when she shall tear
    The lines some younger rival sends,
She'll give me leave to write, I fear,
    And we shall still continue friends.

For, as our different ages move,
    'Tis so ordain'd (would Fate but mend it !)
That I shall be past making love,
    When she begins to comprehend it.

MATTHEW PRIOR

An Epitaph

Stet quicunque volet potens
Aulæ culmine lubrico, etc.

Interr'd beneath this marble stone,
Lie sauntering Jack, and idle Joan.
While rolling threescore years and one
Did round this globe their courses run ;
If human things went ill or well ;
If changing empires rose or fell ;
The morning pass'd, the evening came,
And found this couple still the same.
They walk'd and eat, good folks : what then ?
Why then they walk'd and eat again :
They soundly slept the night away :
They did just nothing all the day :
And having buried children four,
Would not take pains to try for more.
Nor sister either had, nor brother :
They seem'd just tallied for each other.

Their moral and œconomy
Most perfectly they made agree :
Each virtue kept its proper bound,
Nor trespass'd on the other's ground.
Nor fame, nor censure they regarded :
They neither punish'd, nor rewarded :
He car'd not what the footmen did :
Her maids she neither prais'd, nor chid :
So every servant took his course ;
And bad at first, they all grew worse.
Slothful disorder fill'd his stable ;
And sluttish plenty deck'd her table.
Their beer was strong ; their wine was port ;
Their meal was large ; their grace was short.
They gave the poor the remnant meat,
Just when it grew not fit to eat.

MATTHEW PRIOR

They paid the church and parish rate ;
And took, but read not the receipt :
For which they claim'd their Sunday's due
Of slumbering in an upper pew.

No man's defects sought they to know ;
So never made themselves a foe.
No man's good deeds they did commend ;
So never rais'd themselves a friend.
Nor cherish'd they relations poor ;
That might decrease their present store :
Nor barn nor house did they repair ;
That might oblige their future heir.

They neither added, nor confounded :
They neither wanted, nor abounded.
Each Christmas they accompts did clear ;
And wound their bottom round the year.
Nor tear, nor smile did they employ
At news of public grief, or joy.
When bells were rung, and bonfires made,
If ask'd, they ne'er denied their aid :
Their jug was to the ringers carried,
Who ever either died, or married ;
Their billet at the fire was found,
Who ever was depos'd, or crown'd.

Nor good, nor bad, nor fools, nor wise ;
They would not learn, nor could advise :
Without love, hatred, joy, or fear,
They led—a kind of—as it were :
Nor wish'd, nor car'd, nor laugh'd, nor cried :
And so they liv'd ; and so they died.

MATTHEW PRIOR

On My Birthday

I, my dear, was born to-day,
So all my jolly comrades say ;
They bring me music, wreaths, and mirth,
And ask to celebrate my birth :
Little, alas ! my comrades know
That I was born to pain and woe ;
To thy denial, to thy scorn,
Better I had ne'er been born,
I wish to die ev'n whilst I say,
I, my dear, was born to-day.

I, my dear, was born to-day,
Shall I salute the rising ray ?
Wellspring of all my joy and woe,
Clotilda, thou alone dost know.
Shall the wreath surround my hair ?
Or the music please my ear ?
Shall I my comrades' mirth receive,
And bless my birth, and wish to live ?
Then let me see great Venus chase
Imperious anger from thy face ;
Then let me hear thee smiling say,
" Thou, my dear, wert born to-day."

Jinny the Just

Releas'd from the noise of the butcher and baker,
Which, my old friends be thanked, did seldom forsake her,
And from the soft duns of my landlord the Quaker ;

From chiding the footmen and watching the lasses,
From Nell that burn'd milk, and Tom that broke glasses,
(Sad mischiefs through which a good housekeeper passes!);

From some real care, but more fancied vexation,
From a life parti-colour'd, half reason, half passion,
Here lies after all the best wench in the nation.

23

MATTHEW PRIOR

From the Rhine to the Po, from the Thames to the Rhone,
Joanna or Janneton, Jinny or Joan,
'Twas all one to her by what name she was known ;

For the idiom of words very little she heeded,
Provided the matter she drove at succeeded,
She took and gave languages just as she needed ;

So for kitchen and market, for bargain and sale,
She paid English or Dutch or French down on the nail,
But in telling a story she sometimes did fail ;

Then begging excuse, as she happen'd to stammer,
With respect to her betters, but none to her grammar,
Her blush help'd her out, and her jargon became her.

Her habit and mien she endeavour'd to frame
To the different *gout* of the place where she came,
Her outside still chang'd, but her inside the same ;

At the Hague in her slippers, and hair as the mode is,
At Paris all falbalow'd fine as a goddess,
And at censuring London in smock-sleeves and bodice,

She order'd affairs, that few people could tell
In what part about her that mixture did dwell
Of Vrough or Mistress, or Mademoiselle.

For her surname and race let the heralds e'en answer,
Her own proper worth was enough to advance her,
And he who lik'd her, little valu'd her grandsire ;

But from what house so ever her lineage may come,
I wish my own Jinny but out of her tomb,
Though all her relations were there in her room.

Of such terrible beauty she never could boast
As with absolute sway o'er all hearts rules the roast,
When J—— bawls aloud to the Chair for a toast ;

But of good household features her person was made,
Nor by faction cried up, nor of censure afraid,
And her beauty was rather for use than parade ;

Her blood so well mix'd, and flesh so well pasted,
That though her youth faded her comeliness lasted,
The blew was wore off but the plum was well tasted ;

Less smooth than her skin, and less white than her breast,
Was this polish'd stone beneath which she lies press'd ;
Stop, reader, and sigh, while thou thinkst on the rest.

With a just trim of virtue her soul was endu'd,
Not affectedly pious, nor secretly lewd,
She cut even between the coquette and the prude.

Her will with her duty so equally stood,
That, seldom oppos'd, she was commonly good,
And did pretty well, doing just what she would.

Declining all power, she found means to persuade,
Was then most regarded when most she obey'd,
The mistress, in truth, when she seem'd but the maid.

Such care of her own proper actions she took,
That on other folks' lives she had no time to look,
So censure and praise were struck out of her book ;

Her thought still confin'd to its own little sphere,
She minded not who did excel or did err,
But just as the matter related to her ;

Then too when her private tribunal was rear'd,
Her mercy so mix'd with her judgment appear'd
That her foes were condemn'd and her friends always
    clear'd.

Her religion so well with her learning did suit
That in practice sincere, and in controverse mute,
She show'd she knew better to live than dispute ;

Some parts of the Bible by heart she recited,
And much in historical chapters delighted,
But in points about Faith she was something short-sighted ;

So notions and modes she referr'd to the Schools,
And in matters of conscience adher'd to two rules—
To advise with no bigots, and jest with no fools ;

And scrupling but little, enough she believ'd,
By charity ample small sins she retriev'd,
And when she had new clothes she always receiv'd.

Thus still while her morning unseen fled away
In ord'ring the linen, and making the tea,
That she scarce could have time for the Psalms of the day ;

And while after dinner the night came so soon
That half she propos'd very seldom was done,
With twenty " God bless me's, how this day is gone ! "

While she read and accounted and paid and abated,
Eat and drank, play'd and work'd, laugh'd and cried, lov'd
     and hated,
As answer'd the end of her being created ;

In the midst of her age came a cruel disease,
Which neither her julips nor receipts could appease,
So down dropt her clay.   May her soul be at peace.

Retire from this sepulchre all the prophane,
You that love for debauch, or that marry for gain,
Retire lest ye trouble the Manes of Jane.

But thou, that know'st love above int'rest or lust,
Strew the myrtle and rose on this once belov'd dust,
And shed one pious tear upon Jinny the Just.

Tread soft on her grave, and do right to her honour,
Let neither rude hand nor ill tongue light upon her,
Do all the small favours that now can be done her.

And when what thou [lik'st] shall return to her clay,
For so I'm persuaded she must do one day,
Whatever fantastic John Asgill may say ;

When, as I have done now, thou shalt set up a stone
For something however distinguish'd or known,
May some pious friend the misfortune bemoan,
And make thy concern by reflection his own.

Epitaph Extempore

Heralds, and statesmen, by your leave,
Here lie the bones of Matthew Prior ;
The son of Adam and of Eve,
Can Bourbon, or Nassau, go higher ?

For My Own Tombstone

To me 'twas given to die : to thee 'tis given
To live : alas ! one moment sets us even.
Mark ! how impartial is the will of Heaven !

For My Own Monument

As doctors give physic by way of prevention,
  Matt alive and in health of his tomb-stone took care,
For delays are unsafe, and his pious intention
  May haply be never fulfill'd by his heir.

Then take Matt's word for it, the sculptor is paid,
  That the figure is fine, pray believe your own eye,
Yet credit but lightly what more may be said,
  For we flatter ourselves, and teach marble to lie.

Yet counting as far as to fifty his years,
  His virtues and vices were as other men's are,
High hopes he conceiv'd, and he smother'd great fears,
  In a life parti-colour'd, half pleasure, half care.

Not to business a drudge, nor to faction a slave,
   He strove to make int'rest and freedom agree,
In public employments industrious and grave,
   And alone with his friends, Lord, how merry was he.

Now in equipage stately, now humbly on foot,
   Both fortunes he tried, but to neither would trust,
And whirl'd in the round, as the wheel turn'd about,
   He found riches had wings, and knew man was but dust.

This verse little polish'd, though mighty sincere,
   Sets neither his titles nor merit to view,
It says that his relics collected lie here,
   And no mortal yet knows too if this may be true.

Fierce robbers there are that infest the highway,
   So Matt may be kill'd, and his bones never found,
False witness at court, and fierce tempests at sea,
   So Matt may yet chance to be hang'd, or be drown'd.

If his bones lie in earth, roll in sea, fly in air,
   To Fate we must yield, and the thing is the same,
And if passing thou giv'st him a smile, or a tear,
   He cares not—yet prithee be kind to his fame.

Sir JOHN VANBRUGH, Knt. (1664-1726)

Fable

(*From the Comedy of " Aesop."*)

A Band, a Bob-wig, and a Feather,
Attack'd a lady's heart together :
The Band, in a most learned plea,
Made up of deep philosophy,
Told her, if she would please to wed
A reverend beard, and take, instead
  Of vigorous youth,
  Old solemn truth
With books and morals into bed,
  How happy she would be.

Sir JOHN VANBRUGH

The Bob, he talk'd of management,
What wond'rous blessings Heaven sent
On care, and pains, and industry ;
And truly he must be so free,
To own he thought your airy beaux,
With powder'd wigs, and dancing shoes,
Were good for nothing (mend his soul !)
But prate, and talk, and play the fool.
He said, 'twas wealth gave joy and mirth,
  And that to be the dearest wife
  Of one who labour'd all his life
To make a mine of gold his own,
And not spend sixpence, when he'd done,
  Was Heaven upon earth.

When these two blades had done, d'ye see,
The Feather (as it might be me)
Steps out, Sir, from behind the screen,
With such an air, and such a mien :
Look you, old gentleman ! in short,
He quickly spoil'd the statesman's sport.
  It prov'd such charming weather,
That, you must know, at the first beck,
The lady leap'd about his neck,
  And off they went together.

WILLIAM COLEPEPER (16—-1726)

To the Lady Dutry

Dutry, that soul-inspiring fair !
  Improves the poet's story,
With spotless fame and beauty rare
  Surpassing Helen's glory.

Helen, less fair, may boast her art
  A guilty warmth to raise ;
Dutry refines the vanquish'd heart
  To virtue's purer praise.

ANNE FINCH (*née* KINGSMILL), Countess of WINCHILSEA (1666-1720)

To Death

O king of terrors, whose unbounded sway
All that have life must certainly obey ;
The king, the priest, the prophet, all are thine,
Nor would ev'n God (in flesh) thy stroke decline.
My name is on thy roll, and sure I must
Increase thy gloomy kingdom in the dust.
My soul at this no apprehension feels,
But trembles at thy swords, thy racks, thy wheels ;
Thy scorching fevers, which distract the sense,
And snatch us raving, unprepar'd, from hence ;
At thy contagious darts, that wound the heads
Of weeping friends, who wait at dying beds.
Spare these, and let thy time be when it will ;
My business is to die, and thine to kill.
Gently thy fatal sceptre on me lay,
And take to thy cold arms, insensibly, thy prey.

To the Nightingale

Exert thy voice, sweet harbinger of spring !
   This moment is thy time to sing,
   This moment I attend to praise,
And set my numbers to thy lays ;
   Free as thine shall be my song,
   As thy music short, or long.
Poets wild as thee were born,
   Pleasing best when unconfin'd,
   When to please is least design'd,
Soothing but their cares to rest ;
   Cares do still their thoughts molest,
   And still th' unhappy poet's breast,
Like thine, when best he sings, is plac'd against a thorn.

She begins, let all be still !
  Muse, thy promise now fulfill !
Sweet, oh ! sweet, still sweeter yet !
Can thy words such accents fit,
Canst thou syllables refine,
Melt a sense that shall retain
Still some spirit of the brain,
Till with sounds like these it join ?
  'Twill not be ! then change thy note ;
Let division shake thy throat.
Hark ! division now she tries ;
Yet as far the Muse outflies.

Cease then, prithee, cease thy tune ;
  Trifler, wilt thou sing till June ?
Till thy business all lies waste,
And the time of building's past !
  Thus we poets that have speech,
Unlike what thy forests teach,
  If a fluent vein be shown
  That's transcendent to our own,
Criticise, reform, or preach,
Or censure what we cannot reach.

The Atheist and the Acorn

" Methinks this world is oddly made,
  And every thing's amiss,"
A dull, presuming atheist said,
As stretch'd he lay beneath a shade,
  And instanced in this :

" Behold," quoth he, " that mighty thing,
  A pumpkin, large and round,
Is held but by a little string,
Which upwards cannot make it spring,
  Or bear it from the ground.

' Whilst on this oak a fruit so small,
　　So disproportion'd, grows ;
That, who with sense surveys this *All*,
This universal casual ball,
　　Its ill contrivance knows.

" My better judgement would have hung
　　That weight upon a tree,
And left this mast, thus lightly strung,
'Mongst things which on the surface sprung
　　And small and feeble be."

No more the caviller could say,
　　Nor farther faults descry ;
For, as he upwards gazing lay,
An acorn, loosen'd from the stay,
　　Fell down upon his eye.

Th' offended part with tears ran o'er,
　　As punish'd for the sin :
Fool ! had that bough a pumpkin bore,
Thy whimsies must have work'd no more,
　　Nor skull had kept them in !

Life's Progress

How gaily is at first begun
　　Our life's uncertain race !
Whilst yet that sprightly morning sun,
With which we just set out to run,
　　Enlightens all the place.

How smiling the world's prospect lies,
　　How tempting to go through !
Not Canaan to the Prophet's eyes,
From Pisgah with a sweet surprise,
　　Did more inviting shew.

32

LADY WINCHILSEA

How promising's the book of Fate,
  Till throughly understood !
Whilst partial hopes such lots create,
As may the youthful fancy treat
  With all that's great and good.

How soft the first ideas prove,
  Which wander through our minds !
How full the joys, how free the love,
Which does that early season move,
  As flowers the western winds !

Our sighs are then but vernal air ;
  But April-drops our tears,
Which swiftly passing, all grows fair,
Whilst beauty compensates our care,
  And youth each vapour clears.

But oh ! too soon, alas, we climb ;
  Scarce feeling, we ascend
The gently rising hill of Time,
From whence with grief we see that prime,
  And all its sweetness, end.

The die now cast, our station known,
  Fond expectation past ;
The thorns, which former days had sown,
To crops of late repentance grown,
  Through which we toil at last.

Whilst every care's a driving harm,
  That helps us to bear down ;
Which faded smiles no more can charm,
But every tear's a winter-storm,
  And every look's a frown.

Till with succeeding ills opprest,
  For joys we hop'd to find ;
By age, too, rumpled and undrest,
We, gladly sinking down to rest,
  Leave following crowds behind.

D

LADY WINCHILSEA

Jealousy

Vain Love, why dost thou boast of wings,
    That cannot help thee to retire,
When such quick flames Suspicion brings,
    As do the heart about thee fire ?

Still swift to come, but when to go
Thou shouldst be more—Alas ! how slow !

Lord of the World must surely be
    But thy bare title at the most ;
Since Jealousy is lord of thee,
    And makes such havoc on thy coast,

As does thy pleasant land deface,
Yet binds thee faster to the place.

The Tree

Fair tree ! for thy delightful shade
'Tis just that some return be made :
Sure, some return is due from me
To thy cool shadows, and to thee.
When thou to birds dost shelter give,
Thou music dost from them receive ;
If travellers beneath thee stay,
Till storms have worn themselves away,
That time in praising thee they spend,
And thy protecting power commend ;
The shepherd here, from scorching freed,
Tunes to thy dancing leaves his reed,
Whilst his lov'd nymph, in thanks, bestows
Her flowery chaplets on thy boughs.
Shall I then only silent be,
And no return be made by me ?
No ; let this wish upon thee wait,

And still to flourish be thy fate ;
To future ages may'st thou stand
Untouch'd by the rash workman's hand,
Till that large stock of sap is spent,
Which gives thy summer's ornament ;
Till the fierce winds, that vainly strive
To shock thy greatness whilst alive,
Shall on thy lifeless hour attend,
Prevent the axe, and grace thy end ;
Their scatter'd strength together call,
And to the clouds proclaim thy fall ;
Who then their evening-dews may spare,
When thou no longer art their care ;
But shalt, like ancient heroes, burn,
And some bright hearth be made thy urn.

A Nocturnal Reverie

In such a night, when every louder wind
Is to its distant cavern safe confin'd ;
And only gentle Zephyr fans his wings,
And lonely Philomel, still waking, sings ;
Or from some tree, fam'd for the owl's delight,
She, hollowing clear, directs the wanderer right :
In such a night, when passing clouds give place,
Or thinly veil the Heavens' mysterious face ;
When in some river, overhung with green,
The waving moon and trembling leaves are seen ;
When freshen'd grass now bears itself upright,
And makes cool banks to pleasing rest invite,
Whence springs the woodbind, and the bramble-rose,
And where the sleepy cowslip shelter'd grows ;
Whilst now a paler hue the foxglove takes,
Yet chequers still with red the dusky brakes ;
When scatter'd glow-worms, but in twilight fine,
Shew trivial beauties watch their hour to shine,
Whilst Salisb'ry stands the test of every light,

In perfect charm, and perfect virtue bright ;
When odours, which declin'd repelling day,
Through temp'rate air uninterrupted stray ;
When darken'd groves their softest shadows wear,
And falling waters we distinctly hear ;
When through the gloom more venerable shows
Some ancient Fabric, awful in repose,
While sunburnt hills their swarthy looks conceal,
And swelling haycocks thicken up the vale ;
When the loos'd horse now, as his pasture leads,
Comes slowly grazing through th' adjoining meads,
Whose stealing pace, and lengthen'd shade, we fear,
Till torn up forage in his teeth we hear ;
When nibbling sheep at large pursue their food,
And unmolested kine rechew the cud ;
When curlews cry beneath the village-walls,
And to her straggling brood the partridge calls ;
Their shortliv'd jubilee the creatures keep,
Which but endures, whilst tyrant Man does sleep ;
When a sedate content the spirit feels,
And no fierce light disturbs, whilst it reveals ;
But silent musings urge the mind to seek
Something, too high for syllables to speak ;
Till the free Soul to a compos'dness charm'd,
Finding the elements of rage disarm'd,
O'er all below a solemn quiet grown,
Joys in th' inferior world, and thinks it like her own :
In such a night let me abroad remain,
Till morning breaks, and all's confus'd again,
Our cares, our toils, our clamours are renew'd,
Or pleasures, seldom reach'd, again pursu'd.

GEORGE GRANVILLE, Baron LANSDOWNE
(1667-1735)

To Myra,

Loving at First Sight

No warning of th' approaching flame,
Swiftly, like sudden death, it came ;
Like travellers by lightning kill'd,
I burnt the moment I beheld.

In whom so many charms are plac'd,
Is with a mind as nobly grac'd ;
The case, so shining to behold,
Is fill'd with richest gems and gold.

To what my eyes admir'd before
I add a thousand graces more ;
And fancy blows into a flame
The spark that from her beauty came.

The object thus improv'd by thought,
By my own image I am caught ;
Pygmalion so, with fatal art,
Polish'd the form that stung his heart.

Song to Myra

Foolish love, begone, said I,
   Vain are thy attempts on me ;
Thy soft allurements I defy,
Women, those fair dissemblers, fly,
   My heart was never made for thee.

Love heard ; and straight prepar'd a dart ;
   Myra, revenge my cause, said he :
Too sure 'twas shot, I feel the smart,
It rends my brain, and tears my heart ;
   O Love ! my conqu'ror, pity me !

37

LORD LANSDOWNE

Fortune

When Fortune seems to smile, 'tis then I fear
Some lurking ill, and hidden mischief, near :
Us'd to her frowns, I stand upon my guard,
And arm'd in virtue, keep my soul prepar'd.
Fickle and false to others she may be,
I can complain but of her constancy.

Song to Myra

Why should a heart so tender break ?
    O Myra ! give its anguish ease ;
The use of beauty you mistake,
    Not meant to vex, but please.

Those lips for smiling were design'd ;
    That bosom to be prest ;
Your eyes to languish, and look kind ;
    For amorous arms, your waist.

Each thing has its appointed right,
    Establish'd by the powers above :
The sun to give us warmth and light,
    Myra to kindle love.

To Myra

Thoughtful nights, and restless waking,
    O the pains that we endure !
Broken faith, unkind forsaking,
    Ever doubting, never sure.

Hopes deceiving, vain endeavours,
    What a race has Love to run !
False protesting, fleeting favours,
    Every, every way undone.

Still complaining, and defending,
   Both to love, yet not agree ;
Fears tormenting, passion rending,
   O the pangs of jealousy !

From such painful ways of living,
   Ah ! how sweet, could Love be free !
Still presenting, still receiving,
   Fierce, immortal ecstasy.

Song to Myra

Why, cruel creature, why so bent
   To vex a tender heart ?
To gold and title you relent,
   Love throws in vain his dart.

Let glittering fools in courts be great ;
   For pay, let armies move ;
Beauty should have no other bait
   But gentle vows and love.

If on those endless charms you lay
   The value that's their due,
Kings are themselves too poor to pay,
   A thousand worlds too few.

But if a passion without vice,
   Without disguise or art,
Ah Myra ! if true love's your price,
   Behold it in my heart.

Song

The happiest mortals once were we,
I lov'd Myra, Myra me ;
   Each desirous of the blessing,
   Nothing wanting but possessing ;
I lov'd Myra, Myra me,
The happiest mortals once were we.

But since cruel fates dissever,
Torn from love, and torn for ever,
　Tortures end me !
　Death befriend me !
Of all pains the greatest pain
Is to love, and love in vain.

Belinda

Belinda's pride's an arrant cheat,
　A foolish artifice to blind ;
Some honest glance that scorns decei
　Does still reveal her native mind.

With look demure, and forc'd disdain,
　She idly acts the saint ;
We see through this disguise as plain
　As we distinguish paint.

So have I seen grave fools design
　With formal looks to pass for wise ;
But nature is a light will shine,
　And break through all disguise.

Cloe

Cloe's the wonder of her sex,
　'Tis well her heart is tender ;
How might such killing eyes perplex,
　With virtue to defend her ?

But nature, graciously inclin'd
　With liberal hand to please us,
Has to her boundless beauty join'd
　A boundless bent to ease us.

The Rev. JOHN POMFRET (1667-1702)

To his Friend inclined to Marry

I would not have you, Strephon, choose a mate
From too exalted, or too mean, a state :
For in both these we may expect to find
A creeping spirit, or a haughty mind.
Who moves within the middle region, shares
The least disquiets, and the smallest cares.
Let her extraction with true lustre shine,
If somewhat brighter, not too bright for thine :
Her education liberal, not great,
Neither inferior, nor above her state.
Let her have wit ; but let that wit be free
From affectation, pride, and pedantry :
For the effect of woman's wit is such,
Too little is as dangerous as too much.
But chiefly, let her humour close with thine,
Unless where yours does to a fault incline :
The least disparity in this destroys,
Like sulph'rous blasts, the very buds of joys.
Her person amiable, straight, and free
From natural, or chance, deformity.
Let not her years exceed, if equal, thine ;
For women past their vigour, soon decline.
Her fortune competent ; and, if thy sight
Can reach so far, take care 'tis gather'd right.
If thine's enough, then hers may be the less :
Do not aspire to riches in excess.
For that which makes our lives delightful prove,
Is a genteel Sufficiency, and Love.

The Rev. JONATHAN SWIFT, D.D. (1667-1745)

A Description of a City Shower
in imitation of Virgil's Georgics

Careful observers may foretell the hour
(By sure prognostics) when to dread a shower.
While rain depends, the pensive cat gives o'er
Her frolics, and pursues her tail no more.
Returning home at night, you'll find the sink
Strike your offended sense with double stink.
If you be wise, then go not far to dine ;
You'll spend in coach-hire more than save in wine.
A coming shower your shooting corns presage,
Old achës throb, your hollow tooth will rage ;
Sauntering in coffee-house is Dulman seen,
He damns the climate, and complains of spleen.

Meanwhile the South, rising with dabbled wings,
A sable cloud athwart the welkin flings,
That swill'd more liquor than it could contain,
And, like a drunkard, gives it up again.
Brisk Susan whips her linen from the rope,
While the first drizzling shower is borne aslope :
Such is that sprinkling which some careless quean
Flirts on you from her mop, but not so clean :
You fly, invoke the gods ; then, turning, stop
To rail ; she, singing, still whirls on her mop.
Not yet the dust had shunn'd th' unequal strife,
But, aided by the wind, fought still for life,
And wafted with its foe by violent gust,
'Twas doubtful which was rain and which was dust.
Ah ! where must needy poet seek for aid,
When dust and rain at once his coat invade ?
Sole coat ! where dust, cemented by the rain,
Erects the nap, and leaves a cloudy stain !

Now in contiguous drops the flood comes down,
Threatening with deluge this devoted town.
To shops in crowds the daggled females fly,
Pretend to cheapen goods, but nothing buy.
The Templar spruce, while every spout's abroach,

Stays till 'tis fair, yet seems to call a coach.
The tuck'd-up sempstress walks with hasty strides,
While streams run down her oil'd umbrella's sides.
Here various kinds, by various fortunes led,
Commence acquaintance underneath a shed.
Triumphant Tories, and desponding Whigs,
Forget their feuds, and join to save their wigs.
Box'd in a chair the Beau impatient sits,
While spouts run clattering o'er the roof by fits,
And ever and anon with frightful din
The leather sounds ; he trembles from within.
So when Troy chairmen bore the wooden steed,
Pregnant with Greeks impatient to be freed,
(Those bully Greeks, who, as the moderns do,
Instead of paying chairmen, ran them through)
Laocoon struck the outside with his spear,
And each imprison'd hero quak'd for fear.

Now from all parts the swelling kennels flow,
And bear their trophies with them as they go :
Filths of all hues and odour seem to tell
What street they sail'd from, by their sight and smell.
They, as each torrent drives with rapid force,
From Smithfield to St. Pulchre's shape their course,
And, in huge confluence join'd at Snowhill ridge,
Fall from the conduit prone to Holborn bridge.
Sweepings from butchers' stalls, dung, guts, and blood,
Drown'd puppies, stinking sprats, all drench'd in mud,
Dead cats, and turnip-tops come tumbling down the flood.

In Sickness

Written in Ireland in October 1714

'Tis true—then why should I repine
To see my life so fast decline ?
But why obscurely here alone,
Where I am neither lov'd nor known ?
My state of health none care to learn ;
My life is here no soul's concern :

And those with whom I now converse
Without a tear will tend my hearse.
Remov'd from kind Arbuthnot's aid,
Who knows his art but not his trade,
Preferring his regard for me
Before his credit, or his fee,
Some formal visits, looks, and words,
What mere humanity affords,
I meet perhaps from three or four,
From whom I once expected more,
Which those who tend the sick for pay
Can act as decently as they :
But no obliging tender friend
To help at my approaching end.
My life is now a burden grown
To others, ere it be my own.

Ye formal weepers for the sick,
In your last offices be quick ;
And spare my absent friends the grief
To hear, yet give me no relief ;
Expir'd to-day, entomb'd to-morrow,
When known, will save a double sorrow.

Stella's Birthday, 1720

All travellers at first incline
Where'er they see the fairest sign ;
And if they find the chambers neat,
And like the liquor and the meat,
Will call again, and recommend
The Angel Inn to every friend.
What though the painting grows decay'd,
The house will never lose its trade :
Nay, though the treach'rous tapster Thomas
Hangs a new Angel, two doors from us,
As fine as dauber's hands can make it,
In hopes that strangers may mistake it,
We think it both a shame and sin
To quit the true old Angel Inn.

JONATHAN SWIFT

Now this is Stella's case in fact,
An angel's face a little crack'd,
Could poets or could painters fix
How angels look at thirty-six :
This drew us in at first to find
In such a form an angel's mind ;
And every virtue now supplies
The fainting rays of Stella's eyes.
See at her levee crowding swains,
Whom Stella freely entertains
With breeding, humour, wit, and sense,
And puts them but to small expense ;
Their mind so plentifully fills,
And makes such reasonable bills,
So little gets for what she gives,
We really wonder how she lives !
And had her stock been less, no doubt
She must have long ago run out.

Then who can think we'll quit the place,
When Doll hangs out a newer face ?
Or stop and light at Cloe's head,
With scraps and leavings to be fed ?
Then, Cloe, still go on to prate
Of thirty-six and thirty-eight ;
Pursue your trade of scandal-picking,
Your hints, that Stella is no chicken ;
Your innuendoes, when you tell us,
That Stella loves to talk with fellows :
And let me warn you to believe
A truth, for which your soul should grieve :
That should you live to see the day,
When Stella's locks must all be gray,
When age must print a furrow'd trace
On every feature of her face ;
Though you, and all your senseless tribe,
Could Art, or Time, or Nature bribe
To make you look like Beauty's Queen,
And hold for ever at fifteen ;

No bloom of youth can ever blind
The cracks and wrinkles of your mind ;
All men of sense will pass your door,
And crowd to Stella's at four-score.

Stella's Birthday, 1725

As, when a beauteous nymph decays,
We say, she's past her dancing days ;
So poets lose their feet by time,
And can no longer dance in rhyme.
Your annual bard had rather chose
To celebrate your birth in prose :
Yet merry folks, who want by chance
A pair to make a country dance,
Call the old housekeeper, and get her
To fill a place, for want of better.
While Sheridan is off the hooks,
And friend Delany at his books,
That Stella may avoid disgrace,
Once more the Dean supplies their place.
Beauty and wit, too sad a truth !
Have always been confin'd to youth ;
The God of Wit and Beauty's Queen,
He twenty-one and she fifteen,
No poet ever sweetly sung,
Unless he were, like Phœbus, young ;
Nor ever nymph inspir'd to rhyme,
Unless, like Venus, in her prime.
At fifty-six, if this be true,
Am I a poet fit for you ?
Or, at the age of forty-three,
Are you a subject fit for me ?
Adieu ! bright wit, and radiant eyes !
You must be grave, and I be wise.
Our fate in vain we would oppose :
But I'll still be your friend in prose :

Esteem and friendship to express,
Will not require poetic dress ;
And if the Muse deny her aid
To have them sung, they may be said.

But, Stella, say, what evil tongue
Reports you are no longer young ;
That Time sits, with his scythe to mow,
Where erst sat Cupid with his bow ;
That half your locks are turn'd to gray ?
I'll ne'er believe a word they say.
'Tis true, but let it not be known,
My eyes are somewhat dimmish grown ;
For Nature, always in the right,
To your decays adapts my sight ;
And wrinkles undistinguish'd pass,
For I'm asham'd to use a glass ;
And till I see them with these eyes,
Whoever says you have them, lies.
No length of time can make you quit
Honour and virtue, sense and wit :
Thus you may still be young to me,
While I can better hear than see.
O ne'er may Fortune show her spite,
To make me deaf, and mend my sight !

ANTHONY HAMMOND (1668-1738)

The Happy Man

A plain good man without deceit,
Whose virtues only make him great,
Whose learning does to wisdom tend,
Whose wisdom does in goodness end ;
Contented with the humble state,
In which he's plac'd by choice or fate,
To a few honest wise men known,

For ill or folly tax'd by none ;
One who with prudence does enjoy
Pleasures which fill, but never cloy ;
Pleasures above gross sense refin'd,
A true dear friend, a serious mind,
A constant health, a fair kind wife,
Books, quiet, and a country life.
Thus, before age comes on, to fall :
Pleas'd in himself and prais'd by all.

To Clara

Clara, had your lovely face
Fewer beauties, were each grace
Less engaging ; did your eyes
With less force my heart surprise ;
Were less bright or fine your hair,
Or your skin less smooth and fair ;
Were these charms as much below,
As they excel all women's now ;
You have others would control,
Conquer, fix, and charm my soul ;
Your humour innocent and free,
As youth and innocence can be ;
So quick and natural your wit,
While judgment guides and governs it,
That in all you say, or do,
You show your wit and judgment too.
These were charms that would detain
In a strong and grateful chain
Your captive ; were these charms alone,
These would make my heart your own :
But, fairest, when I see you stand
Finish'd thus by nature's hand ;
With such a body, such a mind,
As nature ne'er till now has join'd ;

Oh ! then I burn, I bleed, I die,
For love of you————
Witness all ye powers above,
If ever there was truer love
Than this I vow, may sudden Death
Stop my false and perjur'd breath.

WILLIAM CONGREVE (1670-1729)

Song

False though she be to me and love,
  I'll ne'er pursue revenge ;
For still the charmer I approve,
  Though I deplore her change.

In hours of bliss we oft have met,
  They could not always last ;
And though the present I regret,
  I'm grateful for the past.

Epitaph

*upon Robert Huntingdon, of Stanton Harcourt, Esq., and
Robert his son*

This peaceful tomb does now contain
  Father and son together laid ;
Whose living virtues shall remain,
  When they and this are quite decay'd.

What man should be, to ripeness grown,
  And finish'd worth should do, or shun,
At full was in the father shown ;
  What youth could promise in the son.

49   E

But Death, obdurate, both destroy'd
   The perfect fruit, and opening bud :
First seiz'd the sweets we had enjoy'd,
   Then robb'd us of the coming good.

Song

See, see, she wakes, Sabina wakes !
   And now the sun begins to rise ;
Less glorious is the morn that breaks
   From his bright beams, than her fair eyes.

With light united, day they give,
   But different fates ere night fulfil ;
How many by his warmth will live !
   How many will her coldness kill !

Amoret

Fair Amoret is gone astray ;
   Pursue and seek her, every lover ;
I'll tell the signs by which you may
   The wandering shepherdess discover.

Coquet and coy at once her air,
   Both studied, though both seem neglected ;
Careless she is with artful care,
   Affecting to seem unaffected.

With skill her eyes dart every glance,
   Yet change so soon you'd ne'er suspect them ;
For she'd persuade they wound by chance,
   Though certain aim and art direct them.

She likes herself, yet others hates
　For that which in herself she prizes ;
And, while she laughs at them, forgets
　She is the thing that she despises.

The Rev. THOMAS YALDEN, D.D. (1670-1736)

Advice to a Lover *

For many unsuccessful years
　At Cynthia's feet I lay ;
Battering them often with my tears
　I sigh'd, but durst not pray.
No prostrate wretch, before the shrine
　Of some lov'd saint above,
E'er thought his goddess more divine
　Or paid more awful love.

Still the disdainful nymph look'd down
　With coy insulting pride ;
Receiv'd my passion with a frown,
　Or turn'd her head aside.
Then Cupid whisper'd in my ear,
　" Use more prevailing charms ;
You modest, whining fool, draw near,
　And clasp her in your arms.

" With eager kisses tempt the maid,
　From Cynthia's feet depart ;
The lips he briskly must invade,
　That would possess the heart."
With that I shook off all the slave,
　My better fortunes tried ;
When Cynthia in a moment gave
　What she for years denied.

* This poem has also been attributed—erroneously, I think—to Prior.

JOHN SMITH* (*circa* 1713)

The Roses

Go, lovely pair of roses, go,
This clad in scarlet, that in snow.
Go say to my ungentle fair,
    (If on your forms she deigns to gaze),
You dare not hope to rival her,
    Or match the glories of her face ;
But that you're humbly sent, to prove
A youth undone by Beauty and her love.

The sickly white in this pale rose
My wan and meagre looks disclose :
But that which shines so fiercely bright,
    Whose head in painted flames aspires,
And blushes so with purple light,
    It seems to send forth real fires,
Tell her, that rose's ruddy fires impart
The flames her eyes have kindled in my heart.

Song

I saw Lucinda's bosom bare,
    Transparent was the skin,
As through a crystal, did appear
    A beating heart within.

The beating heart transfix'd I saw,
    And yet the heart was stone ;
I saw it bleed, and by the wound
    I thought it was mine own.

But O ! when I perceiv'd it was
    Enshrin'd within your breast,
I knew 'twas yours : for mine, alas !
    Was never yet so blest !

* Of this writer I know nothing. His poems were written, he says in his preface, when he was a young man. He did not publish them till 1713, but possibly they were written in the Restoration period.

COLLEY CIBBER, Poet Laureate (1671-1757)

The Blind Boy

O, say, what is that thing call'd light,
  Which I can ne'er enjoy ?
What is the blessing of the sight ?
  O, tell your poor blind boy !

You talk of wondrous things you see,
  You say the sun shines bright ;
I feel him warm, but how can he
  Then make it day or night ?

My day or night myself I make,
  Whene'er I wake, or play ;
And could I ever keep awake,
  It would be always day.

With heavy sighs I often hear
  You mourn my hopeless woe :
But, sure, with patience I can bear
  A loss I ne'er can know.

Then let not what I cannot have
  My cheer of mind destroy ;
Whilst thus I sing, I am a king,
  Although a poor blind boy !

The Rt. Hon. JOSEPH ADDISON, M.P. (1672-1719)

An Ode

The spacious firmament on high,
With all the blue ethereal sky,
And spangled heavens, a shining frame,
Their great original proclaim.
Th' unwearied sun, from day to day,
Does his Creator's power display ;
And publishes, to every land,
The work of an almighty hand.

Soon as the evening shades prevail,
The moon takes up the wondrous tale ;
And nightly, to the listening earth,
Repeats the story of her birth :
Whilst all the stars that round her burn,
And all the planets, in their turn,
Confirm the tidings as they roll,
And spread the truth from pole to pole.

What though, in solemn silence, all
Move round the dark terrestrial ball ?
What though nor real voice, nor sound,
Amidst their radiant orbs be found ?
In reason's ear they all rejoice,
And utter forth a glorious voice ;
For ever singing, as they shine,
" The hand that made us is divine."

Paraphrase on Psalm XXIII

The Lord my pasture shall prepare,
And feed me with a shepherd's care ;
His presence shall my want supply,
And guard me with a watchful eye ;
My noon-day walks He shall attend,
And all my midnight hours defend.

When in the sultry glebe I faint,
Or on the thirsty mountain pant ;
To fertile vales and dewy meads
My weary wandering steps He leads ;
Where peaceful rivers, soft and slow,
Amid the verdant landscape flow.

Though in the paths of death I tread,
With gloomy horrors overspread,
My steadfast heart shall fear no ill,
For Thou, O Lord, art with me still ;
Thy friendly crook shall give me aid,
And guide me through the dreadful shade.

Though in a bare and rugged way
Through devious lonely wilds I stray,
Thy bounty shall my wants beguile,
The barren wilderness shall smile,
With sudden greens and herbage crown'd,
And streams shall murmur all around.

Hymn

When all Thy mercies, O my God,
　My rising soul surveys ;
Transported with the view, I'm lost
　In wonder, love and praise.

O how shall words with equal warmth
　The gratitude declare,
That glows within my ravish'd heart !
　But Thou canst read it there.

Thy providence my life sustain'd,
　And all my wants redress'd,
When in the silent womb I lay,
　And hung upon the breast.

To all my weak complaints and cries,
　Thy mercy lent an ear,
Ere yet my feeble thoughts had learnt
　To form themselves in prayer.

Unnumber'd comforts to my soul
　Thy tender care bestow'd,
Before my infant heart conceiv'd
　From whom these comforts flow'd.

When in the slippery path of youth
　With heedless steps I ran,
Thine arm unseen convey'd me safe
　And led me up to man.

Through hidden dangers, toils and death,
   It gently clear'd my way ;
And through the pleasing snares of vice,
   More to be fear'd than they.

When worn with sickness, oft hast Thou
   With health renew'd my face ;
And when in sins and sorrows sunk,
   Reviv'd my soul with grace.

Thy bounteous hand with worldly bliss
   Has made my cup run o'er,
And in a kind and faithful friend
   Has doubled all my store.

Ten thousand thousand precious gifts
   My daily thanks employ ;
Nor is the least a cheerful heart,
   That tastes those gifts with joy.

Through every period of my life,
   Thy goodness I'll pursue ;
And after death, in distant worlds,
   The glorious theme renew.

When Nature fails, and day and night
   Divide Thy works no more,
My ever-grateful heart, O Lord !
   Thy mercy shall adore.

Through all eternity to Thee
   A joyful song I'll raise ;
For, oh ! eternity's too short,
   To utter all Thy praise.

JOSEPH ADDISON

An Ode

How are Thy servants blest, O Lord !
  How sure is their defence !
Eternal wisdom is their guide,
  Their help Omnipotence.

In foreign realms, and lands remote,
  Supported by Thy care,
Through burning climes I pass'd unhurt,
  And breath'd in tainted air.

Thy mercy sweeten'd every soil,
  Made every region please ;
The hoary Alpine hills it warm'd,
  And smooth'd the Tyrrhene seas.

Think, O my soul, devoutly think,
  How, with affrighted eyes,
Thou saw'st the wide-extended deep
  In all its horrors rise.

Confusion dwelt in every face,
  And fear in every heart,
When waves on waves, and gulfs in gulfs,
  O'ercame the pilot's art.

Yet then from all my griefs, O Lord !
  Thy mercy set me free ;
Whilst in the confidence of prayer
  My soul took hold on Thee.

For though in dreadful whirls we hung
  High on the broken wave,
I knew Thou wert not slow to hear,
  Nor impotent to save.

The storm was laid, the winds retir'd,
  Obedient to Thy will ;
The sea, that roar'd at Thy command,
  At Thy command was still.

In midst of dangers, fears and death,
   Thy goodness I'll adore ;
And praise Thee for Thy mercies past,
   And humbly hope for more.

My life, if Thou preserv'st my life,
   Thy sacrifice shall be ;
And death, if death must be my doom,
   Shall join my soul to Thee.

Captain Sir RICHARD STEELE, M.P. (1672-1729)

Song

From " The Tender Husband "

Why, lovely charmer, tell me why,
So very kind, so very shy ?
Why does that cold forbidding air
Give damps of sorrow and despair ?
Or why that smile my soul subdue,
And kindle up my flames anew ?

In vain you strive with all your art,
By turns to freeze and fire my heart :
When I behold a face so fair,
So sweet a look, so soft an air,
My ravish'd soul is charm'd all o'er,
I cannot love thee less nor more.

Love below Stairs

From " The Funeral "

Cynderaxa, kind and good,
   Has all my heart and stomach too ;
She makes me love, not hate, my food,
   As other peevish wenches do.

When Venus leaves her Vulcan's cell,
    Which all but I a coal-hole call ;
Fly, fly, ye that above stairs dwell !
    Her face is wash'd, ye vanish all !

And as she's fair, she can impart
    That beauty to make all things fine ;
Brightens the floor with wondrous art,
    And at her touch the dishes shine.

Song

Me Cupid made a happy slave,
    A merry wretched man :
I slight the nymphs I cannot have,
    Nor doat on those I can.

This constant maxim still I hold,
    To baffle all despair :
The absent, ugly are and old :
    The present, young and fair.

ANONYMOUS (*from Steele's Collection*, 1714)

Love's Relief

A wretch long tortur'd with disdain,
That hourly pin'd, but pin'd in vain,
At length the God of Wine address'd,
The refuge of a wounded breast :

" Vouchsafe, oh Power, thy healing aid,
Teach me to gain the cruel maid ;
Thy juices take the lover's part,
Flush his wan looks, and cheer his heart."

Thus to the jolly God he cried ;
And thus the jolly God replied :
" Give whining o'er, be brisk and gay,
And quaff this sneaking form away.

" With dauntless mien approach the fair ;
The way to conquer is to dare."
The swain pursu'd the God's advice ;
The nymph was now no longer nice.

She smil'd, and spoke the Sex's mind :
" When you grow daring, we grow kind :
Men to themselves are most severe,
And make us tyrants by their fear."

Song

How long will Cynthia own no flame,
 And my warm suit disprove ?
Our ages mutually proclaim,
 'Tis now the time to love.

Ah ! think how swift each minute flies,
 How years will form consume :
No lover, when you wither, dies ;
 We sicken when you bloom.

Minerva, rough and bred in war,
 The nuptial joys declin'd :
But had she been, like Venus, fair,
 She'd been, like Venus, kind.

In vain you force severe replies,
 And willing nature wrong :
While Cupids languish in your eyes,
 Who can believe your tongue ?

Half to forbid, and half comply,
  Nor damps nor blows desire :
In looks, as well as words, deny,
  Or put out fire with fire !

Song

Why will Florella, when I gaze,
  My ravish'd eyes reprove,
And chide them from the only face
  They can behold with love ?

To shun your scorn, and ease my care,
  I seek a nymph more kind :
And, while I range from fair to fair,
  Still gentle usage find.

But, oh ! how faint is every joy
  Where Nature has no part :
New beauties may my eyes employ,
  But you engage my heart.

So restless exiles, as they roam,
  Meet pity everywhere ;
Yet languish for their native home,
  Though death attends them there.

A Sigh

Gentle air, thou breath of lovers,
  Vapour from a secret fire,
Which by thee itself discovers,
  Ere yet daring to aspire.

Softest note of whisper'd anguish,
  Harmony's refined part,
Striking, while thou seem'st to languish,
  Full upon the listener's heart ;

Safest messenger of passion,
  Stealing through a crowd of spies,
Who constrain the outward fashion,
  Close the lips, and watch the eyes :

Shapeless Sigh ! we ne'er can show thee,
  Fram'd but to assault the ear :
Yet, ere to their cost they know thee,
  Every nymph may read thee—here.

On some Snow

that melted on a lady's breast

Those envious flakes came down in haste,
  To prove her breast less fair :
Grieving to find themselves surpass'd,
  Dissolv'd into a tear.

ANONYMOUS (*from "The Merry Musician,"* 1716)

Song

Banish, my Lydia, these sad thoughts,—
  Why sit'st thou musing so,
To hear the ugly rail at faults
  They would, but cannot, do ?
For let the guilt be what it will,
  So small account they bear,
That none yet thought it worth their while
  On such to be severe.

With far more reason thou may'st pine,
  Thyself, for being fair ;
For hadst thou but less glorious been,
  Thou of no faults wouldst hear :
So the great light that shines from far
  Has had its spots set down,
While many a little useless star
  Has not been tax'd with one.

ANONYMOUS (*from Mosse's Miscellany,* 1721)

Song

Ye little Loves, that round her wait,
To bring me tidings of my fate,
As Celia on her pillow lies,
Ah ! gently whisper " Strephon dies."

If this will not her pity move,
And the proud fair disdains to love,
Smile and say " 'Tis all a lie,
And haughty Strephon scorns to die ! "

JOHN OLDMIXON (1673-1742)

Song*

I lately vow'd, but 'twas in haste,
    That I no more would court
The joys which seem, when they are past,
    As dull as they are short.

I oft to hate my mistress swear,
    But soon my weakness find :
I make my oaths, when she's severe,
    And break 'em, when she's kind.

---

* I have not included poems from Oldmixon's volume of 1696.
The text of this song is from *Examen Miscellaneum,* 1702.

ELIZABETH ROWE, *née* SINGER (1674-1737)

A Hymn

In vain the dusky night retires,
   And sullen shadows fly :
In vain the morn with purple light
   Adorns the eastern sky.

In vain the gaudy rising sun
   The wide horizon gilds,
Comes glittering o'er the silver streams,
   And cheers the dewy fields.

In vain, dispensing vernal sweets,
   The morning breezes play :
In vain the birds with cheerful songs
   Salute the new-born day ;

In vain ! unless my Saviour's face
   These gloomy clouds control,
And dissipate the sullen shades
   That press my drooping soul.

O ! visit then Thy servant, Lord,
   With favour from on high ;
Arise, my bright, immortal Sun !
   And all these shades will die.

When, when shall I behold Thy face,
   All radiant and serene,
Without these envious dusky clouds
   That make a veil between ?

When shall that long expected day
   Of sacred vision be,
When my impatient soul shall make
   A near approach to Thee ?

ELIZABETH ROWE

A Laplander's Song to his Mistress *

Shine out, resplendent god of day,
   On my fair Orramoor ;
Her charms thy most propitious ray
   And kindest looks allure.

In mountain, vale, or gloomy grove,
   I'd climb the tallest tree,
Could I from thence my absent love,
   My charming rover see.

I'd venture on a rising cloud,
   Aloft in yielding air ;
From that exalted station proud,
   To view the smiling fair.

Should she in some sequester'd bower,
   Among the branches hide,
I'd tear off every leaf and flower,
   Till she was there descried.

From every bird I'd steal a wing,
   To Orramoor to fly ;
And urg'd by love, would swiftly spring
   Along the lightsome sky.

Return, and bless me with thy charms,
   While yet the sun displays
His fairest beams, and kindly warms
   Us with his vital rays.

Return before the light be gone,
   In which thou shouldst appear ;
Unwelcome night is hast'ning on
   To darken half the year.

* A similar poem is in *The Spectator*. It is described as " from the Lapland Tongue," and has been ascribed to Steele by Anderson. There is also another version by Aaron Hill.

In vain, relentless maid, in vain
    Thou dost a youth forsake,
Whose love shall quickly o'er the plain
    Thy savage flight o'ertake.

Should bars of steel my passage stay,
    They could not thee secure :
I'd through enchantments find a way
    To seize my Orramoor.

NICHOLAS ROWE, Poet Laureate (1674-1718)

The Reconcilement between Jacob Tonson and Mr. Congreve

An imitation of Horace, Book III, Ode IX

TONSON

While at my house in Fleet Street once you lay,
How merrily, dear sir, time pass'd away !
While I partook your wine, your wit, and mirth,
I was the happiest creature on God's yearth.*

CONGREVE

While in your early days of reputation,
You for blue garters had not such a passion ;
While yet you did not use (as now your trade is)
To drink with noble lords, and toast their ladies ;
Thou, Jacob Tonson, wert, to my conceiving,
The cheerfullest, best, honest, fellow living.

TONSON

I'm in with Captain Vanbrugh at the present,
A most sweet-natur'd gentleman, and pleasant ;
He writes your comedies, draws schemes, and models :
And builds dukes' houses upon very odd hills :
For him, so much I dote on him, that I,
If I was sure to go to Heaven, would die.

* Tonson, Sen., his dialect.

CONGREVE

Temple and Dalaval are now my party,
Men that are *tam Mercurio* both *quam Marte ;*
And though for them I shall scarce go to Heaven,
Yet I can drink with them six nights in seven.

TONSON

What if from Van's dear arms I should retire,
And once more warm my bunnians at your fire ;
If I to Bow Street should invite you home,
And set a bed up in my dining room,
Tell me, dear Mr. Congreve, would you come ?

CONGREVE

Though the gay sailor, and the gentle knight,
Were ten times more my joy and heart's delight ;
Though civil persons they, you ruder were,
And had more humours than a dancing-bear ;
Yet for your sake I'd bid 'em both adieu,
And live and die, dear Cob, with only you.

The Contented Shepherd

As on a summer's day
In the greenwood shade I lay,
  The maid that I lov'd,
  As her fancy mov'd,
Came walking forth that way.

And as she passed by
With a scornful glance of her eye,
  What a shame, quoth she,
  For a swain must it be,
Like a lazy loon for to die !

And dost thou nothing heed,
What Pan our god has decreed ;
  What a prize to-day
  Shall be given away,
To the sweetest shepherd's reed ?

There's not a single swain
Of all this fruitful plain,
   But with hopes and fears
   Now busily prepares
The bonny boon to gain.

   Shall another maiden shine
In brighter array than thine ?
   Up, up, dull swain,
   Tune thy pipe once again,
And make the garland mine.

   Alas ! my love, he cried,
What avails this courtly pride ?
   Since thy dear desert
   Is written in my heart,
What is all the world beside ?

   To me thou art more gay
In this homely russet gray,
   Than the nymphs of our green,
   So trim and so sheen,
Or the brightest queen of May.

   What though my fortune frown,
And deny thee a silken gown ;
   My own dear maid,
   Be content with this shade,
And a shepherd all thy own.

Colin's Complaint

Despairing beside a clear stream
   A shepherd forsaken was laid ;
And while a false nymph was his theme,
   A willow supported his head.

The wind that blew over the plain
   To his sighs with a sigh did reply ;
And the brook, in return to his pain,
   Ran mournfully murmuring by.

Alas, silly swain that I was !
   Thus sadly complaining he cried,
When first I beheld that fair face,
   'Twere better by far I had died.
She talk'd, and I bless'd the dear tongue ;
   When she smil'd, 'twas a pleasure too great ;
I listen'd, and cried, when she sung,
   Was nightingale ever so sweet ?

How foolish was I to believe
   She could doat on so lowly a clown,
Or that her fond heart would not grieve,
   To forsake the fine folk of the town ?
To think that a beauty so gay,
   So kind and so constant would prove ;
Or go clad like our maidens in gray,
   Or live in a cottage on love ?

What though I have skill to complain,
   Though the Muses my temples have crown'd ;
What though when they hear my soft strain,
   The virgins sit weeping around.
Ah, Colin, thy hopes are in vain,
   Thy pipe and thy laurel resign ;
Thy false one inclines to a swain,
   Whose music is sweeter than thine.

And you, my companions so dear,
   Who sorrow to see me betray'd,
Whatever I suffer, forbear,
   Forbear to accuse the false maid.

Though through the wide world I should range,
    'Tis in vain from my fortune to fly ;
'Twas hers to be false and to change,
    'Tis mine to be constant and die.

If while my hard fate I sustain,
    In her breast any pity is found,
Let her come with her nymphs of the plain,
    And see me laid low in the ground.
The last humble boon that I crave,
    Is to shade me with Cypress and Yew ;
And when she looks down on my grave,
    Let her own that her shepherd was true.

Then to her new love let her go,
    And deck her in golden array,
Be finest at every fine show,
    And frolic it all the long day ;
While Colin, forgotten and gone,
    No more shall be talk'd of, or seen,
Unless when beneath the pale moon,
    His ghost shall glide over the green.

The Rev. ISAAC WATTS, D.D. (1674-1748)

Divine Songs for Children

I

Against Quarrelling and Fighting

Let dogs delight to bark and bite,
    For God has made them so ;
Let bears and lions growl and fight,
    For 'tis their nature too.

But, children, you should never let
    Such angry passions rise ;
Your little hands were never made
    To tear each other's eyes.

Let love through all your actions run,
　And all your words be mild ;
Live like the blessed Virgin's son,
　That sweet and lovely child.

His soul was gentle as a lamb ;
　And as His stature grew,
He grew in favour both with man
　And God His Father too.

Now Lord of all He reigns above,
　And from His Heavenly throne
He sees what children dwell in love,
　And marks them for His own.

II

Against Idleness and Mischief

How doth the little busy bee
　Improve each shining hour,
And gather honey all the day
　From every opening flower ?

How skilfully she builds her cell !
　How neat she spreads the wax !
And labours hard to store it well
　With the sweet food she makes.

In works of labour or of skill,
　I would be busy too ;
For Satan finds some mischief still
　For idle hands to do.

In books, or work, or healthful play,
　Let my first years be past,
That I may give for every day
　Some good account at last.

III

A Morning Song

My God, who mak'st the sun to know
　His proper hour to rise,
And to give light to all below,
　Dost send him round the skies.

When from the chambers of the east
　His morning race begins,
He never tires, nor stops to rest,
　But round the world he shines.

So, like the sun, would I fulfil
　The business of the day ;
Begin my work betimes, and still
　March on my heavenly way.

Give me, O Lord, Thy early grace,
　Nor let my soul complain
That the young morning of my days
　Has all been spent in vain.

The Sluggard

'Tis the voice of the sluggard ; I hear him complain,
" You have wak'd me too soon, I must slumber again."
As the door on its hinges, so he on his bed,
Turns his sides and his shoulders and his heavy head.

" A little more sleep and a little more slumber " ;
Thus he wastes half his days, and his hours without number ;
And when he gets up, he sits folding his hands,
Or walks about sauntering, or trifling he stands.

I pass'd by his garden, and saw the wild briar,
The thorn and the thistle grow broader and higher ;
His clothes that hang on him are turning to rags :
And his money still wastes till he starves or he begs.

I made him a visit, still hoping to find
He had took better care for improving his mind :
He told me his dreams, talk'd of eating and drinking ;
But he scarce reads his Bible and never loves thinking.

Said I then to my heart, " Here's a lesson to me :
That man's but a picture of what I might be ;
But thanks to my friends for their care in my breeding,
Who taught me betimes to love working and reading."

A Cradle Hymn

Hush, my dear, lie still and slumber,
    Holy Angels guard thy bed !
Heavenly blessings without number
    Gently falling on thy head.

Sleep, my babe ; thy food and raiment,
    House and home thy friends provide ;
All without thy care or payment
    All thy wants are well supplied.

How much better thou'rt attended
    Than the Son of God could be,
When from Heaven He descended,
    And became a child like thee.

Soft and easy is thy cradle :
    Coarse and hard thy Saviour lay :
When His birthplace was a stable,
    And His softest bed was hay.

Blessed Babe ! what glorious features,
    Spotless fair, divinely bright !
Must He dwell with brutal creatures ?
    How could angels bear the sight ?

Was there nothing but a manger
    Cursed sinners could afford,
To receive the heavenly stranger ?
    Did they thus affront their Lord ?

Soft, my child ; I did not chide thee,
   Though my song might sound too hard ;
'Tis thy mother sits beside thee,
   And her arms shall be thy guard.

Yet to read the shameful story,
   How the Jews abus'd their King,
How they serv'd the Lord of Glory,
   Makes me angry while I sing.

See the kinder shepherds round Him,
   Telling wonders from the sky !
Where they sought Him, there they found Him,
   With His virgin mother by.

See the lovely babe a-dressing ;
   Lovely infant, how He smil'd !
When He wept, the mother's blessing
   Sooth'd and hush'd the holy child.

Lo, He slumbers in His manger,
   Where the horned oxen fed ;
Peace, my darling, here's no danger,
   Here's no ox a-near thy bed.

'Twas to save thee, child, from dying,
   Save my dear from burning flame,
Bitter groans and endless crying,
   That thy blest Redeemer came.

May'st thou live to know and fear Him,
   Trust and love Him all thy days ;
Then go dwell for ever near Him,
   See His face, and sing His praise !

I could give thee thousand kisses,
   Hoping what I most desire ;
Not a mother's fondest wishes
   Can to greater joys aspire.

ISAAC WATTS

The Day of Judgment

An Ode Attempted in English Sapphic

When the fierce north wind with his airy forces
Rears up the Baltic to a foaming fury ;
And the red lightning with a storm of hail comes
        Rushing amain down.

How the poor sailors stand amaz'd and tremble !
While the hoarse thunder, like a bloody trumpet,
Roars a loud onset to the gaping waters
        Quick to devour them.

Such shall the noise be, and the wild disorder,
(If things eternal may be like these earthly)
Such the dire terror, when the great Archangel
        Shakes the creation ;

Tears the strong pillars of the vault of Heaven,
Breaks up old marble, the repose of princes ;
See the graves open, and the bones arising,
        Flames all around 'em !

Hark, the shrill outcries of the guilty wretches !
Lively bright horror, and amazing anguish,
Stare through their eyelids, while the living worm lies
        Gnawing within them.

Thoughts, like old vultures, prey upon their heart-strings,
And the smart twinges, when the eye beholds the
Lofty Judge frowning, and a flood of vengeance
        Rolling afore Him.

Hopeless Immortals ! how they scream and shiver,
While devils push them to the pit wide-yawning,
Hideous and gloomy, to receive them headlong
        Down to the centre.

Stop here, my fancy : (all away, ye horrid
Doleful ideas,) come, arise to Jesus ;
How He sits God-like ! and the saints around Him
           Thron'd, yet adoring !

O may I sit there when He comes triumphant,
Dooming the nations ! then ascend to glory,
While our hosannas all along the passage
           Shout the Redeemer.

False Greatness

Mylo, forbear to call him blest
That only boasts a large estate,
Should all the treasures of the West
Meet and conspire to make him great.
I know thy better thoughts, I know
Thy reason can't descend so low.
Let a broad stream with golden sands
   Through all his meadows roll,
He's but a wretch, with all his lands,
   That wears a narrow soul.

He swells amid his wealthy store,
And proudly poising what he weighs,
In his own scale he fondly lays
   Huge heaps of shining ore.
He spreads the balance wide to hold
   His manors and his farms,
And cheats the beam with loads of gold
   He hugs between his arms.
So might the plough-boy climb a tree,
   When Crœsus mounts his throne,
And both stand up, and smile to see
   How long their shadow's grown.
Alas ! how vain their fancies be
   To think that shape their own !

Thus mingled still with wealth and state
Crœsus himself can never know ;
His true dimensions and his weight
Are far inferior to their show.
Were I so tall to reach the Pole,
Or grasp the ocean with my span,
I must be measur'd by my soul :
The Mind's the standard of the Man.

Man Frail and God Eternal

Psalm XC, verses 1-5

Our God, our help in ages past,
   Our hope for years to come,
Our shelter from the stormy blast,
   And our eternal home.

Under the shadow of Thy throne
   Thy Saints have dwelt secure ;
Sufficient is Thine arm alone,
   And our defence is sure.

Before the hills in order stood
   Or earth receiv'd her frame,
From everlasting Thou art God,
   To endless years the same.

Thy word commands our flesh to dust,
   " Return, ye sons of men " :
All nations rose from earth at first,
   And turn to earth again.

A thousand ages in Thy sight
   Are like an evening gone ;
Short as the watch that ends the night
   Before the rising sun.

The busy tribes of flesh and blood
  With all their lives and cares
Are carried downwards by Thy flood,
  And lost in following years.

Time like an ever-rolling stream
  Bears all its sons away ;
They fly forgotten as a dream
  Dies at the opening day.

Like flowery fields the nations stand
  Pleas'd with the morning-light ;
The flowers, beneath the Mower's hand,
  Lie withering e'er 'tis night.

Our God, our help in ages past,
  Our hope for years to come,
Be Thou our guard while troubles last,
  And our eternal home.

AMBROSE PHILIPS (1675 ?-1749)

To Miss Margaret Pulteney

Daughter of Daniel Pulteney, Esq , in the nursery

Dimply damsel, sweetly smiling,
All caressing, none beguiling,
Bud of beauty, fairly blowing,
Every charm to nature owing,
This and that new thing admiring,
Much of this and that enquiring,
Knowledge by degrees attaining,
Day by day some virtue gaining,
Ten years hence, when I leave chiming,
Beardless poets, fondly rhyming,
(Fescu'd now, perhaps in spelling,)
On thy riper beauties dwelling,
Shall accuse each killing feature
Of the cruel charming creature,
Whom I knew complying, willing,
Tender, and averse to killing.

AMBROSE PHILIPS

To Miss Charlotte Pulteney
in her mother's arms, May 1, 1724

Timely blossom, infant fair,
Fondling of a happy pair,
Every morn, and every night,
Their solicitous delight,
Sleeping, waking, still at ease,
Pleasing without skill to please ;
Little gossip, blithe and hale,
Tattling many a broken tale,
Singing many a tuneless song,
Lavish of a heedless tongue ;
Simple maiden, void of art,
Babbling out the very heart,
Yet abandon'd to thy will,
Yet imagining no ill,
Yet too innocent to blush ;
Like the linlet in the bush,
To the mother linnet's note
Moduling her slender throat,
Chirping forth thy petty joys ;
Wanton in the change of toys,
Like the linnet green, in May,
Flitting to each bloomy spray ;
Wearied then, and glad to rest,
Like the linlet in the nest.
This thy present happy lot,
This, in time, will be forgot :
Other pleasures, other cares,
Ever-busy Time prepares ;
And thou shalt in thy daughter see,
This picture, once, resembled thee.

In Answer to the Question, What is Thought ?

The hermit's solace in his cell,
The fire that warms the poet's brain,
The lover's heaven, or his hell,
The madman's sport, the wise man's pain.

79

Song

From White's and Will's
To purling rills
The love-sick Strephon flies ;
There, full of woe,
His numbers flow,
And all in rhyme he dies.

The fair coquet,
With feign'd regret,
Invites him back to town ;
But, when in tears
The youth appears,
She meets him with a frown.

Full oft the maid
This prank had play'd,
Till angry Strephon swore,
And, what is strange,
Though loth to change,
Would never see her more.

Song

Why we love, and why we hate,
    Is not granted us to know ;
Random chance, or wilful fate,
    Guides the shaft from Cupid's bow.

If on me Zelinda frown,
    Madness 'tis in me to grieve :
Since her will is not her own,
    Why should I uneasy live ?

If I for Zelinda die,
    Deaf to poor Mizella's cries,
Ask me not the reason why :
    Seek the riddle in the skies.

AMBROSE PHILIPS

On his Lute

(*From the first ode of Anacreon*)

The line of Atreus will I sing ;
To Cadmus will I tune the string :
But, as from string to string I move,
My lute will only sound of love.

The chords I change through every screw,
And model the whole lute anew ;
Once more in song my voice I raise,
And, Hercules, thy toils I praise :
My lute does still my voice deny,
And in the tones of love reply.
Ye heroes, then, at once farewell :
Loves only echo from my shell.

Song

(*From Sappho*)

Bless'd as th' immortal Gods is he,
The youth who fondly sits by thee ;
And hears and sees thee, all the while,
Softly speak and sweetly smile.

'Twas this depriv'd my soul of rest,
And rais'd such tumults in my breast ;
For, while I gaz'd, in transport toss'd,
My breath was gone, my voice was lost.

My bosom glow'd, the subtle flame
Ran quick through all my vital frame ;
O'er my dim eyes a darkness hung ;
My ears with hollow murmurs rung.

In dewy damps my limbs were chill'd ;
My blood with gentle horrors thrill'd ;
My feeble pulse forgot to play ;
I fainted, sunk, and died away.

WILLIAM SOMERVILLE (1675-1742)

Address to his Elbow-chair,
new-clothed

My dear companion, and my faithful friend !
If Orpheus taught the listening oaks to bend ;
If stones and rubbish, at Amphion's call,
Danc'd into form, and built the Theban wall,
Why shouldst not thou attend my humble lays,
And hear my grateful harp resound thy praise ?

   True, thou art spruce and fine, a very beau ;
But what are trappings and external show ?
To real worth alone I make my court ;
Knaves are my scorn, and coxcombs are my sport.
Once I beheld thee far less trim and gay,
Ragged, disjointed, and to worms a prey ;
The safe retreat of every lurking mouse ;
Derided, shunn'd ; the lumber of my house.
Thy robe how chang'd from what it was before !
Thy velvet robe, which pleas'd my sires of yore !
'Tis thus capricious Fortune wheels us round ;
Aloft we mount—then tumble to the ground.
Yet grateful then, my constancy I prov'd ;
I knew thy worth ; my friend in rags I lov'd :
I lov'd thee more ; nor, like a courtier, spurn'd
My benefactor when the tide was turn'd.
With conscious shame, yet frankly, I confess
That in my youthful days—I lov'd thee less.
Where vanity, where pleasure call'd, I stray'd,
And every wayward appetite obey'd ;
But sage Experience taught me how to prize
Myself, and how this world : she bade me rise
To nobler flights, regardless of a race
Of factious emmets ; pointed where to place
My bliss, and lodg'd me in thy soft embrace.

   Here on thy yielding down I sit secure,
And, patiently, what Heaven has sent endure ;
From all the futile cares of business free,

Not fond of life, but yet content to be ;
Here mark the fleeting hours, regret the past,
And seriously prepare to meet the last.

So safe on shore the pension'd sailor lies,
And all the malice of the storm defies ;
With ease of body bless'd, and peace of mind,
Pities the restless crew he left behind ;
Whilst in his cell he meditates alone
On his great voyage to the world unknown.

On Presenting to a Lady a White Rose and a Red,
on the tenth of June

If this pale rose offend your sight,
   It in your bosom wear,
'Twill blush to find itself less white,
   And turn Lancastrian there.

But, Celia, should the red be chose,
   With gay vermilion bright,
'Twould sicken at each blush that glows,
   And in despair turn white.

Let politicians idly prate,
   Their Babels build in vain ;
As uncontrollable as Fate
   Imperial Love shall reign.

Each haughty faction shall obey,
   And Whigs and Tories join,
Submit to your despotic sway,
   Confess your right divine.

Yet, this, my gracious Monarch ! own,
   They're tyrants that oppress ;
'Tis mercy must support your throne,
   And 'tis like Heaven to bless.

? The Rev. JABEZ EARLE, D.D. (1676-1768)

On the Duchess of Queensberry and her Sister*

Stella and Flavia, every hour,
    Do various hearts surprise ;
In Stella's soul lies all her power,
    And Flavia's in her eyes.

More boundless Flavia's conquests are,
    And Stella's more confin'd ;
All can discern a face that's fair,
    But few a lovely mind.

Stella, like Britain's monarch, reigns
    O'er cultivated lands ;
Like eastern tyrants Flavia deigns
    To rule o'er barren sands.

Then boast, fair Flavia, boast thy face,
    Thy beauties' only store ;
Thy charms will every day decrease,
    Each day gives Stella more.

JOHN HUGHES (1677-1720)

From the French

I die with too transporting joy,
    If she I love rewards my fire ;
If she's inexorably coy,
    With too much passion I expire.

No way the fates afford to shun
    The cruel torment I endure ;
Since I am doom'd to be undone
    By the disease or by the cure.

* This poem has also been attributed, erroneously, to Mrs. Barber and to Mrs. Pilkington. Earle's authorship is not quite certain, but it seems probable. I must admit, however, that none of Earle's acknowledged verse is nearly so well written as this little poem. For the evidence as to this attribution see *The London Mercury* for March 1922.

JOHN HUGHES

The Fair Traveller

In young Astrea's sparkling eye
    Resistless Love has fix'd his throne ;
A thousand lovers bleeding lie
    For her, with wounds they fear to own,
While the coy beauty speeds her flight
    To distant groves from whence she came.
So lightning vanishes from sight,
    But leaves the forest in a flame.

*Song**

Would you gain the tender creature,
Softly—gently—kindly—treat her !
    Suff'ring is the lover's part :
Beauty by constraint possessing,
You enjoy but half the blessing,
    Listless charms without the heart.

Song

Thy origin's divine, I see,
Of mortal race thou canst not be ;
Thy lip a ruby lustre shows ;
Thy purple cheek outshines the rose,
And thy bright eye is brighter far,
Than any planet, any star.
Thy sordid way of life despise,
Above thy slavery, Silvia, rise ;
Display thy beauteous form and mien,
And grow a goddess, or a queen.

On Archeanassa of Colophon
(*From the Greek of Plato, or of Asclepiades*)

Archeanassa's charms inspire
Within my breast a lover's fire ;
Age, its feeble spite displaying,
    Vainly wrinkles all her face,

* This song also occurs in " Acis and Galatea " and may be by Gay.

Cupids, in each wrinkle playing,
   Charm my eyes with lasting grace :
But, before old Time pursu'd her,
   Ere he sunk these little caves,
How I pity those who view'd her,
   And in youth were made her slaves !

GEORGE FARQUHAR (1678-1707)

Song

Tell me, Aurelia, tell me pray,
   How long must Damon sue ?
Prefix the time, and I'll obey,
With patience wait the happy day
   That makes me sure of you.

The sails of time my sighs shall blow,
   And make the minutes glide ;
My tears shall make the current flow,
   And swell the hastening tide.

The wings of love shall fly so fast,
   My hopes mount so sublime ;
The wings of love shall make more haste
   Than the swift wings of time.

A Song on a Trifle

A trifling song you shall hear,
   Begun with a trifle and ended :
All trifling people draw near,
   And I shall be nobly attended.

Were it not for trifles a few,
   That lately have come into play,
The men would want something to do,
   And the women want something to say.

GEORGE FARQUHAR

What makes men trifle in dressing ?
   Because the ladies, they know,
Admire, by often possessing,
   That eminent trifle, a Beau.

When the lover his moments has trifled,
   The trifle of trifles to gain,
No sooner the virgin is rifled
   But a trifle shall part them again.

What mortal man would be able
   At White's half-an-hour to sit ?
Or who could bear a tea-table,
   Without talking trifles for wit ?

The Court is from trifles secure,
   Gold Keys are no trifles, we see ;
White Rods are no trifles, I'm sure,
   Whatever their bearers may be.

But if you will go to the place,
   Where trifles abundantly breed,
The *Levée* will show you his Grace
   Makes promises trifles indeed !

A coach with six footmen behind
   I count neither trifle nor sin
But, ye gods ! how oft do we find
   A scandalous trifle within !

A flask of champagne, people think it
   A trifle, or something as bad ;
But if you'll contrive how to drink it,
   You'll find it no trifle, by gad !

A parson's a trifle at sea,
   A widow's a trifle in sorrow ;
A Peace is a trifle to-day :
   Who knows what may happen to-morrow ?

A Black Coat a trifle may cloak,
   Or to hide it the Red may endeavour ;
But if once the Army is broke,
   We shall then have more trifles than ever.

The stage is a trifle, they say ;
   The reason pray carry along,
Because at ev'ry new play
   The house they with trifles so throng.

But with people's malice to trifle,
   And to set us all on a foot ;
The author of this is a trifle,
   And his song is a trifle to boot.

Mrs. CATHARINE COCKBURN (*née* TROTTER)

(1679-1749)

The Vain Advice

Ah, gaze not on those eyes ! forbear
   That soft enchanting voice to hear :
Not looks of basilisks give surer death,
Nor Syrens sing with more destructive breath.

Fly, if thy freedom thou'dst maintain,
   Alas ! I feel th' advice is vain !
A heart, whose safety but in flight does lie,
Is too far lost to have the power to fly.

The Rev. ABEL EVANS, D.D. (1679-1737)

On Blenheim House *

See, Sir, here's the grand approach,
This way is for his Grace's coach ;
There lies the bridge, and here's the clock :
Observe the lion, and the cock,
The spacious court, the colonnade,
And mark how wide the hall is made !
The chimneys are so well design'd,
They never smoke in any wind.
This gallery's contriv'd for walking,
The windows to retire and talk in ;
The council-chamber for debate,
And all the rest are rooms of state.

Thanks, Sir, cried I, 'tis very fine,
But where d'ye sleep, and where d'ye dine ?
I find by all you have been telling,
That 'tis a house, but not a dwelling.

Epitaph on Sir John Vanbrugh

Under this stone, reader, survey
Dead Sir John Vanbrugh's house of clay.
Lie heavy on him, Earth ! for he
Laid many heavy loads on thee !

On Dr. Tadlow

a very fat man

When Tadlow walks the streets, the paviours cry,
" God bless you, Sir ! " and lay their rammers by.

* This is sometimes attributed to Pope.

Song

When thy beauty appears
In its graces and airs,
All bright as an angel new dropt from the sky ;
   At distance I gaze, and am aw'd by my fears,
   So strangely you dazzle my eye !

But when without art
Your kind thoughts you impart,
When your love runs in blushes through every vein ;
   When it darts from your eyes, when it pants in your heart,
   Then I know you're a woman again.

There's a passion and pride
In our sex (she replied)
And thus (might I gratify both) I would do :
   Still an angel appear to each lover beside,
   But still be a woman to you.

Song

Thyrsis, a young and am'rous swain,
Saw two, the beauties of the plain ;
   Who both his heart subdue :
Gay Cœlia's eyes were dazzling fair,
Sabina's easy shape and air
   With softer magic drew.

He haunts the stream, he haunts the grove,
Lives in a fond romance of love,
   And seems for each to die ;
Till each a little spiteful grown,
Sabina Cœlia's shape ran down,
   And she Sabina's eye.

Their envy made the shepherd find
Those eyes, which only love could blind,
　So set the lover free ;
No more he haunts the grove or stream,
Or with a true-love knot and name
　Engraves a wounded tree.

" Ah Cœlia ! " sly Sabina cried,
" Though neither love, we're both denied ;
Now, to support the sex's pride,
　Let either fix the dart."
" Poor girl ! " says Cœlia, " say no more ;
For should the swain but one adore,
That spite which broke his chains before,
　Would break the other's heart."

Song

My days have been so wondrous free,
　The little birds that fly
With careless ease from tree to tree,
　Were but as bless'd as I.

Ask gliding waters, if a tear
　Of mine increas'd their stream ?
Or ask the flying gales, if e'er
　I lent one sigh to them ?

But now my former days retire,
　And I'm by beauty caught,
The tender chains of sweet desire
　Are fix'd upon my thought.

Ye nightingales, ye twisting pines !
　Ye swains that haunt the grove !
Ye gentle echoes, breezy winds !
　Ye close retreats of love !

With all of nature, all of art,
   Assist the dear design ;
O teach a young, unpractis'd heart,
   To make my Nancy mine.

The very thought of change I hate,
   As much as of despair ;
Nor ever covet to be great,
   Unless it be for her.

'Tis true, the passion in my mind
   Is mix'd with soft distress ;
Yet while the fair I love is kind,
   I cannot wish it less.

An Elegy to an Old Beauty

In vain, poor nymph, to please our youthful sight
You sleep in cream and frontlets all the night,
Your face with patches soil, with paint repair,
Dress with gay gowns, and shade with foreign hair.
If truth in spite of manners must be told,
Why really, fifty-five is something old.

Once you were young ; or one, whose life's so long,
She might have born my mother, tells me wrong.
And once (since envy's dead before you die)
The women own you play'd a sparkling eye,
Taught the light foot a modish little trip,
And pouted with the prettiest purple lip. . . .

To some new charmer are the roses fled,
Which blew to damask all thy cheek with red ;
Youth calls the Graces there to fix their reign,
And Airs by thousands fill their easy train.
So parting summer bids her flowery prime
Attend the sun to dress some foreign clime,
While withering seasons in succession, here,
Strip the gay gardens, and deform the year.

But thou (since nature bids) the world resign,
'Tis now thy daughter's daughter's time to shine.
With more address (or such as pleases more)
She runs her female exercises o'er,
Unfurls or closes, raps or turns the fan,
And smiles, or blushes at the creature man.
With quicker life, as gilded coaches pass,
In sideling courtesy she drops the glass ;
With better strength, on visit-days she bears
To mount her fifty flights of ample stairs.
Her mien, her shape, her temper, eyes and tongue
Are sure to conquer—for the rogue is young ;
And all that's madly wild, or oddly gay,
We call it only pretty Fanny's way.

Let time that makes you homely, make you sage,
The sphere of wisdom is the sphere of age.
'Tis true, when beauty dawns with early fire,
And hears the flattering tongues of soft desire,
If not from virtue, from its gravest ways
The soul with pleasing avocation strays.
But beauty gone, 'tis easier to be wise ;
As harpers better, by the loss of eyes.

Henceforth retire, reduce your roving airs,
Haunt less the plays, and more the public prayers,
Reject the Mechlin head, and gold brocade,
Go pray, in sober Norwich crape array'd.
Thy pendent diamonds let thy Fanny take,
(Their trembling lustre shows how much you shake ;)
Or bid her wear thy necklace row'd with pearl,
You'll find your Fanny an obedient girl.
So for the rest, with less encumbrance hung,
You walk through life, unmingled with the young ;
And view the shade and substance as you pass
With joint endeavour trifling at the glass,
Or Folly dress'd, and rambling all her days,
To meet her counterpart, and grow by praise :
Yet still sedate yourself, and gravely plain,
You neither fret, nor envy at the vain.

'Twas thus (if man with woman we compare)
The wise Athenian cross'd a glittering fair.
Unmov'd by tongues and sights, he walk'd the place,
Through tape, toys, tinsel, gimp, perfume, and lace ;
Then bends from Mars's hill his awful eyes,
And *What a world I never want !* he cries ;
But cries unheard : for folly will be free.
So parts the buzzing gaudy crowd and he :
As careless he for them, as they for him ;
He wrapt in wisdom, and they whirl'd by whim.

A Night-Piece on Death

By the blue taper's trembling light,
No more I waste the wakeful night,
Intent with endless view to pore
The Schoolmen and the Sages o'er :
Their books from wisdom widely stray,
Or point at best the longest way.
I'll seek a readier path, and go
Where wisdom's surely taught below.

How deep yon azure dyes the sky !
Where orbs of gold unnumber'd lie,
While through their ranks in silver pride
The nether crescent seems to glide.
The slumb'ring breeze forgets to breathe,
The lake is smooth and clear beneath,
Where once again the spangled show
Descends to meet our eyes below.
The grounds which on the right aspire,
In dimness from the view retire :
The left presents a place of graves,
Whose wall the silent water laves ;
That steeple guides thy doubtful sight
Among the livid gleams of night.
There pass with melancholy state,
By all the solemn heaps of fate,

And think, as softly-sad you tread
Above the venerable dead,
Time was, like thee they life possest,
And time shall be, that thou shalt rest.

Those graves, with bending osier bound,
That nameless heave the crumbled ground,
Quick to the glancing thought disclose
Where *Toil* and *Poverty* repose.

The flat smooth stones that bear a name,
The chisel's slender help to fame,
(Which e'er our set of friends decay
Their frequent steps may wear away,)
A *middle race* of mortals own,
Men, half ambitious, all unknown.

The marble tombs that rise on high,
Whose dead in vaulted arches lie,
Whose pillars swell with sculptur'd stones,
Arms, angels, epitaphs and bones,
These (all the poor remains of state)
Adorn the *Rich*, or praise the *Great ;*
Who while on earth in fame they live,
Are senseless of the fame they give.

Ha ! while I gaze, pale Cynthia fades,
The bursting earth unveils the shades !
All slow, and wan, and wrapp'd in shrouds,
They rise in visionary crowds,
And all with sober accent cry,
Think, Mortal, what it is to die.

Now from yon black and fun'ral yew
That bathes the charnel house with dew,
Methinks I hear a voice begin ;
(Ye ravens, cease your croaking din,

Ye toiling clocks, no time resound
O'er the long lake and midnight ground),
It sends a peal of hollow groans,
Thus speaking from among the bones.

" When men my scythe and darts supply,
How great a King of Fears am I !
They view me like the last of things :
They make, and then they dread, my stings.
Fools ! if you less provok'd your fears,
No more my spectre-form appears.
Death's but a path that must be trod,
If man would ever pass to God :
A port of calms, a state of ease
From the rough rage of swelling seas.

" Why then thy flowing sable stoles,
Deep pendent cypress, mourning poles,
Loose scarfs to fall athwart thy weeds,
Long palls, drawn hearses, cover'd steeds,
And plumes of black, that, as they tread,
Nod o'er the 'scutcheons of the dead ?

" Nor can the parted body know,
Nor wants the soul, these forms of woe :
As men who long in prison dwell,
With lamps that glimmer round the cell,
Whene'er their suffering years are run,
Spring forth to greet the glitt'ring sun :
Such joy, though far transcending sense,
Have pious souls at parting hence.
On earth, and in the body plac'd,
A few, and evil, years they waste :
But when their chains are cast aside,
See the glad scene unfolding wide,
Clap the glad wing and tow'r away,
And mingle with the blaze of day."

THOMAS BREREWOOD (*died* 1748)

Autumn

Though the seasons must alter, ah ! yet let me find
    What all must confess to be rare,
A female still cheerful, and faithful and kind,
    The blessings of autumn to share.

Let one side of our cottage a flourishing vine
    O'erspread with its branches and shade ;
Whose clusters appear more transparent and fine,
    As its leaves are beginning to fade.

When the fruit makes the branches bend down with its
       load,
    In our orchard surrounded with pales :
In a bed of clean straw let our apples be stow'd,
    For a tart that in winter regales.

When the vapours that rise from the earth in the morn
    Seem to hang on its surface like smoke,
Till dispers'd by the sun that gilds over the corn,
    Within doors let us prattle and joke.

But when we see clear all the hues of the leaves,
    And at work in the fields all the hands,
Some in reaping the wheat, others binding the sheaves,
    Let us carelessly stroll o'er the lands.

How pleasing the sight of the toiling they make,
    To collect what kind nature has sent !
Heaven grant we may not of their labour partake ;
    But, O ! give us their happy content.

And sometimes on a bank, under shade, by a brook,
    Let us silently sit at our ease,
And there gaze on the stream, till the fish on the hook
    Struggles hard to procure its release.

THOMAS BREREWOOD

And now when the husbandman sings harvest home,
  And the corn's all got into the house ;
When the long wish'd for time of their meeting is come,
  To frolic, and feast, and carouse :

When the leaves from the trees are begun to be shed,
  And are leaving the branches all bare,
Either strew'd at the roots, shrivell'd, wither'd, and dead,
  Or else blown to and fro in the air :

When the ways are so miry, that bogs they might seem,
  And the axle-tree's ready to break ;
While the waggoner whistles in stopping his team,
  And then claps the poor jades on the neck :

In the morning let's follow the cry of the hounds,
  Or the fearful young covey beset ;
Which, though skulking in stubble and weeds on the ground,
  Are becoming a prey to the net.

Let's enjoy all the pleasure retirement affords,
  Still amus'd with these innocent sports,
Nor once envy the pomp of fine ladies and lords,
  With their grand entertainments at courts.

In the evening when lovers are leaning on stiles,
  Deep engag'd in some amorous chat,
And 'tis very well known by his grin, and her smiles,
  What they both have a mind to be at ;

To our dwelling, though homely, well-pleas'd to repair,
  Let our mutual endearments revive,
And let no single action, or look, but declare
  How contented and happy we live.

Should ideas arise that may ruffle the soul,
  Let soft music the phantoms remove,
For 'tis harmony only has force to control
  And unite all the passions in love.

With her eyes but half open, her cap all awry,
   When the lass is preparing for bed ;
And the sleepy dull clown, who sits nodding just by,
   Sometimes rouses and scratches his head ;

In the night when 'tis cloudy and rainy and dark,
   And the labourers snore as they lie,
Not a noise to disturb us, unless a dog bark
   In the farm, or the village hard by ;

At the time of sweet rest, and of quiet like this,
   Ere our eyes are clos'd up in their lids,
Let us welcome the season, and taste of that bliss,
   Which the sunshine and daylight forbids.

BARTON BOOTH* (1681-1733)

Song

Am I then condemn'd by Love,
Still to wander, still to rove ;
Ever searching, never finding,
Hearing, swearing oaths not binding ;
Still pursuing, still astray,
Hunting truth that flies away ?

Yet I the chase can never leave,
But still my own fond hopes deceive :
Till Mira, soft, inviting fair !
   By Nature form'd to bless my arms,
Shall stop me in my full career,
   A victim to her friendly charms ;
Observe her blushes, and her sighs,
Mark not her words, but watch her eyes !

* A well-known actor,

Truth is in her tender breast ;
   Her looks are sweet, and full of love ;
My soul in her alone would rest,
   Nor any further trial prove :
But if my wish I fail to gain,
   No disappointment I'll deplore ;
But swear, and lie, and still remain
   The wand'ring thing I was before.

WILLIAM BEDINGFIELD (fl. 1720)

*Beauty**

An Ode

Fair rival of the god of day,
Beauty, to thy celestial ray
   A thousand sprightly fruits we owe :
Gay wit, and moving eloquence,
And every art t' improve the sense,
   And every grace that shines below.

Not Phœbus does our songs inspire,
Nor did Cylenius form the lyre ;
   'Tis thou art music's living spring :
To thee the poet tunes his lays,
And sweetly warbling Beauty's praise,
   Describes the power that makes him sing.

Painters from thee their skill derive,
By thee their works to ages live,
   For when thy shadows give surprise,—
As when we view in crystal streams,
The morning sun, and rising beams,
   That seem to shoot from other skies,—

* This poem was attributed to John Hughes, in the post-humous editions of his work. This was, I think, an error. The present attribution is that in Anthony Hammond's Miscellany, 1720.

WILLIAM BEDINGFIELD

Enchanting vision ! who can be
Unmov'd, that turns his eyes on thee ?
    Yet brighter still thy glories shine,
And double charms thy power improve,
When Beauty dress'd in smiles of love
    Grows like its parent Heaven divine.

ELIJAH FENTON (1683-1730)

To a Lady Sitting Before Her Glass

So smooth and clear the fountain was,
    In which his face Narcissus spied,
When, gazing in that liquid glass,
    He for himself despair'd and died :
Nor, Chloris, can you safer see
Your own perfections here than he.

The lark before the mirror plays,
    Which some deceitful swain has set,
Pleas'd with herself she fondly stays
    To die deluded in the net !
Love may such frauds for you prepare,
Yourself the captive, and the snare.

But, Chloris, whilst you there review
    Those graces opening in their bloom,
Think how disease and age pursue,
    Your riper glories to consume :
Then sighing you would wish your glass
Could show to Chloris what she was.

Let Pride no more give Nature law,
   But free the youth your power enslaves :
Her form, like yours, bright Cynthia saw
   Reflected in the crystal waves,
Yet priz'd not all her charms above
The pleasure of Endymion's love.

No longer let your glass supply
   Too just an emblem of your breast ;
Where oft to my deluded eye
   Love's image has appear'd imprest ;
But play'd so lightly on your mind,
It left no lasting print behind.

The Rose

See, Sylvia, see, this new-blown rose,
   The image of thy blush,
Mark how it smiles upon the bush,
   And triumphs as it grows.
" Oh, pluck it not ! we'll come anon,"
Thou say'st. Alas ! 'twill then be gone.
   Now its purple beauty's spread ;
Soon it will drop and fall,
And soon it will not be at all ;
   No fine things draw a length of thread.
Then tell me, seems it not to say,
" Come on, and crop me whilst you may ? "

ANONYMOUS POEMS

From Miscellaneous Poems (1726)
Edited by David Lewis* (1683 ?-1760), *some of them possibly by him*

Translation from the Ancient British

(*Song to Winifreda*)

Away ! let nought to Love displeasing,
    My Winifreda, move your care ;
Let nought delay the heavenly blessing,
    Nor squeamish pride, nor gloomy fear.

What though no grants of royal donors
    With pompous titles grace our blood :
We'll shine in more substantial honours,
    And to be noble, we'll be good.

Our name, while virtue thus we tender,
    Will sweetly sound where'er 'tis spoke :
And all the great ones, they shall wonder
    How they respect such little folk !

What though from Fortune's lavish bounty
    No mighty treasures we possess :
We'll find, within our pittance, plenty,
    And be content, without excess.

Still shall each kind returning season
    Sufficient for our wishes give ;
For we will live a life of reason,
    And that's the only life to live !

Through youth and age, in love excelling,
    We'll hand in hand together tread ;
Sweet-smiling Peace shall crown our dwelling,
    And babes, sweet-smiling babes, our bed.

* It seems to me possible that David Lewis was one of the greatest of our unknown poets. He was a Welshman and may quite well have written a translation " from the ancient British," to say nothing of some others of these charming anonymous poems. A poem known to be by him is quoted in Boswell's Johnson.

How should I love the pretty creatures,
  While round my knees they fondly clung !
To see them look their mother's features !
  To hear them lisp their mother's tongue !

And when, with envy, Time, transported,
  Shall think to rob us of our joys,
You'll in your girls again be courted,
  And I'll go wooing in my boys.

Epitaph on Tom D'Urfey

Here lies the Lyric, who, with tale and song,
Did life to three-score years and ten prolong :
His tale was pleasant, and his song was sweet ;
His heart was cheerful—but his thirst was great.
Grieve, reader, grieve, that he, too soon grown old,
His song has ended, and his tale has told.

Song

Forgive, fair creature, form'd to please,
  Forgive a wond'ring youth's desire :
Those charms, those virtues when he sees,
  How can he see and not admire ?

While each the other still improves,
  The fairest face, the fairest mind ;
Not, with the proverb, he that loves,
  But he that loves you not, is blind.

On the Death of Penkethman

The crowded theatre's delight,
  Poor Pinky ! has play'd out his play ;
His Exit, his last Exit, made !
  Say, Comic Mirth, and Laughter, say,
    Alas ! poor Pinky !

Whene'er his face, that matchless face,
  Poor Pinky's face, which now is clay,
In merry likeness shall be seen,
  With pleasing kind remembrance say,
    Alas ! poor Pinky !
The heaving sigh, and falling tear,
  If near poor Pinky's grave you stray,
Would sorrow too expensive be ;
  Grieve only with a smile, and say,
    Alas ! poor Pinky !

ANONYMOUS POEMS

From David Lewis's Second Collection of Miscellaneous Poems (1730)

The Retirement*

'Tis weak and worldly to conclude
Retirement all a solitude ;
The wise and good will always own
That man is never less alone
Than when alone ; 'tis so with me,
When in my own large company.

Withdrawn and pensive while I move
Beneath the shade of yonder grove,
Monarchs, that triple circles wear,
Feel not the weight of half my care :
In sighs and prayers my soul I bend,
But rise to transports in the end.

When from the world retir'd apart
To dress the temple of my heart,
To make it beautiful and fair,
Fit for the God residing there ;
'Tis then, and only then, I live,
Enjoying all this globe can give.

* Can this be an eighteenth century poem ? I think so ; but do not feel positive that it is not a seventeenth century poem, which I have failed to run to earth.

Think'st thou to treat Almighty Power
Is but the business of an hour ?
Or who, that gets so dear a guest
But once enshrin'd within his breast,
Would, for the world's impertinence,
Neglect him there, or drive him thence ?

My Eden then be my abode,
And the great visitant, my God !
He only my companion be,
From whom I hope Eternity !
They, who below their Heaven fore-date,
Ne'er dread th' uplifted Hand of Fate,
Tasting the glories that shall crown
An endless Life, when this is done.

Epitaph from the Greek

Accept this tomb, dear friend of mine,
Of mighty love the little sign ;
Love, which my heart can ne'er forego !
Do thou remember me below ;
If friendship privilege may take,
Oh ! drink no Lethe for my sake !

On an Open Grave

Laborious passenger, look down,
    Behold thy journey's end ;
See ! whither all thy weary steps,
    'Tis hither, see ! they tend.

Observe the distance, mark how small,
    But six foot deep or less,
A measure scarce beyond thy own,
    That leads from pain to ease !

Nor here alone, but wheresoe'er
   Thy toilsome footsteps sound,
Thy length and breadth will show the spot
   Where rest is to be found.

Then, patient, the fatigues of life
   With this reflection bear :
That journey can't be over-long,
   Whose end is every where.

Song

Though, Flavia, to my warm desire
   You mean no kind return ;
Yet still with undiminish'd fire
   You wish to see me burn.

Averse my anguish to remove,
   You think it wondrous right
That I love on, for ever love,
   And you for ever slight.

But you and I shall ne'er agree,
   So, gentle Nymph ! adieu !
Since you no pleasure have for me,
   I'll have no pain for you.

Song

You tell me 'tis dissembled love,
   Whene'er I speak my pain ;
My prayers have lost the power to move,
   And all my vows are vain.

But why betrays my soul surprise,
   As those bright charms appear ?
Why dwell on you alone my eyes
   Amidst a thousand fair ?

Mark how I roam from place to place,
   Yet anxious find no rest ;
Think, whence the paleness in my face,
   And panting of my breast.

Yes, yes, dear girl ! no credit pay
   To ought that may deceive ;
Grant still no faith to what I say,
   But what you see believe.

The Hon. SIMON HARCOURT (1684-1720) or
MATTHEW PRIOR ?

The Female Phaeton

Thus Kitty,* beautiful and young,
   And wild as colt untam'd,
Bespoke the fair from whom she sprung,
   With little rage inflam'd.

Inflam'd with rage at sad restraint,
   Which wise Mamma ordain'd ;
And sorely vex'd to play the saint,
   Whilst wit and beauty reign'd.

" Shall I thumb holy books, confin'd
   With Abigals forsaken !
Kitty's for other things design'd,
   Or else I'm much mistaken.

" Must Lady Jenny frisk about,
   And visit with her cousins ?
At balls must she make all the rout,
   And bring home hearts by dozens ?

* Lady Katherine Hyde, afterward Duchess of Queensberry.
See also under Horace Walpole.

" What has she better, pray, than I ?
  What hidden charms to boast,
That all mankind for her should die,
  Whilst I am scarce a toast ?

" Dearest Mamma, for once let me,
  Unchain'd, my fortune try ;
I'll have my Earl as well as she,
  Or know the reason why.

" I'll soon with Jenny's pride quit score,
  Make all her lovers fall ;
They'll grieve I was not loos'd before,
  She, I was loos'd at all."

Fondness prevail'd, Mamma gave way ;
  Kitty, at heart's desire,
Obtain'd the chariot for a day,
  And set the world on fire.

The Judgment of Venus

When Kneller's works of various grace
  Were to fair Venus shown,
The goddess spied in every face
  Some features of her own.

" Just so," (and pointing with her hand)*
  " So shone," says she, " my eyes,
When from two goddesses I gain'd
  An apple for a prize.

" When in the glass and river too
  My face I lately view'd,
Such was I, if the glass be true,
  If true the crystal flood.

* To the picture of Lady Ranelaugh.

" In colours of this glorious kind*
   Apelles painted me ;
My hair thus flowing with the wind,
   Sprung from my native sea.

" Like this, disorder'd, wild, forlorn,†
   Big with ten thousand fears,
Thee, my Adonis, did I mourn,
   Ev'n beautiful in tears."

But viewing Myra plac'd apart,
   " I fear," says she, " I fear,
Apelles, that Sir Godfrey's art
   Has far surpass'd thine here.

" Or I, a goddess of the skies,
   By Myra am outdone,
And must to her resign the prize,
   The apple which I won."

But as soon as she had Myra seen
   Majestically fair,
The sparkling eyes, the look serene,
   The gay and easy air ;

With fiery emulation fill'd,
   The wondering goddess cried,
" Apelles must to Kneller yield,
   Or Venus must to Hyde."

* Picture of Lady Salisbury.
† Lady Jane Douglas, sister to the Duke of Douglas.

JOSEPH MITCHELL (1684-1738)

Song

Leave kindred and friends, sweet lady,
　　Leave kindred and friends for me,
Assur'd thy servant is steady
　　To Love, to Honour, and thee.
The gifts of Nature, and Fortune,
　　May fly by chance, as they came !
They are grounds the Destinies sport on,
　　But Virtue is ever the same.

Although my fancy were roving,
　　Thy charms so heavenly appear,
That, other beauties disproving,
　　I'd worship thine only, my dear,
And should life's sorrows embitter
　　The pleasure we promise our loves,
To share them, together, is fitter,
　　Than moan asunder like doves.

Oh ! were I but once so blessed,
　　To grasp my love in my arms !
By thee to be grasp'd, and kissed !
　　And live on thy Heaven of charms !
I'd laugh at Fortune's caprices,
　　Should Fortune capricious prove ;
Though Death should tear me to pieces,
　　I'd die a martyr to Love.

WILLIAM PULTENEY, Earl of Bath (1684-1764)

Strawberry Hill

Some cry up Gunnersbury,
　　For Sion some declare,
Some say, that with Chiswick House
　　No villa can compare ;
But ask the beaux of Middlesex,
　　Who know the country well,
If Strawberry-hill, if Strawberry-hill,
　　Don't bear away the bell ?

WILLIAM PULTENEY

Some love to roll down Greenwich-hill,
    For this thing and for that,
And some prefer sweet Marble-hill,
    Though sure 'tis somewhat flat ;
Yet Marble-hill and Greenwich-hill,
    If Kitty Clive can tell,
From Strawberry-hill, from Strawberry-hill,
    Will never bear the bell.

Though Surrey boasts its Oatlands,
    And Clermont kept so jim,
And some prefer sweet Southcoats,
    'Tis but a dainty whim ;
But ask the gallant Bristol,
    Who doth in taste excel,
If Strawberry-hill, if Strawberry-hill,
    Don't bear away the bell.

Since Denham sung of Cooper's,
    There's scarce a hill around,
But what in song or ditty,
    Is turn'd to fairy ground.
Ah ! peace be with their memory,
    I wish them wondrous well,
But Strawberry-hill, but Strawberry-hill,
    Will ever bear the bell.

Great William dwells at Windsor,
    As Edward did of old,
And many a Gaul and many a Scot
    Have found him full as bold.
On lofty hills like Windsor
    Such heroes ought to dwell ;
Yet the little folks on Strawberry-hill
    Like Strawberry-hill as well.

The Rt. Rev. GEORGE BERKELEY, D.D.,
Bishop of Cloyne (1685-1753)

Verses on the Prospect of Planting Arts and Learning in America

The Muse, disgusted at an age and clime
    Barren of every glorious theme,
In distant lands now waits a better time,
    Producing subjects worthy fame :

In happy climes, where from the genial sun
    And virgin earth such scenes ensue,
The force of art by nature seems outdone,
    And fancied beauties by the true :

In happy climes, the seat of innocence,
    Where nature guides and virtue rules,
Where men shall not impose for truth and sense
    The pedantry of courts and schools :

There shall be sung another golden age,
    The rise of empire and of arts,
The good and great inspiring epic rage,
    The wisest heads, and noblest hearts.

Not such as Europe breeds in her decay ;
    Such as she bred when fresh and young,
When heavenly flame did animate her clay,
    By future poets shall be sung.

Westward the course of empire takes its way ;
    The four first acts already past,
A fifth shall close the drama with the day ;
    Time's noblest offspring is the last.

I

JOHN GAY (1685-1732)

Songs from " The Beggar's Opera "

I

If the heart of a man is depress'd with cares,
The mist is dispell'd when a woman appears ;
Like the notes of a fiddle, she sweetly, sweetly,
Raises the spirits, and charms our ears.
Roses and lilies her cheeks disclose,
But her ripe lips are more sweet than those ;
> Press her,
> Caress her,
> With blisses,
> Her kisses
Dissolve us in pleasure and soft repose.

II

Youth's the season made for joys,
> Love is then our duty ;
She alone who that employs,
> Well deserves her beauty.
> > Let's be gay
> > While we may,
> Beauty's a flower despis'd in decay.

Let us drink and sport to-day,
> Our's is not to-morrow ;
Love with youth flies swift away,
> Age is nought but sorrow.
> > Dance and sing,
> > Time's on the wing,
> Life never knows the return of spring.

III

MACHEATH

Were I laid on Greenland's coast,
> And in my arms embrac'd my lass,
Warm amidst eternal frost,
> Too soon the half-year's night would pass.

POLLY

Were I sold on Indian soil,
　　Soon as the burning day was clos'd,
I could mock the sultry toil,
　　When on my charmer's breast repos'd.

MACHEATH

And I would love you all the day,

POLLY

Every night would kiss and play ;

MACHEATH

If with me you'd fondly stray

POLLY

Over the hills and far away.

Songs from " Polly "

I

The crow or daw through all the year
　　No fowler seeks to ruin ;
But birds of voice or feather rare
　　He's all day long pursuing.
Beware, fair maids, to 'scape the net
　　That other beauties fell in ;
For sure at heart was never yet
　　So great a wretch as Helen !

II

Sleep, O sleep,
With thy rod of incantation,
Charm my imagination,
Then, only then, I cease to weep.

By thy power,
The virgin by time o'ertaken,
For years forlorn, forsaken,
Enjoys the happy hour.

What's to sleep ?
'Tis a visionary blessing ;
A dream that's past expressing,
Our utmost wish possessing ;
So may I always keep.

III

The sportsmen keep hawks, and their quarry they gain ;
Thus the woodcock, the partridge, the pheasant, is slain.
What care and expense for their hounds are employ'd !
Thus the fox and the hare and the stag are destroy'd.
The spaniel they cherish, whose flattering way
Can as well as their masters cringe, fawn, and betray.
Thus staunch politicians, look all the world round,
Love the men who can serve as hawk, spaniel or hound.

Songs from " Acis and Galatea "

I

Love in her eyes sits playing,
    And sheds delicious death ;
Love in her lips is straying,
    And warbling in her breath :
Love on her breasts sits panting,
    And swells with soft desire ;
Nor grace, nor charm, is wanting
    To set the heart on fire.

II

Polyphemus' Song

I rage, I melt, I burn,
The feeble god has stabb'd me to the heart.
    Thou trusty pine,
Prop of my god-like steps, I lay thee by.
Bring me a hundred reeds, of decent growth,
To make a pipe for my capacious mouth ;
In soft enchanting accents let me breathe
Sweet Galatea's beauty, and my love.

O ruddier than the cherry !
O sweeter than the berry !
O nymph more bright
Than moonshine night,
Like kidlings blithe and merry !
Ripe as the melting cluster !
No lily has such lustre ;
Yet hard to tame
As raging flame,
And fierce as storms that bluster !

Sweet William's Farewell to Black-Eyed Susan

A Ballad

All in the Downs the fleet was moor'd,
The streamers waving in the wind,
When black-eyed Susan came aboard :
" Oh ! where shall I my true love find ?
Tell me, ye jovial sailors, tell me true,
If my sweet William sails among the crew."

William, who high upon the yard
Rock'd with the billow to and fro,
Soon as her well-known voice he heard,
He sigh'd and cast his eyes below :
The cord slides swiftly through his glowing hands
And (quick as lightning) on the deck he stands.

So the sweet lark, high-pois'd in air,
Shuts close his pinions to his breast
(If, chance, his mate's shrill call he hear)
And drops at once into her nest.
The noblest captain in the British fleet,
Might envy William's lip those kisses sweet.

" Oh ! Susan, Susan, lovely dear,
　　My vows shall ever true remain ;
Let me kiss off that falling tear,
　　We only part to meet again.
Change, as ye list, ye winds ; my heart shall be
The faithful compass that still points to thee.

" Believe not what the landmen say,
　　Who tempt with doubts thy constant mind :
They'll tell thee sailors, when away,
　　In every port a mistress find.
Yes, yes, believe them when they tell thee so,
For thou art present wheresoe'er I go.

" If to far India's coast we sail,
　　Thy eyes are seen in diamonds bright ;
Thy breath is Afric's spicy gale,
　　Thy skin is ivory, so white.
Thus every beauteous object that I view,
Wakes in my soul some charm of lovely Sue.

" Though battle call me from thy arms,
　　Let not my pretty Susan mourn ;
Though cannons roar, yet safe from harms,
　　William shall to his dear return.
Love turns aside the balls that round me fly,
Lest precious tears should drop from Susan's eye."

The boatswain gave the dreadful word,
　　The sails their swelling bosom spread,
No longer must she stay aboard :
　　They kiss'd, she sigh'd, he hung his head ;
Her lessening boat unwilling rows to land :
" Adieu ! " she cries ; and wav'd her lily hand.

A Ballad,

from " The What D'ye Call It."

'Twas when the seas were roaring
  With hollow blasts of wind ;
A damsel lay deploring,
  All on a rock reclin'd.
Wide o'er the rolling billows
  She cast a wistful look ;
Her head was crown'd with willows
  That tremble o'er the brook.

" Twelve months are gone and over,
  And nine long tedious days.
Why didst thou, vent'rous lover,
  Why didst thou trust the seas ?
Cease, cease, thou cruel ocean,
  And let my lover rest :
Ah ! what's thy troubled motion
  To that within my breast ?

" The merchant, robb'd of pleasure,
  Sees tempests in despair ;
But what's the loss of treasure
  To losing of my dear ?
Should you some coast be laid on
  Where gold and diamonds grow,
You'd find a richer maiden,
  But none that loves you so.

" How can they say that nature
  Has nothing made in vain ;
Why then beneath the water
  Should hideous rocks remain ?
No eyes the rocks discover
  That lurk beneath the deep,
To wreck the wandering lover,
  And leave the maid to weep."

All melancholy lying,
   Thus wail'd she for her dear ;
Repaid each blast with sighing,
   Each billow with a tear ;
When, o'er the white wave stooping,
   His floating corpse she spied ;
Then like a lily drooping,
   She bow'd her head and died.

Molly Mog :

or, The Fair Maid of the Inn

A Ballad

Says my uncle, " I pray you discover
   What hath been the cause of your woes,
Why you pine and you whine like a lover? "—
   " I have seen Molly Mog of the Rose."

" O nephew ! your grief is but folly,
   In town you may find better prog ;
Half-a-crown there will get you a Molly,
   A Molly much better than Mog."

I know that by wits 'tis recited
   That women at best are a clog ;
But I am not so easily frighted
   From loving of sweet Molly Mog.

The school-boy's desire is a play-day ;
   The schoolmaster's joy is to flog ;
The milk-maid's delight is on May-day,
   But mine is on sweet Molly Mog.

Will-a-wisp leads the trav'ller a-gadding
   Through ditch, and through quagmire, and bog;
But no light can set me a-madding
   Like the eyes of my sweet Molly Mog.

For guineas in other men's breeches
　Your gamesters will palm and will cog ;
But I envy them none of their riches,
　So I may win sweet Molly Mog.

The heart when half-wounded is changing,
　It here and there leaps like a frog ;
But my heart can never be ranging,
　'Tis so fixt upon sweet Molly Mog.

Who follows all ladies of pleasure,
　In pleasure is thought but a hog ;
All the sex cannot give so good measure
　Of joys as my sweet Molly Mog.

I feel I'm in love to distraction,
　My senses all lost in a fog ;
And nothing can give satisfaction
　But thinking of sweet Molly Mog.

A letter when I am inditing,
　Comes Cupid and gives me a jog,
And I fill all the paper with writing
　Of nothing but sweet Molly Mog.

If I would not give up the three Graces,
　I wish I were hang'd like a dog,
And at court all the drawing-room faces,
　For a glance of my sweet Molly Mog.

Those faces want nature and spirit,
　And seem as cut out of a log ;
Juno, Venus, and Pallas's merit
　Unite in my sweet Molly Mog.

Those who toast all the Family Royal,
　In bumpers of Hogan and Nog,
Have hearts not more true or more loyal
　Than mine to my sweet Molly Mog.

Were Virgil alive with his Phillis,
    And writing another eclogue ;
Both his Phillis and fair Amaryllis
    He'd give up for sweet Molly Mog.

When she smiles on each guest like her liquor,
    Then jealousy sets me agog ;
To be sure she's a bit for the Vicar,
    And so I shall lose Molly Mog.

On a Miscellany of Poems. To Bernard Lintott

*Ipsa varietate tentamus efficere ut alia aliis ; quædam
    fortasse omnibus placeant*—Plinii *Epistolae.*

As when some skilful cook, to please each guest,
Would in one mixture comprehend a feast,
With due proportion and judicious care
He fills each dish with different sorts of fare,
Fishes and fowls deliciously unite,
To feast at once the taste, the smell, and sight.

So, Bernard, must a miscellany be
Compounded of all kinds of poetry ;
The Muses' olio, which all tastes may fit,
And treat each reader with his darling wit.

Wouldst thou for miscellanies raise thy fame,
And bravely rival Jacob's mighty name ;
Let all the Muses in the piece conspire,
The lyric bard must strike th' harmonious lyre ;
Heroic strains must here and there be found,
And nervous sense be sung in lofty sound ;
Let elegy in moving numbers flow,
And fill some pages with melodious woe ;
Let not your am'rous songs too numerous prove,
Nor glut thy reader with abundant love ;
Satire must interfere, whose pointed rage
May lash the madness of a vicious age ;

JOHN GAY

Satire, the Muse that never fails to hit,
For if there's scandal, to be sure there's wit.
Tire not our patience with Pindaric lays,
Those swell the piece, but very rarely please ;
Let short-breath'd epigram its force confine,
And strike at follies in a single line.
Translations should throughout the work be sown,
And Homer's god-like Muse be made our own ;
Horace in useful numbers should be sung,
And Virgil's thoughts adorn the British tongue ;
Let Ovid tell Corinna's hard disdain,
And at her door in melting notes complain :
His tender accents pitying virgins move,
And charm the listening ear with tales of love.
Let every classic in the volume shine,
And each contribute to thy great design :
Through various subjects let the reader range,
And raise his fancy with a grateful change ;
Variety's the source of joy below,
From whence still fresh revolving pleasures flow.
In books and love, the mind one end pursues,
And only change th' expiring flame renews.

Where Buckingham will condescend to give,
That honour'd piece to distant times must live ;
When noble Sheffield strikes the trembling strings,
The little loves rejoice and clap their wings.
" Anacreon lives," they cry, " th' harmonious swain
Retunes the lyre, and tries his wonted strain,
'Tis he,—our lost Anacreon lives again."
But when th' illustrious poet soars above
The sportive revels of the god of love,
Like Maro's Muse he takes a loftier flight,
And towers beyond the wondering Cupid's sight.

If thou wouldst have thy volume stand the test,
And of all others be reputed best,
Let Congreve teach the listening groves to mourn,
As when he wept o'er fair Pastora's urn.

JOHN GAY

Let Prior's Muse with softening accents move,
Soft as the strains of constant Emma's love :
Or let his fancy choose some jovial theme,
As when he told Hans Carvel's jealous dream ;
Prior th' admiring reader entertains,
With Chaucer's humour, and with Spenser's strains.

Waller in Granville lives ; when Mira sings
With Waller's hand he strikes the sounding strings,
With sprightly turns his noble genius shines,
And manly sense adorns his easy lines.

On Addison's sweet lays attention waits,
And silence guards the place while he repeats ;
His Muse alike on every subject charms,
Whether she paints the god of love, or arms ;
In him pathetic Ovid sings again,
And Homer's *Iliad* shines in his *Campaign*.

Whenever Garth shall raise his sprightly song,
Sense flows in easy numbers from his tongue ;
Great Phœbus in his learned son we see,
Alike in physic, as in poetry.

When Pope's harmonious Muse with pleasure roves
Amidst the plains, the murmuring streams and groves,
Attentive Echo, pleas'd to hear his songs,
Through the glad vale each warbling note prolongs ;
His various numbers charm our ravish'd ears,
His steady judgment far out-shoots his years,
And early in the youth the god appears.

From these successful bards collect thy strains,
And praise with profit shall reward thy pains :
Then, while calves-leather binding bears the sway,
And sheep-skin to its sleeker gloss gives way ;
While neat old Elzevir is reckon'd better
Than pirate Hills' brown sheets and scurvy letter :
While print admirers careful Aldus choose
Before John Morphew, or the weekly news :
So long shall live thy praise in books of fame,
And Tonson yield to Lintott's lofty name.

JOHN GAY

The Fable of the Sick Man and the Angel

" Is there no hope ? " the sick man said.
The silent doctor shook his head,
And took his way with signs of sorrow,
Despairing of his fee to-morrow.

When thus the man with gasping breath :
" I feel the chilling wound of death :
Since I must bid the world adieu,
Let me my former life review.
I grant, my bargains well were made,
But all men overreach in trade ;
'Tis self-defence in each profession,
Sure self-defence is no transgression.
The little portion in my hands,
By good security on lands,
Is well increas'd. If, unawares,
My justice to myself and heirs
Hath let my debtor rot in jail,
For want of good sufficient bail ;
If I by writ, or bond, or deed,
Reduc'd a family to need,
My will hath made the world amends ;
My hope on charity depends.
When I am number'd with the dead,
And all my pious gifts are read,
By heaven and earth 'twill then be known,
My charities were amply shown."

An Angel came. " Ah, friend ! " he cried,
" No more in flattering hope confide.
Can thy good deeds in former times
Outweigh the balance of thy crimes ?
What widow or what orphan prays
To crown thy life with length of days ?
A pious action's in thy power ;
Embrace with joy the happy hour.

Now, while you draw the vital air,
Prove your intention is sincere.
This instant give a hundred pound ;
Your neighbours want, and you abound."

" But why such haste," the sick man whines ;
" Who knows as yet what Heaven designs ?
Perhaps I may recover still ;
That sum and more are in my will."

" Fool," says the Vision, " now 'tis plain,
Your life, your soul, your heaven was gain ;
From every side, with all your might,
You scrap'd, and scrap'd beyond your right ;
And after death would fain atone,
By giving what is not your own."

" Where there is life, there's hope," he cried ;
" Then why such haste ? " So groan'd, and died.

The Fable of the Fox at the Point of Death

A fox, in life's extreme decay,
Weak, sick, and faint, expiring lay ;
All appetite had left his maw,
And age disarm'd his mumbling jaw.
His numerous race around him stand
To learn their dying sire's command :
He rais'd his head with whining moan,
And thus was heard the feeble tone :

" Ah, sons ! from evil ways depart ;
My crimes lie heavy on my heart.
See, see, the murder'd geese appear !
Why are those bleeding turkeys there ?
Why all around this cackling train,
Who haunt my ears for chicken slain ? "

The hungry foxes round them star'd,
And for the promis'd feast prepar'd.

" Where, sir, is all this dainty cheer ?
No turkey, goose, nor hen is here.
These are the phantoms of your brain,
And your sons lick their lips in vain."

" O gluttons ! " says the drooping sire,
" Restrain inordinate desire.
Your liqu'rish taste you shall deplore,
When peace of conscience is no more.
Does not the hound betray our pace,
And gins and guns destroy our race ?
Thieves dread the searching eye of power,
And never feel the quiet hour.
Old age (which few of us shall know)
Now puts a period to my woe.
Would you true happiness attain,
Let honesty your passions rein ;
So live in credit and esteem,
And the good name you lost, redeem."

" The counsel's good," a fox replies,
" Could we perform what you advise.
Think what our ancestors have done ;
A line of thieves from son to son :
To us descends the long disgrace,
And infamy hath mark'd our race.
Though we, like harmless sheep, should feed,
Honest in thought, in word, and deed,
Whatever hen-roost is decreas'd,
We shall be thought to share the feast.
The change shall never be believ'd.
A lost good name is ne'er retriev'd."

" Nay then," replies the feeble fox,
" (But hark ! I hear a hen that clocks)
Go, but be moderate in your food ;
A chicken too might do me good."

JOHN GAY

My Own Epitaph

Life is a jest ; and all things show it.
I thought so once ; but now I know it.

WILLIAM HARRISON (1685-1713)

To a Very Young Lady

Florella, when those eyes I see,
So innocently kind and free,
Ever fix'd, and fix'd on me ;

Say, why should I my time misspend,
With idle fears so long attend,
And lose the lover in the friend ?

A year, or two, I could forbear ;
But that some happier youth, I fear,
May gain thy heart, and triumph there.

Then, dearest girl, with me retire ;
What Age should give, Love shall inspire,
And thou shalt ripen by my fire.

AARON HILL (1685-1750)

Epitaph

On a young Lady, who died unmarried

Ripe in virtue, green in years,
  Here a matchless maid lies low :
None could read, and spare their tears,
  Did they but her sweetness know.

Humbly wise, and meekly good,
  No earthly lover's arms she bless'd ;
But, full of grace, her Saviour woo'd,
  And hides her blushes in His breast.

AARON HILL

The Journey

As in a journey just begun,
    We think the distance vast,
Yet while we travel gaily on,
    Insensibly 'tis past.

So in our youth we measure slow
    Long views of promis'd breath :
Till like a shadow out we go,
    And vanish into death.

An Epitaph

Why in such thoughtless haste ? Oh stay, and know
The dust, now mouldering here, once hurried so !
If will to serve, or art to please mankind ;
If being just, and of a generous mind ;
If harmless mirth, free friendship, stingless truth,
Unswerving judgment, and unerring youth ;
If these could e'er have brib'd the dart of death,
This grave's gay tenant still had kept his breath :
Stay then ! and lend one sigh to mourn his fate !
So may your loss be griev'd, so may your death be late.

JABEZ HUGHES* (1685 ?-1731)

The Morning Apparition

Written at Wallington House, 1719

All things were hush'd, as noise itself were dead ;
No midnight mice stirr'd round my silent bed ;
Not even a gnat disturb'd the peace profound ;
Dumb, o'er my pillow, hung my watch unwound ;
No ticking death-worm told a fancied doom,
Nor hidden cricket chirrup in the room.
No breeze the casement shook, or fann'd the leaves,

* Brother of John Hughes.

Nor drops of rain fell soft from off the eaves,
Nor noisy splinter made the candle weep,
But the dim watch-light seem'd itself asleep,
When tir'd I clos'd my eyes—how long I lay
In slumber wrapt, I list not now to say ;
When hark, a sudden noise !—see—open flies
The yielding door—I, starting, rubb'd my eyes,
Fast-clos'd awhile, and, as their lids I rear'd,
Full at my feet a tall thin form appear'd,
While through my parted curtains rushing broke
A light like day, ere yet the figure spoke.
Cold sweats bedew'd my limbs—nor did I dream ;
(Hear, mortals, hear ! for real truth's my theme ;)
And now more bold I rais'd my trembling bones
To look—when lo ! 'twas honest Master Jones,*
Who wav'd his hand, to banish fears and sorrow,
Well-charg'd with toast and sack, and cried " Good-
    morrow ! "

EUSTACE BUDGELL† (1686-1737)

Song

I'm not one of your fops, who, to please a coy lass,
Can lie whining and pining, and look like an ass :
Life is dull without love, and not worth the possessing,
But fools make a curse, what was meant for a blessing.
While his godship's not rude, I'll allow him my breast,
But, by Jove ! out he goes, should he once break my rest !
I can toy with a girl for an hour, to allay
The fluster of youth, or the ferment of May ;
But must beg her excuse not to bear pains or anguish,
For that's not to love, by her leave, but to languish.

* The butler.
† A cousin of Addison's.

THOMAS TICKELL (1686-1740)

To the Earl of Warwick, on the Death of
Mr. Addison

If, dumb too long, the drooping Muse hath stay'd,
And left her debt to Addison unpaid,
Blame not her silence, Warwick, but bemoan,
And judge, oh judge, my bosom by your own.
What mourner ever felt poetic fires !
Slow comes the verse that real woe inspires :
Grief unaffected suits but ill with art,
Or flowing numbers with a bleeding heart.
  Can I forget the dismal night that gave
My soul's best part for ever to the grave !
How silent did his old companions tread,
By midnight lamps, the mansions of the dead,
Through breathing statues, then unheeded things,
Through rows of warriors, and through walks of kings !
What awe did the slow solemn knell inspire ;
The pealing organ, and the pausing choir ;
The duties by the lawn-rob'd prelate paid ;
And the last words, that dust to dust convey'd !
While speechless o'er thy closing grave we bend,
Accept these tears, thou dear departed friend ;
Oh gone for ever, take this long adieu ;
And sleep in peace, next thy lov'd Montague.
  To strew fresh laurels let the task be mine,
A frequent pilgrim, at thy sacred shrine ;
Mine with true sighs thy absence to bemoan,
And grave with faithful epitaphs thy stone.
If e'er from me thy lov'd memorial part,
May shame afflict this alienated heart ;
Of thee forgetful if I form a song,
My lyre be broken, and untun'd my tongue ;
My grief be doubled, from thy image free ;
And mirth a torment, unchastis'd by thee.
  Oft let me range the gloomy aisles alone,
Sad luxury ! to vulgar minds unknown,
Along the walls where speaking marbles show
What worthies form the hallow'd mould below ;

Proud names, who once the reins of empire held ;
In arms who triumph'd ; or in arts excell'd ;
Chiefs, grac'd with scars, and prodigal of blood ;
Stern patriots, who for sacred freedom stood ;
Just men, by whom impartial laws were given ;
And saints who taught, and led, the way to Heaven ;
Ne'er to these chambers, where the mighty rest,
Since their foundation came a nobler guest ;
Nor e'er was to the bowers of bliss convey'd
A fairer spirit or more welcome shade.
　　In what new region, to the just assign'd,
What new employments please th' unbodied mind ?
A winged Virtue, through the ethereal sky
From world to world unwearied does he fly ?
Or curious trace the long laborious maze
Of Heaven's decrees, where wondering Angels gaze ?
Does he delight to hear bold Seraphs tell
How Michael battled and the dragon fell ?
Or mixt with milder Cherubim, to glow
In hymns of love, not ill essay'd below ?
Or dost thou warn poor mortals left behind,
A task well suited to thy gentle mind ?
Oh ! if sometimes thy spotless form descend,
To me thy aid, thou guardian genius, lend !
When rage misguides me, or when fear alarms,
When pain distresses, or when pleasure charms,
In silent whisperings purer thoughts impart,
And turn from ill a frail and feeble heart ;
Lead through the paths thy virtue trod before,
Till bliss shall join, nor death can part us more.
　　That awful form, which, so ye Heavens decree,
Must still be lov'd and still deplor'd by me,
In nightly visions seldom fails to rise,
Or, rous'd by fancy, meets my waking eyes.
If business calls, or crowded courts invite,
Th' unblemish'd statesman seems to strike my sight ;
If in the stage I seek to soothe my care,
I meet his soul which breathes in Cato there ;
If pensive to the rural shades I rove,

His shape o'ertakes me in the lonely grove :
'Twas there of just and good he reason'd strong,
Clear'd some great truth, or rais'd some serious song ;
There patient show'd us the wise course to steer,
A candid censor, and a friend severe ;
There taught us how to live ; and, oh ! too high
The price for knowledge, taught us how to die.

Thou hill, whose brow the antique structures grace,
Rear'd by bold chiefs of Warwick's noble race ;
Why, once so lov'd, when'er thy bower appears,
O'er my dim eye-balls glance the sudden tears ?
How sweet were once thy prospects fresh and fair,
Thy sloping walks, and unpolluted air !
How sweet the glooms beneath thy aged trees,
Thy noon-tide shadow, and thy evening breeze !
His image thy forsaken bowers restore ;
Thy walks and airy prospects charm no more ;
No more the summer in thy glooms allay'd,
Thy evening breezes, and thy noon-day shade.

From other ills, however fortune frown'd,
Some refuge in the Muse's art I found ;
Reluctant now I touch the trembling string
Bereft of him, who taught me how to sing ;
And these sad accents, murmur'd o'er his urn,
Betray that absence they attempt to mourn.
Oh ! must I then, (now fresh my bosom bleeds,
And Craggs in death to Addison succeeds),
The verse, begun to one lost friend, prolong,
And weep a second in th' unfinish'd song !

These works divine, which on his death-bed laid
To thee, Oh Craggs, th' expiring sage convey'd,
Great, but ill-omen'd, monument of fame,
Nor he surviv'd to give, nor thou to claim.
Swift after him thy social spirit flies,
And close to his, how soon ! thy coffin lies.
Blest pair ! whose union future bards shall tell
In future tongues : each other's boast ! farewell !
Farewell ! whom join'd in fame, in friendship tried,
No chance could sever, nor the grave divide.

THOMAS TICKELL

Colin and Lucy

A Ballad

Of Leinster, fam'd for maidens fair,
  Bright Lucy was the grace ;
Nor e'er did Liffy's limpid stream
  Reflect so sweet a face :
Till luckless love, and pining care,
  Impair'd her rosy hue,
Her coral lips, and damask cheeks,
  And eyes of glossy blue.

Oh ! have you seen a lily pale,
  When beating rains descend ?
So droop'd the slow-consuming maid,
  Her life now near its end.
By Lucy warn'd, of flattering swains
  Take heed, ye easy fair :
Of vengeance due to broken vows,
  Ye perjur'd swains, beware.

Three times, all in the dead of night,
  A bell was heard to ring ;
And shrieking at her window thrice,
  The raven flapp'd his wing.
Too well the love-lorn maiden knew
  The solemn boding sound ;
And thus, in dying words, bespoke
  The virgins weeping round :

" I hear a voice, you cannot hear,
  Which says, I must not stay ;
I see a hand, you cannot see,
  Which beckons me away.
By a false heart, and broken vows,
  In early youth I die :
Was I to blame, because his bride
  Was thrice as rich as I ?

" Ah Colin ! give not her thy vows,
   Vows due to me alone :
Nor thou, fond maid, receive his kiss,
   Nor think him all thy own.
To-morrow, in the church to wed,
   Impatient, both prepare !
But know, fond maid ; and know, false man,
   That Lucy will be there !

" Then bear my corse, my comrades, bear,
   This bridegroom blithe to meet,
He in his wedding trim so gay,
   I in my winding sheet.''
She spoke ; she died ; her corse was borne
   The bridegroom blithe to meet,
He in his wedding trim so gay,
   She in her winding sheet.

Then what were perjur'd Colin's thoughts ?
   How were these nuptials kept ?
The bridesmen flock'd round Lucy dead,
   And all the village wept.
Confusion, shame, remorse, despair,
   At once his bosom swell :
The damps of death bedew'd his brow,
   He shook, he groan'd, he fell.

From the vain bride, ah bride no more !
   The varying crimson fled,
When, stretch'd before her rival's corse,
   She saw her husband dead.
Then to his Lucy's new-made grave,
   Convey'd by trembling swains,
One mould with her, beneath one sod,
   For ever he remains.

Oft at this grave the constant hind
   And plighted maid are seen ;
With garlands gay, and true-love knots,
   They deck the sacred green ;

135

But, swain forsworn, whoe'er thou art,
    This hallow'd spot forbear ;
Remember Colin's dreadful fate,
    And fear to meet him there.

On the Death of the Earl of Cadogan

Of Marlb'rough's captains and Eugenio's friends,
The last, Cadogan, to the grave descends :
Low lies each hand, whence Blenheim's glory sprung,
The chiefs who conquer'd, and the bards who sung.
From his cold corse though every friend be fled,
Lo ! Envy waits, that lover of the dead :
Thus did she feign o'er Nassau's hearse to mourn ;
Thus wept insidious, Churchill, o'er thy urn ;
To blast the living, gave the dead their due,
And wreaths, herself had tainted, trimm'd anew.
Thou, yet unnam'd to fill his empty place,
And lead to war thy country's growing race,
Take every wish a British heart can frame,
Add palm to palm, and rise from fame to fame.

An hour must come, when thou shalt hear with rage
Thyself traduc'd, and curse a thankless age :
Nor yet for this decline the generous strife,
These ills, brave man, shall quit thee with thy life ;
Alive though stain'd by every abject slave,
Secure of Fame, and Justice in the grave.
Ah ! no—when once the mortal yields to fate,
The blast of Fame's sweet trumpet sounds too late,
Too late to stay the spirit on its flight,
Or soothe the new inhabitant of light ;
Who hears regardless, while fond man, distress'd,
Hangs on the absent, and laments the blest.

Farewell then Fame, ill sought through fields and blood,
Farewell unfaithful promiser of good ;
Thou music, warbling to the deafen'd ear !
Thou incense, wasted on the funeral bier !
Through life pursu'd in vain, by death obtain'd,
When ask'd, denied us, and, when given, disdain'd.

The Rev. THOMAS SHERIDAN, D.D. (1687-1738)

A New Simile for the Ladies

" To make a writer miss his end
You've nothing else to do but mend."

I often tried in vain to find
A simile for womankind,
A simile I meant to fit 'em,
In every circumstance to hit 'em.
Through every beast and bird I went,
I ransack'd every element ;
And, after peeping through all nature
To find so whimsical a creature,
A cloud presented to my view,,
And straight this parallel I drew :

Clouds turn with every wind about,
They keep us in suspense and doubt,
Yet oft perverse, like womankind,
Are seen to scud against the wind :
And are not women just the same ?
For who can tell at what they aim ?

Clouds keep the stoutest mortals under,
When bellowing they discharge their thunder :
So when alarum bell is rung
Of Xanti's everlasting tongue,
The husband dreads its loudness more
Than lightning's flash, or thunder's roar.

Clouds weep, as they do, without pain :
And what are tears but women's rain ?

The clouds about the welkin roam :
And ladies never stay at home.

The clouds build castles in the air,—
A thing peculiar to the fair,
For all the schemes of their forecasting
Are not more solid nor more lasting.

A cloud is light by turns, and dark,
Such is a lady with her spark ;
Now with a sudden pouting gloom
She seems to darken all the room ;
Again she's pleas'd, his fears beguil'd,
And all is clear when she has smil'd.
In this they're wondrously alike,
(I hope the simile will strike)
Though in the darkest dumps you view them,
Stay but a moment, you'll see through them.

The clouds are apt to make reflection,
And frequently produce infection :
So Cœlia, with small provocation,
Blasts every neighbour's reputation.

The clouds delight in gaudy show,
(For they, like ladies, have their bow) :
The gravest matron will confess
That she herself is fond of dress.

Observe the clouds in pomp array'd,
What various colours are display'd,
The pink, the rose, the violet's dye,
In that great drawing-room the sky :
How do these differ from our Graces,
In garden-silks, brocades, and laces ?
Are they not such another sight,
When met upon a birth-day night ?

The clouds delight to change their fashion :
(Dear ladies, be not in a passion !)
Nor let this whim to you seem strange,
Who every hour delight in change.

In them and you alike are seen
The sullen symptoms of the spleen ;
The moment that your vapours rise,
We see them dropping from your eyes.

In evening fair you may behold
The clouds are fring'd with borrow'd gold :
And this is many a lady's case,
Who flaunts about in borrow'd lace.

Grave matrons are like clouds of snow,
Their words fall thick, and soft, and slow ;
While brisk coquettes, like rattling hail,
Our ears on every side assail.

Clouds, when they intercept our sight,
Deprive us of celestial light :
So, when my Chloe I pursue,
No Heaven besides I have in view.

Thus on comparison you see,
In every instance they agree ;
So like, so very much the same,
That one may go by t'other's name.
Let me proclaim it then aloud,
That every woman is a cloud.

The Rev. LAURENCE EUSDEN,* Poet Laureate
(1688-1730)

On a Lady

who is the most beautiful and witty when she is angry

Long had I known the soft enchanting wiles,
Which Cupid practis'd in Aurelia's smiles.
Till by degrees, like the fam'd Asian, taught,
Safely I drank the sweet, though poisonous, draught.
Love, vex'd to see his favours vainly shown,
The peevish urchin murder'd with a frown.
What cautious youth would thence have fear'd surprise ?

* I print these two examples of Eusden's verse, partly because
of his position as Poet Laureate, and partly to show his curious
gift of lighting up rather bad poems with occasional really good
lines.

Can beauty from deformity arise ?
In cloudless nights do lightnings harmless fly,
And only blast from a tempestuous sky ?
Mild Venus haunts the shades and peaceful groves,
Her thoughts, her looks, are tender as her doves ;
Smooth'd were the waves, and every Triton sung,
When from old Ocean first the Goddess sprung.
Aurelia shuns the calm, and loves the storm,
Ruffles her passions to improve her form ;
She, by some art to th' artful sex unknown,
Has all the graces, when the rest have none.
Th' unsated victor seeks new triumphs still,
And whom her eyes but wound, her tongue must kill.
No hope of safety, if inflam'd her breast ;
At once the charmer looks and talks the best.
So Dryden sweetest sung, by envy fir'd,
Thirst of revenge, when Phœbus fail'd, inspir'd ;
His Anthony did Sedley's muse o'ertake,
And Absolom was writ for Zimri's sake ;
New injuries fresh laurels did presage,
And a Mac-Flecknoe was the child of rage.

To Mr. ——

You ask, my friend, how I can Delia prize,
When Myra's shape I view, or Cynthia's eyes :
No tedious answer shall create you pain,
For beauty, if but beauty, I disdain.
'Tis not a mien that can my will control,
A speaking body with a silent soul.
The loveliest face to me not lovely shows,
From the sweet lips if melting nonsense flows ;
Nor must the tuneful Chloris be my choice,
An earthly mind ill suits a heavenly voice.

What though my Delia not decay'd appears,
She wants, you cry, the gaudy bloom of years.
True ; but good sense perpetual joys will bring ;

Her wit is ever youthful as the spring.
Those fluttering sparks, who fashionably burn,
And hourly for some fair Dorinda mourn,
Soon as the fancied goddess is enjoy'd,
To find her woman, sicken, and are cloy'd.
Not so my Delia shall consume her charms,
But rise each morn more beauteous from my arms.
With envious swiftness rolling years may move,
Impair her glories, not impair my love :
Time's wasteful rage the husband shall despise,
And view the wife still with the bridegroom's eyes.
So kneels, at some fam'd antiquated shrine,
The pious pilgrim to the Power Divine.
Around he sees wild rugged heaps of stone,
Where Parian marble once, and jasper shone :
Yet, conscious what those ruins were of old,
Dares not, unmov'd, the mossy walls behold ;
But trembles at the Deity's abode,
And owns the powerful presence of the God.

ALEXANDER POPE (1688-1744)

Summer : or, Alexis

A Pastoral

A shepherd boy (he seeks no better name)
Led forth his flocks along the silver Thame,
Where dancing sunbeams on the waters play'd,
And verdant alders form'd a quivering shade ;
Soft as he mourn'd, the streams forgot to flow,
The flocks around a dumb compassion show,
The Naiads wept in every watery bower,
And Jove consented in a silent shower.

Accept, O Garth ! the Muse's early lays,
That adds this wreath of ivy to thy bays ;
Hear what from love unpractis'd hearts endure,
From love, the sole disease thou canst not cure.

Ye shady beeches, and ye cooling streams,
Defence from Phœbus', not from Cupid's beams,
To you I mourn ; nor to the deaf I sing,
" The woods shall answer, and their echo ring."
The hills and rocks attend my doleful lay,
Why art thou prouder and more hard than they ?
The bleating sheep with my complaints agree,
They parch'd with heat, and I inflam'd by thee.
The sultry Sirius burns the thirsty plains,
While in thy heart eternal winter reigns.

Where stray ye, Muses, in what lawn or grove,
While your Alexis pines in hopeless love ?
In those fair fields where sacred Isis glides,
Or else where Cam his winding vales divides ?
As in the crystal stream I view my face,
Fresh rising blushes paint the watery glass ;
But since those graces please thy eyes no more,
I shun the fountains which I sought before.
Once I was skill'd in every herb that grew,
And every plant that drinks the morning dew ;
Ah wretched shepherd, what avails thy art,
To cure thy lambs, but not to heal thy heart !

Let other swains attend the rural care,
Feed fairer flocks, or richer fleeces shear :
But nigh yon mountain let me tune my lays,
Embrace my love, and bind my brows with bays.
That flute is mine which Colin's tuneful breath
Inspir'd when living, and bequeath'd in death :
He said : Alexis, take this pipe, the same
That taught the groves my Rosalinda's name :
But now the reeds shall hang on yonder tree,
For ever silent, since despis'd by thee.
Oh ! were I made by some transforming power
The captive bird that sings within thy bower !
Then might my voice thy listening ears employ,
And I those kisses he receives enjoy.

And yet my numbers please the rural throng,
Rough satyrs dance, and Pan applauds the song :
The nymphs, forsaking every cave and spring,
Their early fruit, and milk-white turtles bring !
Each am'rous nymph prefers her gifts in vain,
On you their gifts are all bestow'd again.
For you the swains their fairest flowers design,
And in one garland all their beauties join ;
Accept the wreath which you deserve alone,
In whom all beauties are compris'd in one.

See what delights in sylvan scenes appear !
Descending gods have found Elysium here.
In woods bright Venus and Adonis stray'd ;
And chaste Diana haunts the forest-shade.
Come, lovely nymph, and bless the silent hours,
When swains from shearing seek their nightly bowers ;
When weary reapers quit the sultry field,
And crown'd with corn their thanks to Ceres yield.
This harmless grove no lurking viper hides,
But in my breast the serpent love abides,
Here bees from blossoms sip the rosy dew,
But your Alexis knows no sweets but you.
O deign to visit our forsaken seats,
The mossy fountains, and the green retreats !
Where'er you walk, cool gales shall fan the glade ;
Trees, where you sit, shall crowd into a shade ;
Where'er you tread, the blushing flowers shall rise,
And all things flourish where you turn your eyes.
O ! how I long with you to pass my days,
Invoke the Muses, and resound your praise !
Your praise the birds shall chant in every grove,
And winds shall waft it to the powers above.
But would you sing, and rival Orpheus' strain,
The wondering forests soon should dance again,
The moving mountains hear the powerful call,
And headlong streams hang listening in their fall.
    But see, the shepherds shun the noon-day heat,
The lowing herds to murm'ring brooks retreat,

To closer shades the panting flocks remove ;
Ye gods ! and is there no relief for love ?
But soon the sun with milder rays descends
To the cool ocean, where his journey ends :
On me love's fiercer flames for ever prey,
By night he scorches, as he burns by day.

Elegy

to the memory of an Unfortunate Lady

What beck'ning ghost, along the moon-light shade
Invites my steps, and points to yonder glade ?
'Tis she !—but why that bleeding bosom gor'd ?
Why dimly gleams the visionary sword ?
Oh ever beauteous, ever friendly ! tell,
Is it, in Heaven, a crime to love too well ?
To bear too tender, or too firm a heart,
To act a lover's or a Roman's part ?
Is there no bright reversion in the sky,
For those who greatly think, or bravely die ?

Why bade ye else, ye powers ! her soul aspire
Above the vulgar flight of low desire ?
Ambition first sprung from your bless'd abodes ;
The glorious fault of angels and of gods :
Thence to their images on earth it flows,
And in the breasts of kings and heroes glows.
Most souls, 'tis true, but peep out once an age,
Dull sullen pris'ners in the body's cage :
Dim lights of life, that burn a length of years
Useless, unseen, as lamps in sepulchres ;
Like Eastern kings a lazy state they keep,
And, close confin'd to their own palace, sleep.

From these perhaps (ere nature bade her die
Fate snatch'd her early to the pitying sky.
As into air the purer spirits flow,

And sep'rate from their kindred dregs below ;
So flew the soul to its congenial place,
Nor left one virtue to redeem her race.

But thou, false guardian of a charge too good,
Thou mean deserter of thy brother's blood !
See on these ruby lips the trembling breath,
These cheeks now fading at the blast of death ;
Cold is that breast which warm'd the world before,
And those love-darting eyes must roll no more.
Thus, if eternal justice rules the ball,
Thus shall your wives, and thus your children fall :
On all the line a sudden vengeance waits,
And frequent hearses shall besiege your gates ;
There passengers shall stand, and pointing say,
(While the long fun'rals blacken all the way)
" Lo ! these were they, whose souls the furies steel'd,
And curs'd with hearts unknowing how to yield."
Thus unlamented pass the proud away,
The gaze of fools, and pageant of a day !
So perish all, whose breast ne'er learn'd to glow
For others' good, or melt at others' woe.

What can atone, oh ever-injur'd shade !
Thy fate unpitied, and thy rites unpaid ?
No friend's complaint, no kind domestic tear
Pleas'd thy pale ghost, or grac'd thy mournful bier.
By foreign hands thy dying eyes were clos'd,
By foreign hands thy decent limbs compos'd,
By foreign hands thy humble grave adorn'd,
By strangers honour'd, and by strangers mourn'd !
What though no friends in sable weeds appear,
Grieve for an hour, perhaps, then mourn a year,
And bear about the mockery of woe
To midnight dances, and the public show ?
What though no weeping loves thy ashes grace,
Nor polish'd marble emulate thy face ?
What though no sacred earth allow thee room,
Nor hallow'd dirge be mutter'd o'er thy tomb ?

Yet shall thy grave with rising flowers be dress'd,
And the green turf lie lightly on thy breast :
There shall the morn her earliest tears bestow,
There the first roses of the year shall blow ;
While angels with their silver wings o'ershade
The ground, now sacred by thy relics made.

So peaceful rests, without a stone, a name,
What once had beauty, titles, wealth, and fame.
How lov'd, how honour'd once, avails thee not,
To whom related, or by whom begot ;
A heap of dust alone remains of thee ;
'Tis all thou art, and all the proud shall be !

Poets themselves must fall like those they sung,
Deaf the prais'd ear, and mute the tuneful tongue.
Ev'n he, whose soul now melts in mournful lays,
Shall shortly want the gen'rous tear he pays ;
Then from his closing eyes thy form shall part,
And the last pang shall tear thee from his heart,
Life's idle business at one gasp be o'er,
The muse forgot, and thou belov'd no more !

Epistle to Mr. Jervas,

with Dryden's translation of Fresnoy's " Art of Painting"

This verse be thine, my friend, nor thou refuse
This, from no venal or ungrateful muse.
Whether thy hand strike out some free design,
Where Life awakes, and dawns at every line ;
Or blend in beauteous tints the colour'd mass,
And from the canvas call the mimic face :
Read these instructive leaves, in which conspire
Fresnoy's close art, and Dryden's native fire :
And reading wish, like theirs our fate and fame,
So mix'd our studies, and so join'd our name :
Like them to shine through long succeeding age,
So just thy skill, so regular my rage.

ALEXANDER POPE

Smit with the love of sister arts we came,
And met congenial, mingling flame with flame ;
Like friendly colours found them both unite,
And each from each contract new strength and light.
How oft in pleasing tasks we wear the day,
While summer suns roll unperceiv'd away !
How oft our slowly-growing works impart,
While images reflect from art to art ;
How oft review ; each finding like a friend
Something to blame, and something to commend !

What flattering scenes our wandering fancy wrought,
Rome's pompous glories rising to our thought !
Together o'er the Alps methinks we fly,
Fir'd with ideas of fair Italy.
With thee on Raphael's monument I mourn,
Or wait inspiring dreams at Maro's urn :
With thee repose where Tully once was laid,
Or seek some ruin's formidable shade :
While Fancy brings the vanish'd piles to view,
And builds imaginary Rome anew.
Here thy well studied marbles fix our eye :
A fading fresco here demands a sigh :
Each heavenly piece unwearied we compare,
Match Raphael's grace with thy lov'd Guido's air,
Carraci's strength, Correggio's softer line,
Paulo's free stroke, and Titian's warmth divine.

How finish'd with illustrious toil appears
This small well-polish'd gem, the work of years.
Yet still how faint by precept is express'd
The living image in the painter's breast ?
Thence endless streams of fair ideas flow,
Strike in the sketch, or in the picture glow ;
Thence Beauty, waking all her forms, supplies
An Angel's sweetness, or Bridgewater's eyes.

Muse ! at that name thy sacred sorrows shed,
Those tears eternal, that embalm the dead :

Call round her tomb each object of desire,
Each purer frame inform'd with purer fire ;
Bid her be all that cheers or softens life,
The tender sister, daughter, friend and wife :
Bid her be all that makes mankind adore,
Then view this marble, and be vain no more !

Yet still her charms in breathing paint engage ;
Her modest cheek shall warm a future age.
Beauty, frail flower that every season fears,
Blooms in thy colours for a thousand years.
Thus Churchill's race shall other hearts surprise,
And other beauties envy Worsley's eyes ;
Each pleasing Blount shall endless smiles bestow,
And soft Belinda's blush for ever glow.

Oh lasting as those colours may they shine,
Free as thy stroke, yet faultless as thy line,
New graces yearly like thy works display,
Soft without weakness, without glaring gay ;
Led by some rule that guides, but not constrains ;
And finish'd more through happiness than pains.
The kindred Arts shall in their praise conspire,
One dip the pencil, and one string the lyre.
Yet should the Graces all thy figures place,
And breathe an air divine on every face ;
Yet should the Muses bid my numbers roll
Strong as their charms, and gentle as their soul ;
With Zeuxis' Helen thy Bridgewater vie,
And these be sung till Granville's Myra die :
Alas ! how little from the grave we claim,
Thou but preserv'st a face, and I a name.

ALEXANDER POPE

Epistle to Miss Martha Blount

on her leaving town after the Coronation

As some fond virgin, whom her mother's care
Drags from the town to wholesome country air,
Just when she learns to roll a melting eye,
And hear a spark, yet think no danger nigh ;
From the dear man unwilling she must sever,
Yet takes one kiss before she parts for ever :
Thus from the world fair Zephalinda flew,
Saw others happy, and with sighs withdrew ;
Not that their pleasures caus'd her discontent,
She sigh'd not that they stay'd, but that she went.

She went to plain-work, and to purling brooks,
Old-fashion'd halls, dull aunts, and croaking rooks ;
She went from Opera, Park, Assembly, Play,
To morning walks, and prayers three hours a day ;
To part her time 'twixt reading and bohea,
To muse, and spill her solitary tea,
Or o'er cold coffee trifle with a spoon,
Count the slow clock, and dine exact at noon ;
Divert her eyes with pictures in the fire,
Hum half a tune, tell stories to the squire ;
Up to her godly garret after seven,
There starve and pray, for that's the way to Heaven.

Some squire, perhaps, you take delight to rack,
Whose game is whisk, whose treat a toast in sack ;
Who visits with a gun, presents you birds,
Then gives a smacking buss, and cries—" No words ! "
Or with his hounds comes hallooing from the stable,
Makes love with nods and knees beneath a table ;
Whose laughs are hearty, though his jests are coarse,
And loves you best of all things—but his horse.

In some fair evening, on your elbow laid,
You dream of triumphs in the rural shade ;
In pensive thought recall the fancied scene,
See coronations rise on every green ;
Before you pass the imaginary sights
Of lords, and earls, and dukes, and garter'd knights,
While the spread fan o'ershades your closing eyes ;
Then give one flirt, and all the vision flies.
Thus vanish sceptres, coronets, and balls,
And leave you in lone woods or empty walls.

So when your slave, at some dear idle time,
(Not plagu'd with head-aches, or the want of rhyme,)
Stands in the streets, abstracted from the crew,
And while he seems to study, thinks of you ;
Just when his fancy points your sprightly eyes,
Or sees the blush of soft Parthenia rise,
Gay pats my shoulder, and you vanish quite,
Streets, chairs, and coxcombs rush upon my sight ;
Vex'd to be still in town, I knit my brow,
Look sour, and hum a tune, as you may now.

Epitaph on John Gay
in Westminster Abbey, 1732

Of manners gentle, of affections mild ;
In wit, a man ; simplicity, a child :
With native humour temp'ring virtuous rage,
Form'd to delight at once and lash the age :
Above temptation, in a low estate,
And uncorrupted, ev'n among the great :
A safe companion, and an easy friend,
Unblam'd through life, lamented in thy end.
These are thy honours ! not that here thy bust
Is mix'd with heroes, or with kings thy dust ;
But that the worthy and the good shall say,
Striking their pensive bosoms,—*Here* lies Gay.

ALEXANDER POPE

A Prologue to a Play for Mr. Dennis's Benefit, in 1733,

when he was old, blind, and in great distress, a little before his death

As when that hero, who in each campaign
Had brav'd the Goth, and many a Vandal slain,
Lay fortune-struck, a spectacle of woe !
Wept by each friend, forgiv'n by every foe :
Was there a gen'rous, a reflecting mind,
But pitied Belisarius, old and blind ?
Was there a chief but melted at the sight ?
A common soldier, but who clubb'd his mite ?
Such, such emotions should in Britons rise,
When press'd by want and weakness Dennis lies ;
Dennis who long had warr'd with modern Huns,
Their quibbles routed, and defied their puns ;
A desp'rate bulwark, sturdy, firm, and fierce
Against the Gothic sons of frozen verse :
How chang'd from him who made the boxes groan,
And shook the stage with thunders all his own !
Stood up to dash each vain Pretender's hope,
Maul the French tyrant, or pull down the Pope !
If there's a Briton then, true bred and born,
Who holds Dragoons and wooden shoes in scorn :
If there's a critic of distinguish'd rage ;
If there's a Senior, who contemns this age ;
Let him to-night his just assistance lend,
And be the Critic's, Briton's, Old Man's friend.

The Dying Christian to his Soul

Vital spark of heavenly flame !
Quit, oh quit this mortal frame :
Trembling, hoping, ling'ring, flying,
Oh the pain, the bliss of dying !
Cease, fond Nature, cease thy strife,
And let me languish into life.

Hark ! they whisper ; Angels say,
" Sister Spirit, come away."
What is this absorbs me quite ?
Steals my senses, shuts my sight,
Drowns my spirits, draws my breath ?
Tell me, my Soul, can this be Death ?

The world recedes ; it disappears !
Heav'n opens on my eyes ! my ears
　　With sounds seraphic ring :
Lend, lend your wings ! I mount ! I fly !
O Grave ! where is thy victory ?
　　O Death ! where is thy sting ?

Ode on Solitude

Happy the man whose wish and care
　　A few paternal acres bound,
Content to breathe his native air,
　　　　In his own ground.

Whose herds with milk, whose fields with bread,
　　Whose flocks supply him with attire,
Whose trees in summer yield him shade,
　　　　In winter fire.

Blest, who can unconcern'dly find
　　Hours, days, and years slide soft away,
In health of body, peace of mind,
　　　　Quiet by day,

Sound sleep by night ; study and ease,
　　Together mixt ; sweet recreation ;
And Innocence, which most does please
　　　　With meditation.

Thus let me live, unseen, unknown,
　　Thus unlamented let me die,
Steal from the world, and not a stone
　　　　Tell where I lie.

ALEXANDER POPE

On a Certain Lady at Court

I know the thing that's most uncommon,
  (Envy, be silent, and attend !) ;
I know a reasonable woman,
  Handsome and witty, yet a friend.

Not warp'd by passion, aw'd by rumour,
  Not grave through pride, or gay through folly,
An equal mixture of good humour,
  And sensible soft melancholy.

" Has she no faults then " (Envy says) " Sir ? "
  Yes, she has one, I must aver ;
When all the world conspires to praise her,
  The woman's deaf, and does not hear.

The Rev. JOHN STRAIGHT (1688 ?-1736)

The Poet to his False Mistress

Wonder not, faithless woman, if you see,
Yourself so chang'd, so great a change in me.
With shame I own it, I was once your slave,
Ador'd myself the beauties which I gave ;
For know, deceiv'd deceitful, that 'twas I
Gave thy form grace, and lustre to thine eye :
Thy tongue, thy fingers, I their magic taught,
And spread the net in which myself was caught.
So pagan priests first form and dress the wood,
Then prostrate fall before the senseless god.
But now, curs'd woman, thy last sentence hear :
I call'd thy beauty forth, I bid it disappear.
I'll strip thee of thy borrow'd plumes ; undress,
And show thee in thy native ugliness.
Those eyes have shone by me, by me that chin
The seat of wanton Cupids long has been :
Ye fires, go out—ye wanton Cupids, fly—
Of every beam disarm her haggard eye :
'Tis I recall ye ; my known voice obey—
And naught of beauty but the falsehood stay !

LEONARD WELSTED (1688-1747)

A Song

While in the bower, with Beauty blest,
   The lov'd Amintor lies ;
While sinking on Zelinda's breast,
   He fondly kiss'd her eyes ;

A wakeful nightingale, who long
   Had mourn'd within the shade,
Sweetly renew'd her plaintive song,
   And warbled through the glade.

" Melodious Songstress," cried the swain,
   " To shades less happy go ;
Or if with us thou wilt remain,
   Forbear thy tuneful woe.

" While in Zelinda's arms I lie,
   To song I am not free ;
On her soft bosom while I sigh,
   I discord find in thee.

" Zelinda gives me perfect joys :
   Then cease thy fond intrusion ;
Be silent ; Music now is noise,
   Variety confusion."

HENRY CAREY (16 . . .—1743)

On his Daughter Rachel
who died on her father's birthday

That fatal day, which lent my earliest breath,
Gave my dear girl to the cold arms of Death :
Others in triumph may their birth-day keep ;
Mine calls aloud for tears, and bids me weep.

HENRY CAREY

Sally in Our Alley

Of all the girls that are so smart
   There's none like pretty Sally,
She is the darling of my heart,
   And she lives in our alley.
There is no lady in the land
   Is half so sweet as Sally,
She is the darling of my heart,
   And she lives in our alley.

Her father he makes cabbage-nets,
   And through the streets does cry 'em :
Her mother she sells laces long,
   To such as please to buy 'em :
But sure such folks could ne'er beget
   So sweet a girl as Sally !
She is the darling of my heart,
   And she lives in our alley.

When she is by I leave my work,
   (I love her so sincerely)
My master comes like any Turk,
   And bangs me most severely ;
But, let him bang his belly-full,
   I'll bear it all for Sally ;
She is the darling of my heart,
   And she lives in our alley.

Of all the days that's in the week,
   I dearly love but one day,
And that's the day that comes betwixt
   A Saturday and Monday ;
For then I'm drest, all in my best,
   To walk abroad with Sally ;
She is the darling of my heart,
   And she lives in our alley.

HENRY CAREY

My master carries me to Church,
  And often am I blamed,
Because I leave him in the lurch,
  As soon as text is named :
I leave the church in sermon time,
  And slink away with Sally ;
She is the darling of my heart,
  And she lives in our alley.

When Christmas comes about again,
  O then I shall have money ;
I'll hoard it up, and box and all
  I'll give it to my honey ;
And, would it were ten thousand pounds,
  I'd give it all to Sally ;
She is the darling of my heart,
  And she lives in our alley.

My master and the neighbours all
  Make game of me and Sally ;
And (but for her) I'd better be
  A slave and row a galley :
But when my seven long years are out,
  O then I'll marry Sally !
O then we'll wed and then we'll bed,
  But not in our alley.

LADY MARY WORTLEY MONTAGU (1689-1762)

Verses

written in a Garden

See how that pair of billing doves
With open murmurs own their loves ;
And heedless of censorious eyes
Pursue their unpolluted joys :
No fears of future want molest
The downy quiet of their nest ;
No int'rest join'd the happy pair,
Securely blest in Nature's care,
While her dear dictates they pursue :
For constancy is nature too.

Can all the doctrine of our schools,
Our maxims, our religious rules,
Can learning to our lives ensure
Virtue so bright, or bliss so pure ?
The great Creator's happy ends
Virtue and pleasure ever blends :
In vain the church and court have tried
Th' united essence to divide ;
Alike they find their wild mistake,
The pedant priest, and giddy rake.

A Hymn to the Moon

Written in July, in an arbour

Thou silver deity of secret night,
  Direct my footsteps through the woodland shade ;
Thou conscious witness of unknown delight,
  The lover's guardian, and the Muses' aid !
By thy pale beams I solitary rove,
  To thee my tender grief confide ;
Serenely sweet you gild the silent grove,
  My friend, my goddess, and my guide.
E'en thee, fair queen, from thy amazing height,
  The charms of young Endymion drew ;
Veil'd with the mantle of concealing night ;
  With all thy greatness, and thy coldness too.

LADY MARY MONTAGU

A Receipt to Cure the Vapours

Why will Delia thus retire,
   And idly languish life away ?
While the sighing crowd admire,
   'Tis too soon for hartshorn tea :

All those dismal looks and fretting
   Cannot Damon's life restore ;
Long ago the worms have eat him,
   You can never see him more.

Once again consult your toilette,
   In the glass your face review :
So much weeping soon will spoil it,
   And no spring your charms renew.

I, like you, was born a woman,
   Well I know what vapours mean :
The disease, alas ! is common ;
   Single, we have all the spleen.

All the morals that they tell us
   Never cur'd the sorrow yet :
Choose, among the pretty fellows,
   One of honour, youth, and wit.

Prithee hear him every morning
   At the least an hour or two ;
Once again at night returning—
   I believe the dose will do.

Farewell to Bath

To all you ladies now at Bath,
   And eke, ye beaus, to you,
With aching heart, and watery eyes,
   I bid my last adieu.

LADY MARY MONTAGU

Farewell, ye nymphs, who waters sip
   Hot reeking from the pumps,
While music lends her friendly aid,
   To cheer you from the dumps.

Farewell, ye wits, who prating stand,
   And criticise the fair ;
Yourselves the joke of men of sense,
   Who hate a coxcomb's air.

Farewell to Deard's, and all her toys,
   Which glitter in her shop,
Deluding traps to girls and boys,
   The warehouse of the fop.

Lindsay's and Hayes's both farewell,
   Where in the spacious hall,
With bounding steps, and sprightly air,
   I've led up many a ball.

Where Somerville of courteous mien
   Was partner in the dance,
With swimming Haws, and Brownlow blithe,
   And Britton pink of France.

Poor Nash, farewell ! may fortune smile,
   Thy drooping soul revive ;
My heart is full, I can no more—
   John, bid the coachman drive.

The Rev. WILLIAM BROOME, LL.D. (1689-1745)

The Rose-Bud :

To the Right Honourable The Lady Jane Wharton

Queen of fragrance, lovely rose,
The beauties of thy leaves disclose !
The Winter's past, the tempests fly,
Soft gales breathe gently through the sky ;
The lark sweet warbling on the wing
Salutes the gay return of spring :
The silver dews, the vernal showers,
Call forth a bloomy waste of flowers ;
The joyous fields, the shady woods,
Are cloth'd with green, or swell with buds ;
Then haste thy beauties to disclose,
Queen of fragrance, lovely rose !

Thou, beauteous flower, a welcome guest,
Shalt flourish on the fair one's breast,
Shalt grace her hand, or deck her hair,
The flower most sweet, the nymph most fair ;
Breathe soft, ye winds ! be calm, ye skies !
Arise ye flowery race, arise !
And haste thy beauties to disclose,
Queen of fragrance, lovely rose !

But thou, fair nymph, thyself survey
In this sweet offspring of a day ;
That miracle of face must fail,
Thy charms are sweet, but charms are frail :
Swift as the short-liv'd flower they fly,
At morn they bloom, at evening die ;
Though sickness yet a while forbears,
Yet time destroys what sickness spares ;
Now Helen lives alone in fame,
And Cleopatra's but a name ;
Time must indent that heavenly brow,
And thou must be what they are now.

This moral to the fair disclose,
Queen of fragrance, lovely rose.

WILLIAM BROOME

To a Lady of Thirty

No more let youth its beauty boast,
S——n at thirty reigns a toast :
And like the sun as he declines,
More mildly, but more sweetly, shines.

The hand of time alone disarms
Her face of its superfluous charms :
But adds, for every grace resign'd,
A thousand to adorn her mind.

Youth was her too inflaming time ;
This, her more habitable clime ;
How must she then each heart engage,
Who blooms like youth, is wise like age ?

Thus the rich orange-trees produce
At once both ornament and use ;
Here opening blossoms we behold,
There fragrant orbs of ripen'd gold.

Poverty and Poetry

'Twas sung of old how one Amphion
Could by his verses tame a lion ;
And by his strange enchanting tunes,
Make bears and wolves dance rigadoons :
His songs could call the timber down,
And form it into house or town ;
But it is plain that in these times
No house is rais'd by poet's rhymes ;
They for themselves can only rear
A few wild castles in the air ;
Poor are the brethren of the bays,
Down from high strains, to ekes and ayes.
The Muses too are virgins yet,
And may be—till they portions get.

WILLIAM BROOME

Yet still the doating rhymer dreams,
And sings of Helicon's bright streams,
But Helicon, for all his clatter,
Yields only uninspiring water ;
Yet even athirst he sweetly sings
Of Nectar, and Elysian springs.

What dire malignant planet sheds,
Ye bards, his influence on your heads ?
Lawyers, by endless controversies,
Consume unthinking clients' purses,
As Pharaoh's kine, which strange and odd is,
Devour'd the plump and well-fed bodies.

The grave physician, who by physic,
Like Death, dispatches him that is sick,
Pursues a sure and thriving trade,
Though patients die, the doctor's paid ;
Licens'd to kill, he gains a palace,
For what another mounts the gallows.

In shady groves the Muses stray,
And love in flowery meads to play ;
An idle crew ! whose only trade is
To shine in trifles, like our ladies ;
In dressing, dancing, toying, singing,
While wiser Pallas thrives by spinning ;
Thus they gain nothing to bequeath
Their votaries, but a laurel wreath.

But love rewards the bard ! the fair
Attend his song, and ease his care :
Alas ! fond youth, your plea you urge ill
Without a jointure, though a Virgil ;
Could you like Phœbus sing, in vain
You nobly swell the lofty strain,
Coy Daphne flies, and you will find as
Hard hearts as hers in your Belindas.

But then some say you purchase fame,
And gain that envied prize, a name ;
Great recompense ! like his who sells
A diamond for beads and bells ;
Will fame be thought sufficient bail
To keep the poet from the gaol ?

Thus the brave soldier, in the wars,
Gets empty praise and aching scars :
Is paid with fame and wooden legs,
And starv'd, the glorious vagrant begs.

THOMAS CATESBY PAGET, Baron PAGET
(1689-1742)

The Character of Almenon

Out of an old manuscript

Almenon had a sort of merit :
Some sense, good humour, wit and spirit,
But then he had a strange weak side :
He hated roguery and pride ;
Nor saw at Court, without a sneer,
The mummeries he met with there.
　　To senates by his country sent,
He serv'd them well in Parliament ;
Nor would, for tawdry toys or pelf,
Betray his trust and sell himself.
　　Sincere and friendly, not punctilious ;
No mamamouche, nor supercilious ;
In conversation gay and free,
But lik'd not too much company.
　　No toping sot, nor noted rake,
But yet would too much pleasure take ;
Though he ne'er hurt estate nor fame,

Nor brought a scandal on the name :
Good books he priz'd from earliest youth,
And valu'd men for worth and truth ;
Chitchat he lov'd, but could not bear
Dull jokes nor spiteful tales to hear ;
And rather chose to spend the day
Alone in his amusing way,
Than barter time, and health, and quiet,
For idle news and noisy riot.
He could not fawn on fools or knaves,
Nor live with sycophants and slaves ;
But still preferred the lone retreat,
To being, that way, rich and great.

Say, what became of this odd creature,
So out of fashion, out of nature ?

Luck he had little, favour less,
Nor did much worldly means possess,
Though born to title and estate,
(So whimsically odd his fate).
Yet he with joy gave all he could
To do his needy neighbours good ;
To studious ease was much inclin'd,
And bless'd with a contented mind ;
Obscure, a peaceful life he led—
Nor envied those who better sped.

GEORGE SEWELL, M.D. (*circa* 1690 ?-1726)

Verses Written at Hampstead
shortly before his death

Why, Damon, with the forward day,
Dost thou thy little spot survey ?
From tree to tree, with doubtful cheer,
Pursue the progress of the year ;
What winds arise, what rains descend,
When thou before that year shalt end ?

What do thy noon-day walks avail,
To clear the leaf, and pick the snail,
Then wantonly to death decree
An insect usefuller than thee ?
    Thou and the worm art brother-kind,
    As low, as earthy, and as blind.

Vain wretch ! canst thou expect to see
The downy peach make court to thee ?
Or that thy sense shall ever meet
The bean-flower's deep-embosom'd sweet,
    Exhaling with an evening's blast ?
    Thy evenings then will all be past.

Thy narrow pride, thy fancied green,
(For vanity's in little seen)
All must be left when Death appears,
In spite of wishes, groans, and tears ;
    Nor one of all thy plants that grow,
    But Rosemary, will with thee go.

The Hon. Mrs. MARY MONK (*née* MOLESWORTH)
(16—1715)

An Epitaph on a Gallant Lady

O'er this Marble drop a tear,
    Here lies fair Rosalinde.
All mankind was pleas'd with her,
    And she with all mankind.

MARY MONK

Verses written on her Death-bed at Bath to her Husband in London

Thou who dost all my worldly thoughts employ,
Thou pleasing source of all my earthly joy,
Thou tenderest husband and thou dearest friend,
To thee this first, this last adieu I send !
At length the conqueror Death asserts his right,
And will for ever veil me from thy sight ;
He woos me to him with a cheerful grace,
And not one terror clouds his meagre face ;
He promises a lasting rest from pain,
And shows that all life's fleeting joys are vain ;
Th' eternal scenes of Heaven he sets in view,
And tells me that no other joys are true.
But love, fond love, would yet resist his power,
Would fain awhile defer the parting hour ;
He brings thy mourning image to my eyes,
And would obstruct my journey to the skies.
But say, thou dearest, thou unwearied friend !
Say, shouldst thou grieve to see my sorrows end ?
Thou know'st a painful pilgrimage I've pass'd ;
And shouldst thou grieve that rest is come at last ?
Rather rejoice to see me shake off life,
And die as I have liv'd, thy faithful wife.

Mrs. MARY BARBER (1690 ?-1757)

An Epigram

on " The Battle of the Books "

Swift for the Ancients has argu'd so well,
'Tis apparent from thence, that the Moderns excel.

MARY BARBER

An Epigram
on a small collection taken for charity

So little giv'n at Chapel door—
This people doubtless must be poor ;
So much at gaming thrown away—
No nation sure so rich as they.
Britons, 'twere greatly for your glory,
Should those, who shall transmit your story,
Their notions of your grandeur frame,
Not as you *give*, but as you *game*.

HENRY NEEDLER (1690-1718)
On Arithmetic and Geometry

Hail, heavenly pair ! by whose conspiring aid
The beauteous fabric of the world was made !
Led on by you, audacious men forget
The narrow bounds by envious Nature set ;
To yon bright mansions soar with happy flight,
Survey the starry realms, and range through worlds of light !

Mrs. MARTHA SANSOM (*née* FOWKE), " CLIO "
(1690-1736)
Song

Foolish eyes, thy streams give over,
Wine, not water, binds the lover,
At the table then be shining,
Gay coquette, and all designing.
To th' addressing foplings bowing,
And thy smile, or hand, allowing,
Whine no more thy sacred passion,
Out of nature, out of fashion.

Let him, disappointed, find thee
False as he, nor dream to bind thee,
While he breaks all tender measures,
Murdering love, and all its pleasures.

Shall a look or word deceive thee,
Which he once an age will give thee ?
Oh ! no more, no more, excuse him,
Like a dull deserter use him.

The Invitation from a Country Cottage

Close to the fire-side confin'd,
By the cold fogs, and piercing wind,
Bless'd with my dog, and peace of mind.
The cheerful rustics all sit round,
Whose careful hands improve the ground,
After the labour of the day,
Upon the clean-swept hearth, and play ;
The well-us'd pack of cards was found,
Grown soil'd with often dealing round ;
No ceremony, here, they use,
But frankly wrangle, when they lose ;
The hand that deals to all the rest,
Returns not back to Colin's breast,
As among finer gamesters seen,
Nor is the table lin'd with green,
But a plain, honest, cleanly board,
Such as these humble shades afford :
No gold upon the table shines,
But chalk the homely game confines ;
Some lad, more am'rous than the rest,
Sings a sad ditty to their guest,
Of some false damsel, most ingrate,
Or melancholy *Bateman's* fate.
Believe, it pleases me, my friend,
To see the artless tears descend ;
Their eyes, that ne'er were *taught* to grieve,
Their hearts, which nat'ral passions heave,
Show lovely nature all undress'd,
And charm my undesigning breast ;
O ! come, my friend, and see *one* place,
Where all things wear an honest face.

JOSEPH THURSTON (*floruit circa* 1729)

Song

Phyllis, would you have me love you,
   Truce with that affected scorn !
Artless if I fail to move you,
   I shall never learn to mourn.

Fops may ogle, sigh, and languish,
   Swear you life or death can give ;
Though your rigour cause me anguish,
   Yet, believe me, I shall live.

You are but yourself disarming,
   While you give your lover pain ;
Beauty ceases to be charming
   Once 'tis tainted with disdain.

Use me kindly, fairest creature,
   You shall ever find me true ;
Yet, so stubborn is my nature,
   Slighted, I can bid adieu.

GEORGE BUBB DODINGTON, Baron MELCOMBE (1691-1762)

Verses sent to Dr. Young,
not long before his lordship's death

Kind companion of my youth,
Lov'd for genius, worth and truth !
Take what friendship can impart,
Tribute of a feeling heart ;
Take the Muse's latest spark,
Ere we drop into the dark.
He, who parts and virtue gave,
Bad thee look beyond thy grave :
Genius soars, and Virtue guides,
Where the love of God presides.
There's a gulf 'twixt us and God ;

Let the gloomy path be trod :
Why stand shivering on the shore ?
Why not boldly venture o'er ?
Where unerring Virtue guides,
Let us brave the winds and tides :
Safe, through seas of doubts and fears,
Rides the bark which Virtue steers.

The Rev. SAMUEL WESLEY, the younger* (1691-1739)

An Hymn to God the Father

Hail, Father ! whose creating call
    Unnumber'd worlds attend ;
JEHOVAH ! comprehending all,
    Whom none can comprehend.

In light unsearchable enthron'd,
    Which Angels dimly see ;
The Fountain of the Godhead own'd,
    And foremost of the Three.

From whom through an eternal Now
    The Son Thy offspring flow'd,
An everlasting Father Thou,
    An everlasting God !

Nor quite display'd to worlds above,
    Nor quite on earth conceal'd ;
By wondrous unexhausted Love
    To mortal man reveal'd !

Supreme and all-sufficient God,
    When nature shall expire ;
When worlds, created by Thy nod,
    Shall perish by Thy fire.

Thy Name, JEHOVAH ! be ador'd
    By creatures without end !
Whom none but Thy essential Word
    And Spirit comprehend.

* Elder brother of John and Charles Wesley.

SAMUEL WESLEY

Epitaph on an Infant

Beneath a sleeping infant lies,
   To earth whose ashes lent,
More glorious shall hereafter rise,
   Though not more innocent.

When the Archangel's Trump shall blow,
   And souls and bodies join,
What crowds will wish their lives below
   Had been as short as thine !

An Epitaph

Here lie I, once a witty fair,
   Ill loving and ill lov'd ;
Whose heedless beauty was my snare,
   Whose wit my folly prov'd.

Reader, should any curious stay
   To ask my luckless name,
Tell them, the grave that hides my clay
   Conceals me from my shame.

Tell them, I mourn'd for guilt of sin,
   More than for pleasure spent :
Tell them : whate'er my morn had been,
   My noon was penitent.

An Epitaph

A clergyman his labour ends,
   And weary sleeps at rest below ;
Who, though his fortune found not friends,
   In person hardly knew a foe.

Minding no business but his own,
   For party never loud to strive ;
His flock not only mourn him gone,
   But even lov'd him when alive.

A conscience clean his forehead cheer'd,
　　Unsour'd by poverty was he ;
And always prais'd, though not prefer'd,
　　By every prelate in the see.

But good men view with small regard
　　The treatment here on earth they find ;
Secure in Heaven to meet reward
　　From the Great Bishop of Mankind.

From a Hint in the Minor Poets

No ! not for those of women born,
　　Not so unlike the die is cast ;
For, after all our vaunt and scorn,
　　How very small the odds at last !

Him rais'd to Fortune's utmost top,
　　With him beneath her feet compare ;
And one has nothing more to hope,
　　And one has nothing more to fear.

An Anacreontick
on parting with a little child.

Dear, farewell a little while,
Easy parting with a smile ;
Every object in thy way
Makes thee innocently gay ;
All that thou canst hear or see,
All is novelty to thee.
Thoughts of parents left behind
Vex not yet thine infant mind ;
Why should then their hearts repine ?
Mournful theirs, and merry thine.
'Tis the world ; the seeming wise
Toil to make their children rise ;

While the heir that reaps their gains
Thankless thinks not of their pains.
Sportive youth in haste to live
Heeds not ills that years may give :
Age in woe and wisdom grey
Vainly mourns for them that play.

Song

How do they err, who throw their love
    On fate or fortune wholly ;
Whom only rants and flights can move,
    And rapture join'd with folly !

For how can pleasure solid be
    Where thought is out of season ?
Do I love you, or you love me,
    My dear, without a reason ?

Our sense then rightly we'll employ,
    No paradise expecting ;
Yet envying none the trifling joy,
    That will not bear reflecting.

For wisdom's power (since after all
    Ev'n life is past the curing)
Softens the worst that can befall,
    And makes the best enduring.

The Monument

Post Funera Virtus

A monster, in a course of vice grown old,
Leaves to his gaping heir his ill-gain'd gold :
Straight breathes his bust, straight are his virtues shown,
Their date commencing with the sculptur'd stone.
If on his specious marble we rely,
Pity a worth like his should ever die !
If credit to his real life we give,
Pity a wretch like him should ever live !

SAMUEL WESLEY

On the Setting Up of Mr. Butler's Monument in Westminster Abbey

While Butler, needy wretch ! was yet alive,
No generous patron would a dinner give :
See him, when starv'd to death and turn'd to dust,
Presented with a monumental bust !
The poet's fate is here in emblem shown,
He ask'd for bread, and he receiv'd a stone !

JOHN BYROM (1692-1763)

A Pastoral

My time, O ye Muses ! was happily spent,
When Phebe went with me wherever I went,
Ten thousand sweet pleasures I felt in my breast,
Sure, never fond shepherd like Colin was blest !
But now she is gone, and has left me behind,
What a marvellous change on a sudden I find !
When things were as fine as could possibly be,
I thought 'twas the spring ; but, alas ! it was she !

With such a companion, to tend a few sheep,
To rise up and play, or to lie down and sleep ;
I was so good-humour'd, so cheerful and gay,
My heart was as light as a feather all day !
But now I so cross and so peevish am grown,
So strangely uneasy, as never was known !
My fair one is gone, and my joys are all drown'd,
And my heart—I am sure it weighs more than a pound !

The fountain, that wont to run sweetly along,
And dance to soft murmurs the pebbles among,
Thou know'st, little Cupid ! if Phebe was there,
'Twas pleasure to look at ! 'twas music to hear !
But now she is absent, I walk by its side,
And still, as it murmurs, do nothing but chide !
" Must you be so cheerful, while I go in pain ?
Peace there, with your bubbling, and hear me complain!"

174

My lambkins around me would oftentimes play,
And Phebe and I were as joyful as they ;
How pleasant their sporting, how happy their time,
When Spring, Love, and Beauty were all in their prime !
But now, in their frolics when by me they pass,
I fling at their fleeces an handful of grass !
" Be still then ! " I cry, " for it makes me quite mad,
To see you so merry, while I am so sad ! "

My dog I was ever well-pleased to see
Come wagging his tail to my fair one and me ;
And Phebe was pleas'd too, and to my dog said,
" Come hither, poor fellow ! " and patted his head.
But now when he's fawning, I, with a sour look,
Cry, " Sirrah ! " and give him a blow with my crook :
And I'll give him another ! For why should not Tray
Be as dull as his master, when Phebe's away ?

When walking with Phebe, what sights have I seen !
How fair was the flower ! how fresh was the green !
What a lovely appearance the trees and the shade,
The cornfields and hedges, and every thing, made !
But now she has left me, though all are still there,
They none of them now so delightful appear ;
'Twas naught but the magic, I find, of her eyes
Made so many beautiful prospects arise !

Sweet music went with us both, all the wood through,
The lark, linnet, throstle, and nightingale too.
Winds over us whisper'd. Flocks by us did bleat ;
And chirp went the grasshopper under our feet.
But now she is absent, though still they sing on,
The woods are but lonely, the melody's gone ;
Her voice, in the consort, as now I have found,
Gave everything else its agreeable sound.

Rose ! what is become of thy delicate hue ?
And where is the violet's beautiful blue ?
Does aught of its sweetness the blossom beguile ?
That meadow, those daisies, why do they not smile ?

Ah ! rivals ! I see what it was, that you drest
And made yourselves fine for ! A place in her breast !
You put on your colours, to pleasure her eye ;
To be pluck'd by her hand, on her bosom to die !

How slowly Time creeps, till my Phebe return,
While amidst the soft Zephyr's cool breezes I burn ;
Methinks, if I knew whereabouts he would tread,
I could breathe on his wings, and 'twould melt down
    the lead.
Fly swifter, ye minutes ! bring hither my dear !
And rest so much longer for't, when she is here.
" Ah ! Colin ! old Time is full of delay ;
Nor will budge one foot faster, for all thou canst say ! "

Will no pitying Power, that hears me complain,
Or cure my disquiet, or soften my pain ?
" To be cur'd, thou must, Colin ! thy passion remove ;
But what swain is so silly to live without love ? "
No, Deity ! bid the dear nymph to return !
For ne'er was poor shepherd so sadly forlorn.
Ah ! what shall I do ? I shall die with despair !
Take heed, all ye swains ! how ye part with your fair !

On Clergymen Preaching Politics

Indeed, Sir Peter, I could wish, I own,
That parsons would let politics alone !
Plead, if they will, the customary plea
For such like talk, when o'er a dish of tea ;
But when they tease us with it from the Pulpit,
I own, Sir Peter, that I cannot gulp it.

If on their rules a Justice should intrench,
And preach, suppose, a sermon from the Bench,
Would you not think your brother magistrate
Was touch'd a little in his hinder pate ?
Now, which is worse, Sir Peter, on the total,—
The lay vagary, or the sacerdotal ?

In ancient times, when preachers preach'd indeed
Their sermons, ere the learned learnt to read,
Another Spirit and another Life
Shut the Church doors against all party strife.
Since then, how often heard from sacred rostrums
The lifeless din of Whig and Tory nostrums !

' Tis wrong, Sir Peter, I insist upon't ;
To common sense 'tis plainly an affront.
The parson leaves the Christian in the lurch,
Whene'er he brings his politics to church.
His cant, on either side, if he calls preaching,
The man's wrong-headed, and his brains want bleaching.

Recall the time from conquering William's reign,
And guess the fruits of such a preaching vein :
How oft its nonsense must have veer'd about,
Just as the politics were in or out ;—
The Pulpit govern'd by no Gospel *data,*
But new Success still mending old *Errata.*

Were I a King (God bless me !) I should hate
My chaplains meddling with affairs of state ;
Nor would my subjects, I should think, be fond,
Whenever theirs the Bible went beyond.
How well, methinks, we both should live together,
If these good folks would keep within their tether !

Epigrams

I

On a Monopoly for Grinding Corn in Manchester,

Bone and Skin,
Two millers thin,
Would starve the town, or near it ;
But be it known
To Skin and Bone,
That Flesh and Blood can't bear it.

II

On Handel and Bononcini

Some say, compar'd to Bononcini,
That Mynheer Handel's but a ninny ;
Others aver, that he to Handel
Is scarcely fit to hold a candle.
Strange all this difference should be
'Twixt Tweedle-dum and Tweedle-dee !

III

God bless the King !—I mean the Faith's defender :
God bless—no harm in blessing—the Pretender !
But who Pretender is, or who is King—
God bless us all ! that's quite another thing !

The Soul's Tendency towards its True Centre

Stones towards the earth descend ;
    Rivers to the ocean roll ;
Ev'ry motion has some end ;—
    What is thine, beloved Soul ?

" Mine is, where my Saviour is ;
    There with Him I hope to dwell.
Jesus is the Central Bliss,
    Love the force that doth impel."

Truly, thou hast answer'd right.
    Now, may Heav'n's Attractive Grace
Tow'rds the Source of thy delight
    Speed along thy quick'ning pace !

" Thank thee for thy gen'rous care !
    Heav'n that did the wish inspire
Through thy instrumental prayer
    Plumes the wings of my desire.

" Now, methinks, aloft I fly ;
  Now, with Angels bear a part.
Glory be to God on High,
  Peace to ev'ry Christian heart ! "

Procrastination

If gold be offer'd thee, thou dost not say,
" To-morrow I will take it, not To-day."
Salvation offer'd, why art thou so cool,
To let thyself become To-morrow's Fool ?

HILDEBRAND JACOB (1693-1739)

Epitaph on My Lady ——

Beneath this marble lays a load
Of earth, which once was flesh and blood,
Warm'd with a spirit strangely prone
To hate all notions but her own :
Her person fair, of moderate size,
Her mind, as moderately wise ;
Not very dull, nor mighty smart ;
But hated wit with all her heart :
Not very silent, nor a scold ;
Extremely chaste, extremely cold,
Loyal, and pious to excess,
And truly humble in distress,
She liv'd in fear, and died in hope,
Renouncing Satan, Whig, and Pope.

Epigram

Titus reads neither prose, nor rhyme ;
He writes himself ; he has no time.

MARY MASTERS* (1694 ?-1771)

The Resolution Broke

Stunn'd with the clamours of the noisy town,
The Muse her humblest vot'ry did disown :
From sad Maria's breast she took her flight,
And charg'd the pensive maid no more to write :
I heard the charge, which was pronounc'd aloud,
And straight a lasting firm obedience vow'd.
Yet one half-day from smoke and strife remov'd,
To tread the earth and breathe the air I lov'd,
I felt a power, too strong to be suppress'd,
Move with poetic rapture in my breast.
Scenes all-transporting set my soul on fire,
And fields and meads their wonted thoughts inspire.
Each fruitful hedge inviting themes supplies,
" In every field harmonious numbers rise."

Here the green wheat dispos'd in even rows
(A pleasing view !) on genial ridges grows,
Its cluster'd heads on lofty spires ascend,
And frequent with delightful wavings bend ;
There younger barley shoots a tender blade,
And spreads a level plain with verdant shade.
The wreathing pea extends its bloomy pride,
And flowery borders smile on either side.

Whate'er I see, does admiration draw,
And strikes my soul with a religious awe.
The annual offspring of the pregnant year
Does well the great Creator's love declare.
For our support the field produces bread,
And 'tis for us the flowery scene is spread.
In all His works His providence I scan,
His never-ceasing care to thankless man.
Prostrate on earth, myself I humbly fling,
In adoration of th' Almighty King.
My grateful heart dissolves in mental prayer,
And thoughts too big for words are lab'ring there.

* This remarkable writer was originally a domestic servant.

Again I rise from off the fertile ground,
Again I view the pleasing prospects round ;
Where'er I turn, instructive scenes arise,
And with new wonders meet my ravish'd eyes.
The feather'd songsters well deserve a lay,
And murm'ring streams in flowing verse should stray.

But hold, the pleasing lyre must be unstrung,
And thousand beauties must remain unsung :
For should I through each gaudy meadow rove,
And paint the varied greens in every grove,
Sing with each bird, and purl with every stream,
I might enlarge, but never end my theme.

Emblems of Clemene

Oft have I seen, with ravish'd eyes,
The beauty of unclouded skies,
When the pure light its lustre sheds,
And o'er the spotless azure spreads.
Such is Clemene's peaceful breast,
When every passion's lull'd to rest :
Her smiles, her lucid eyes impart
Transports to every gazer's heart.

Oft have I seen the troubled air,
When sable clouds were gathering there ;
Darkness the face of Heaven deforms,
Presage of thunder and of storms.
So, when the chang'd Clemene shows
Displeasure on her bended brows ;
When angry looks and frowns appear,
To shade the Heaven of Beauty there ;
Trembling, we view her threatening eye,
And dread the tempest that is nigh.

As fairest, and as sweetest flowers,
Prest with the weight of many showers,
Bend down the melancholy head,
And beautiful in ruin fade :
Such is Clemene, when her mind
Is to invading grief resign'd,
And tears steal forth, herself serene,
As if they meant to fall unseen :
While all, that view the pensive fair,
Would gladly half her sorrow bear :
Nay, the whole burden of her grief,
Would it but give her soul relief.

To Lucinda

Lucinda, you in vain dissuade
  Two hearts from mutual love.
What am'rous youth, or tender maid,
  Could e'er their flames remove ?

What, if the charms in him I see
  Only exist in thought :
Yet Cupid's, like the Medes', decree
  Is firm and changeth not.

Seek not to know my passion's spring,
  The reason to discover :
For reason is a useless thing,
  When we've commenc'd the lover.

Should lovers quarrel with their fate,
  And ask the reason why
They are condemn'd to doat on *that*,
  Or for *this* object die ?

They must not hope for a reply,
  And this is all they know ;
They sigh, and weep, and rave, and die,
  Because it must be so.

Love is a mighty god, you know,
   That rules with potent sway ;
And, when he draws his awful bow,
   We mortals must obey.

Since you the fatal strife endur'd,
   And yielded to his dart ;
How can I hope to be secur'd,
   And guard a weaker heart ?

PHILIP DORMER STANHOPE, EARL OF CHESTERFIELD (1694-1773)

Verses,

written in a Lady's Sherlock upon Death

Mistaken fair, lay Sherlock by,
   His doctrine is deceiving ;
For whilst he teaches us to die,
   He cheats us of our living.

To die's a lesson we shall know
   Too soon without a master ;
Then let us only study now
   How we may live the faster.

To live's to love, to bless, be bless'd
   With mutual inclination ;
Share then my ardour in your breast,
   And kindly meet my passion.

But if thus bless'd I may not live,
   And pity you deny,
To me at least your Sherlock give,
   'Tis I must learn to die.

Song

(*On Lady Frances Shirley*)

When Fanny blooming fair
   First caught my ravish'd sight,
Struck with her shape and air,
   I felt a strange delight :
Whilst eagerly I gaz'd,
   Admiring every part,
And every feature prais'd,
   She stole into my heart.

In her bewitching eyes
   Ten thousand loves appear ;
There Cupid basking lies,
   His shafts are hoarded there ;
Her blooming cheeks are dy'd
   With colour all their own,
Excelling far the pride
   Of roses newly blown.

Her well-turn'd limbs confess
   The lucky hand of Jove ;
Her features all express
   The beauteous Queen of Love :
What flames my nerves invade,
   When I behold the breast
Of that too charming maid
   Rise, suing to be press'd !

Venus round Fanny's waist
   Has her own cestus bound,
With guardian Cupids grac'd,
   Who dance the circle round.
How happy must he be,
   Who shall her zone unloose !
That bliss to all, but me,
   May Heaven and she refuse !

LORD CHESTERFIELD

Advice to a Lady in Autumn

Asses' milk, half a pint, take at sev'n, or before,
Then sleep for an hour or two, and no more.
At nine stretch your arms, and oh ! think when alone,
There's no pleasure in bed.—Mary, bring me my gown !
Slip on that ere you rise ; let your caution be such :
Keep all cold from your breast, there's already too much ;
Your pinners set right, your twitcher tied on,
Your prayers at an end, and your breakfast quite done,
Retire to some author, improving and gay,
And with sense like your own, set your mind for the day.
At twelve you may walk, for at this time o' the year,
The sun, like your wit, is as mild as 'tis clear :
But mark in the meadows the ruin of time ;
Take the hint, and let life be improv'd in its prime.
Return not in haste, nor of dressing take heed ;
For beauty, like yours, no assistance can need.
With an appetite, thus, down to dinner you sit,
Where the chief of the feast is the flow of your wit :
Let this be indulg'd, and let laughter go round ;
As it pleases your mind, to your health 'twill redound.
After dinner two glasses at least, I approve,
Name the first to the King, and the last to your love :
Thus cheerful with wisdom, with innocence gay,
And calm with your joys gently glide through the day.
The dews of the evening most carefully shun ;
Those tears of the sky for the loss of the sun.
Then in chat, or at play, with a dance, or a song,
Let the night, like the day, pass with pleasure along.
All cares, but of love, banish far from the mind ;
And those you may end, when you please to be kind.

LORD CHESTERFIELD

*On Mr. Nash's Picture**

*at full length between the busts of Sir Isaac Newton and
Mr. Pope, at Bath*

The old Egyptians hid their wit
  In hieroglyphic dress,
To give men pains in search of it,
  And please themselves with guess.

Moderns, to hit the self-same path,
  And exercise their parts,
Place figures in a room at Bath :
  Forgive them, God of arts !

Newton, if I can judge aright,
  All wisdom does express ;
His knowledge gives mankind delight,
  Adds to their happiness.

Pope is the emblem of true wit,
  The sunshine of the mind ;
Read o'er his works in search of it,
  You'll endless pleasure find.

Nash represents man in the mass,
  Made up of wrong and right ;
Sometimes a knave, sometimes an ass ;
  Now blunt, and now polite.

The picture plac'd the busts between,
  Adds to the thought much strength ;
Wisdom and Wit are little seen,
  But Folly's at full length.

*This poem has also been attributed, almost certainly erroneously,
to Jane Brereton.

ELIZABETH TOLLET (1694-1754)

On a Death's Head

On this resemblance, where we find
A portrait drawn for all mankind,
Fond lover ! gaze awhile, to see
What beauty's idol charms shall be.
Where are the balls that once could dart
Quick lightning through the wounded heart ?
The skin, whose teint could once unite
The glowing red, and polish'd white ?
The lip in brighter ruby drest ?
The cheek with dimpled smiles imprest ?
The rising front, where Beauty sate
Thron'd in her residence of state ;
Which, half-disclos'd and half-conceal'd,
The hair in flowing ringlets veil'd ?
'Tis vanish'd all ! remains alone
The eyeless scalp of naked bone ;
The vacant orbits sunk within ;
The jaw that offers at a grin.
Is this the object then that claims
The tribute of our youthful flames ?
Must amorous hopes and fancied bliss,
Too dear delusions, end in this ?
How high does Melancholy swell !
Which sighs can more than language tell ;
Till Love can only grieve or fear :
Reflect awhile, then drop a tear
For all that's beautiful and dear.

Song

Be still, ye winds ! let ev'ry breath,
    Let ev'ry whisper cease :
As in the quiet cave of Death,
    Thou babbling Echo ! peace !

ELIZABETH TOLLET

Ye streams, without a murmur glide
   To nourish deep despair ;
No trembling osiers by your side
   Disturb the midnight air.

Ye conscious stars, that roll above
   To fix our fate below,
In solemn silence as you move
   Be witness to my woe :

Be witness to the vows I made,
   The tears I still must pay ;
While, like a melancholy shade,
   I shun the face of day.

The Rev. THOMAS FITZGERALD* (1695 ?-1752)

On an Over-Vain Poetical Friend

Dear Frank, with fancy, fire and style
   Form'd a consummate poet,
Burns with impatience all the while
   That all the world should know it.

Where'er he goes, with pompous boast
   His talent he displays ;
No, not a tittle shall be lost
   Of his minutest praise !

Then let's be candid to our friend,
   And own his just pretence ;
Nor yet, whilst we his wit commend,
   Despise his want of sense.

* For many years a master at Westminster School. Later
Rector of Wotton and of Abinger.

THOMAS FITZGERALD

An Ode

No, no, 'tis in vain in this turbulent town
   To expect either pleasure or rest ;
To hurry and nonsense still tying us down,
   'Tis an overgrown prison at best.

From hence to the country escaping away,
   Leave the crowd and the bustle behind ;
And there you'll see liberal Nature display
   A thousand delights to Mankind.

The change of the seasons, the sports of the fields,
   The sweetly-diversified scene,
The groves, and the gardens—nay ev'ry thing yields
   A happiness ever serene.

Here, here from ambition and avarice free,
   My days may I quietly spend ;
Whilst the cits and the courtiers, unenvied for me,
   May gather up wealth without end.

No, I thank 'em, I'll never, to add to my store,
   My peace and my freedom resign ;
For who, for the sake of possessing the ore,
   Would be sentenc'd to dig in the mine ?

Song

The charms which blooming Beauty shows
   From faces heav'nly fair,
We to the lily and the rose
   With semblance apt compare :

With semblance apt, for ah, how soon,
   How soon they all decay !
The lily droops, the rose is gone,
   And Beauty fades away.

But when bright Virtue shines confess'd,
    With sweet Discretion join'd ;
When Mildness calms the peaceful breast,
    And Wisdom guides the mind ;

When charms like these, dear maid, conspire
    Thy person to approve,
They kindle generous chaste desire,
    And everlasting love.

Beyond the reach of Time or Fate
    These graces shall endure ;
Still, like the passion they create,
    Eternal, constant, pure.

MATTHEW GREEN (1696-1737)

The Sparrow and Diamond

A Song

I lately saw, what now I sing,
    Fair Lucia's hand display'd ;
This finger grac'd a diamond ring,
    On that a sparrow play'd.

The feather'd plaything she caress'd,
    She strok'd its head and wings ;
And while it nestled on her breast,
    She lisp'd the dearest things.

With chisel bill a spark ill-set
    He loosen'd from the rest,
And swallow'd down to grind his meat,
    The easier to digest.

She seiz'd his bill with wild affright,
    Her diamond to descry :
'Twas gone ! she sicken'd at the sight,
    Moaning her bird would die.

MATTHEW GREEN

The tongue-tied knocker none might use,
    The curtains none undraw,
The footmen went without their shoes,
    The street was laid with straw.

The doctor us'd his oily art
    Of strong emetic kind,
The apothecary play'd his part,
    And engineer'd behind.

When Physic ceas'd to spend its store,
    To bring away the stone,
Dicky, like people given o'er,
    Picks up, when let alone.

His eyes dispell'd their sickly dews,
    He peck'd behind his wing ;
Lucia, recovering at the news,
    Relapses for the ring.

Meanwhile within her beauteous breast
    Two different passions strove ;
When av'rice ended the contest,
    And triumph'd over love.

Poor little, pretty, fluttering thing,
    Thy pains the sex display,
Who only to repair a ring
    Could take thy life away.

Drive av'rice from your breasts, ye fair,
    Monster of foulest mien :
Ye would not let it harbour there,
    Could but its form be seen.

It made a virgin put on guile,
    Truth's image break her word,
A Lucia's face forbear to smile,
    A Venus kill her bird.

MATTHEW GREEN

An Epigram

*on the Reverend Mr. Laurence Echard's, and Bishop
Gilbert Burnet's Histories.*

Gil's history appears to me
Political anatomy,
A case of skeletons well done,
And malefactors every one.
His sharp and strong incision pen
Historically cuts up men,
And does with lucid skill impart
Their inward ails of head and heart.
Laurence proceeds another way,
And well-dress'd figures doth display :
His characters are all in flesh,
Their hands are fair, their faces fresh ;
And from his sweetening art derive
A better scent than when alive.
He wax-work made to please the sons,
Whose fathers were Gil's skeletons.

WILLIAM OLDYS (1696-1761)

On a Fly Drinking out of his Cup

Busy, curious, thirsty fly !
Drink with me and drink as I :
Freely welcome to my cup ,
Couldst thou sip and sip it up :
Make the most of life you may,
Life is short and wears away.

Just alike, both mine and thine,
Hasten quick to their decline :
Thine's a summer, mine no more,
Though repeated to three-score.
Three-score summers, when they're gone,
Will appear as short as one !

CHARLES HAMILTON, LORD BINNING (1697-1733)

A Pastoral Ballad

Did ever swain a nymph adore
   As I ungrateful Nanny do ?
Was ever shepherd's heart so sore ?
   Was ever broken heart so true ?
My eyes are swell'd with tears ; but she
Has never shed a tear for me.

If Nanny call'd, did Robin stay,
   Or linger when she bid me run ?
She only had the word to say,
   And all she ask'd was quickly done :
I always thought on her ; but she
Would ne'er bestow a thought on me.

To let her cows my clover taste,
   Have I not rose by break of day ?
When did her heifers ever fast,
   If Robin in his yard had hay ?
Though to my fields they welcome were,
I never welcome was to her !

If Nanny ever lost a sheep,
   I cheerfully did give her two :
Did not her lambs in safety sleep
   Within my folds in frost and snow ?
Have they not there from cold been free ?
But Nanny still is cold to me.

Whene'er I climb'd our orchard trees,
   The ripest fruit was kept for Nan ;
Oh, how those hands that drown'd her bees
   Were stung, I'll ne'er forget the pain !
Sweet were the combs, as sweet could be ;
But Nanny ne'er look'd sweet on me.

If Nanny to the well did come,
   'Twas I that did her pitchers fill :
Full as they were I brought them home,
   Her corn I carried to the mill.
My back did bear her sacks ; but she
Would never bear the sight of me.

To Nanny's poultry oats I gave,
   I'm sure they always had the best :
Within this week her pigeons have
   Eat up a peck of peas at least.
Her little pigeons kiss ; but she
Would never take a kiss from me.

Must Robin always Nanny woo ?
   And Nanny still on Robin frown ?
Alas ! poor wretch ! what shall I do,
   If Nanny does not love me soon ?
If no relief to me she'll bring,
I'll hang me in her apron-string !

RICHARD SAVAGE (1697 ?-1743)

Verses to a Young Lady

Polly ! from me, though now a love-sick youth,
Nay, though a poet, hear the voice of truth !

Polly ! you're not a beauty, yet you're pretty ;
So grave, yet gay ; so silly, yet so witty ;
A heart of softness, yet a tongue of satire ;
You've cruelty, yet, e'en with that, good nature.
Now you are free, and now reserv'd awhile ;
Now a forc'd frown betrays a willing smile.
Reproach'd for absence, yet your sight denied ;
My tongue you silence, yet my silence chide.
How would you praise me, should your sex defame ;
Yet, should they praise, grow jealous and exclaim.
If I despair, with some kind look you bless ;

But if I hope, at once all hope suppress.
You scorn ; yet, should my passion change or fail,
Too late you'd whimper out a softer tale.
You love, yet from your lover's wish retire ;
Doubt, yet discern ; deny, and yet desire.

Such, Polly ! are your sex : part truth, part fiction ;
Some thought, much whim, and all a contradiction !

HENRY BAKER, F.R.S. (1698-1774)

The Declaimer

"Woman ! thoughtless, giddy creature !
    Laughing, idle, flutt'ring thing !
Most fantastic work of Nature !
    Still, like Fancy, on the wing !

" Slave to every changing passion ;
    Loving, hating, in extreme ;
Fond of every foolish fashion ;
    And at best a pleasing dream !

" Lovely trifle ! Dear illusion !
    Conquering weakness ! Wish'd-for pain !
Man's chief glory and confusion !
    Of all vanity, most vain ! "

Thus, deriding Beauty's power,
    Bevil call'd it all a cheat ;
But, in less than half an hour,
    Kneel'd and whin'd at Celia's feet !

On a Spider

Artist, who underneath my table
   Thy curious texture hast display'd !
Who, if we may believe the fable,
   Wert once a lovely blooming maid !

Insidious, restless, watchful spider,
   Fear no officious damsel's broom ;
Extend thy artful fabric wider,
   And spread thy banners round my room.

Swept from the rich man's costly ceiling,
   Thou'rt welcome to my homely roof ;
Here may'st thou find a peaceful dwelling,
   And undisturb'd attend thy woof.

Whilst I thy wondrous fabric stare at,
   And think on hapless poet's fate ;
Like thee confin'd to lonely garret,
   And rudely banish'd rooms of state.

And as from out thy tortur'd body
   Thou draw'st thy slender string with pain ;
So does he labour, like a noddy,
   To spin materials from his brain.

He for some fluttering tawdry creature,
   That spreads her charms before his eye ;
And that's a conquest little better
   Than thine o'er captive butterfly.

Thus far 'tis plain we both agree,
   Perhaps our deaths may better show it ;
'Tis ten to one but penury
   Ends both the spider and the poet.

THOMAS EDWARDS (1699-1757)

To Richard Owen Cambridge

Cambridge, with whom, my pilot and my guide,
   Pleas'd I have travers'd thy Sabrina's flood,
    Both where she foams impetuous, soil'd with mud,
And where she peaceful rolls her golden tide ;

Never, O never let ambition's pride
   (Too oft pretexted with our country's good)
    And tinsel'd pomp, despis'd when understood,
Or thirst of wealth thee from her banks divide.

Reflect how calmly, like her infant wave,
   Flows the clear current of a private life ;
    See the wide public stream by tempests toss'd
Of every changing wind the sport, or slave,
   Soil'd with corruption, vex'd with party strife,
    Cover'd with wrecks of peace and honour lost.

Sonnet

My gracious God, whose kind conducting hand
   Has steer'd me through this life's tumultuous sea,
   From many a rock, and many a tempest free,
Which prudence could not shun, nor strength withstand,

And brought at length almost in sight of land,
   That quiet haven where I long to be,
   Only the straits of Death betwixt, which we
Are doom'd to pass, ere reach the heavenly strand ;

Be this short passage boisterous, rough, and rude,
   Or smooth, and calm—Father, Thy Will be done—
    Support me only in the troublous stour ;
My sins all pardon'd through my Saviour's blood,
   Let Faith, and Hope, and Patience still hold on
    Unshaken, and Joy crown my latest hour !

The Hon. THOMAS HERVEY (1699-1775), or
The Hon. HENRY HERVEY*

Epitaph on Mrs. A. J——s

Entomb'd here lies sweet smiling Nan,
Ravish'd by death, ne'er touch'd by man ;
Near her the faithful youth's† interr'd,
Who death with her to life preferr'd ;
In him death's utmost power behold,
Since, laid near her, he can be cold.

HENRIETTA KNIGHT, née ST. JOHN, LADY LUXBOROUGH (1699-1756)

The Bullfinch in Town

Hark to the blackbird's pleasing note :
    Sweet usher of the vocal throng !
Nature directs his warbling throat,
    And all that hear admire the song.

Yon bullfinch, with unvaried tone,
    Of cadence harsh, and accent shrill,
Has brighter plumage to atone
    For want of harmony and skill.

Yet, discontent with nature's boon,
    Like man, to mimic art he flies ;
On opera-pinions hoping soon
    Unrivall'd he shall mount the skies.

And while, to please some courtly fair,
    He one dull tune with labour learns,
A well-gilt cage, remote from air,
    And faded plumes, is all he earns !

* " He was a vicious man, but very kind to me. If you call a
dog Hervey, I shall love him."—*Johnson*.
  † Mr. Fielding.

Go, hapless captive ! still repeat
   The sounds which nature never taught ;
Go, listening fair ! and call them sweet,
   Because you know them dearly bought.

Unenvied both ! go hear and sing
   Your studied music o'er and o'er ;
Whilst I attend th' inviting spring,
   In fields where birds unfetter'd soar.

The Rev. CHRISTOPHER PITT (1699-1748)

On the Death of a Young Gentleman

With joy, blest youth, we saw thee reach thy goal ;
Fair was thy frame, and beautiful thy soul ;
The Graces and the Muses came combin'd,
These to adorn the body, those the mind ;
'Twas there we saw the softest manners meet,
Truth, sweetness, judgment, innocence and wit.
So form'd, he flew his race ; 'twas quickly won,
'Twas but a step, and finish'd when begun.
Nature herself surpris'd would add no more,—
His life complete in all its parts before,—
But his few years with pleasing wonder told,
By virtues, not by days, and thought him old.
So far beyond his age those virtues ran,
That in a boy she found him more than man.

For years let wretches importune the skies,
Till, at the long expense of anguish wise,
They live to count their days by miseries.
Those win the prize, who soonest run the race,
And life burns brightest in the shortest space.
So to the convex glass embodied run,
Drawn to a point, the glories of the sun ;
At once the glittering beams intensely glow,
And through the straiten'd circle fiercely flow :
In one strong flame conspire the blended rays,
Run to a fire, and crowd into a blaze.

CHRISTOPHER PITT

On Mrs. Walker's Poems,
particularly that on the author

Blush, Wilmot, blush ; a female Muse,
  Without one guilty line,
The tender theme of love pursues
  In softer strains than thine.

'Tis thine the passion to blaspheme,
  'Tis hers with wit and ease
(Where a mere nothing is the theme)
  Beyond thyself to please.

Then be to her the prize decreed,
  Whose merit has prevail'd ;
For what male poet can succeed,
  If Rochester has fail'd ?

Since Phœbus quite forgetful grows,
  And has not yet thought fit,
In his high wisdom, to impose
  A salique law on wit ;

Since of your thoughts he takes no care,
  Ye Priors, Popes, and Gays ;
'Tis hard !—but let the women wear
  The breeches and the bays.

The Rev. JOHN DYER (1700 ?-1758)

The Enquiry

Ye poor little sheep, ah well may ye stray,
While sad is your shepherd, and Clio away !
Tell where have you been, have you met with my love,
On the mountain, or valley, or meadow, or grove ?
Alas-a-day, no—ye are starv'd and half dead,
Ye saw not my love, or ye all had been fed.

JOHN DYER

Oh, Sun, did you see her ? Ay surely you did :
'Mong what willows, or woodbines, or reeds, is she hid ?
Ye tall, whistling pines, that on yonder hill grow,
And o'erlook the beautiful valley below,
Did you see her a-roving in wood or in brake ?
Or bathing her fair limbs in some silent lake ?

Ye mountains, that look on the vigorous east,
And the north, and the south, and the wearisome west,
Pray tell where she hides her, you surely do know,
And let not her lover pine after her so.

Oh, had I the wings of an eagle, I'd fly,
Along with bright Phœbus all over the sky.
Like an eagle, look down, with my wings wide display'd,
And dart in my eyes at each whisp'ring shade :
I'd search every tuft in my diligent tour,
I'd unravel the woodbines, and look in each bower,
Till I found out my Clio, and ended my pain,
And made myself quiet, and happy again.

Grongar Hill

Silent Nymph, with curious eye !
Who, the purple evening, lie
On the mountain's lonely van,
Beyond the noise of busy man,
Painting fair the form of things,
While the yellow linnet sings ;
Or the tuneful nightingale
Charms the forest with her tale ;
Come with all thy various hues,
Come, and aid thy sister Muse ;
Now while Phœbus riding high
Gives lustre to the land and sky !
Grongar Hill invites my song,
Draw the landscape bright and strong ;
Grongar, in whose mossy cells
Sweetly musing Quiet dwells ;

JOHN DYER

Grongar, in whose silent shade,
For the modest Muses made,
So oft I have, the evening still,
At the fountain of a rill,
Sate upon a flowery bed,
With my hand beneath my head ;
While stray'd my eyes o'er Towy's flood,
Over mead, and over wood,
From house to house, from hill to hill,
Till Contemplation had her fill.

About his chequer'd sides I wind,
And leave his brooks and meads behind,
And groves, and grottoes where I lay,
And vistoes shooting beams of day :
Wide and wider spreads the vale ;
As circles on a smooth canal :
The mountains round, unhappy fate !
Sooner or later, of all height,
Withdraw their summits from the skies,
And lessen as the others rise :
Still the prospect wider spreads,
Adds a thousand woods and meads,
Still it widens, widens still,
And sinks the newly-risen hill.

Now, I gain the mountain's brow,
What a landscape lies below !
No clouds, no vapours intervene,
But the gay, the open scene
Does the face of nature show,
In all the hues of heaven's bow !
And, swelling to embrace the light,
Spreads around beneath the sight.

Old castles on the cliffs arise,
Proudly towering in the skies !
Rushing from the woods, the spires
Seem from hence ascending fires !

JOHN DYER

Half his beams Apollo sheds
On the yellow mountain heads !
Gilds the fleeces of the flocks :
And glitters on the broken rocks !

Below me trees unnumber'd rise,
Beautiful in various dyes :
The gloomy pine, the poplar blue,
The yellow beech, the sable yew,
The slender fir, that taper grows,
The sturdy oak with broad-spread boughs.
And beyond the purple grove,
Haunt of Phillis, queen of love !
Gaudy as the opening dawn,
Lies a long and level lawn,
On which a dark hill, steep and high,
Holds and charms the wand'ring eye !
Deep are his feet in Towy's flood,
His sides are cloth'd with waving wood,
And ancient towers crown his brow,
That cast an awful look below ;
Whose ragged walls the ivy creeps,
And with her arms from falling keeps ;
So both a safety from the wind
On mutual dependence find.

'Tis now the raven's bleak abode ;
'Tis now th' apartment of the toad ;
And there the fox securely feeds ;
And there the pois'nous adder breeds,
Conceal'd in ruins, moss and weeds ;
While, ever and anon, there falls
Huge heaps of hoary moulder'd walls.
Yet Time has seen, that lifts the low,
And level lays the lofty brow,
Has seen this broken pile compleat,
Big with the vanity of state ;
But transient is the smile of fate !

JOHN DYER

A little rule, a little sway,
A sun-beam in a winter's day,
Is all the proud and mighty have
Between the cradle and the grave.

And see the rivers how they run,
Through woods and meads, in shade and sun,
Sometimes swift, sometimes slow,
Wave succeeding wave, they go
A various journey to the deep,
Like human life to endless sleep !
Thus is nature's vesture wrought,
To instruct our wandering thought ;
Thus she dresses green and gay,
To disperse our cares away.

Ever charming, ever new,
When will the landscape tire the view !
The fountain's fall, the river's flow,
The woody valleys, warm and low ;
The windy summit, wild and high,
Roughly rushing on the sky !
The pleasant seat, the ruin'd tower,
The naked rock, the shady bower ;
The town and village, dome and farm,
Each give to each a double charm,
As pearls upon an Æthiop's arm.

See on the mountain's southern side,
Where the prospect opens wide,
Where the evening gilds the tide ;
How close and small the ridges lie !
What streaks of meadows cross the eye !
A step methinks may pass the stream,
So little distant dangers seem ;
So we mistake the future's face,
Eyed through hope's deluding glass ;

JOHN DYER

As yon summits soft and fair,
Clad in colours of the air,
Which to those who journey near,
Barren, brown, and rough appear ;
Still we tread the same coarse way,
The present's still a cloudy day.

O may I with myself agree,
And never covet what I see :
Content me with an humble shade,
My passions tam'd, my wishes laid ;
For while our wishes wildly roll,
We banish quiet from the soul :
'Tis thus the busy beat the air ;
And misers gather wealth and care.

Now, ev'n now, my joys run high,
As on the mountain turf I lie ;
While the wanton Zephyr sings,
And in the vale perfumes his wings ;
While the waters murmur deep ;
While the shepherd charms his sheep ;
While the birds unbounded fly,
And with music fill the sky,
Now, ev'n now, my joys run high.

Be full, ye courts, be great who will ;
Search for Peace with all your skill :
Open wide the lofty door,
Seek her on the marble floor,
In vain ye search, she is not there ;
In vain ye search the domes of care !
Grass and flowers Quiet treads,
On the meads, and mountain-heads,
Along with Pleasure, close allied,
Ever by each other's side :
And often, by the murm'ring rill,
Hears the thrush, while all is still,
Within the groves of Grongar Hill.

Mrs. B-LL M-RT-N (*circa* 1725)

*The Humble Wish**

I ask not wit, nor beauty do I crave,
Nor wealth, nor pompous titles wish to have ;
But since 'tis doom'd, in all degrees of life,
(Whether a daughter, sister, or a wife,)
That females shall the stronger males obey,
And yield perforce to their tyrannic sway ;
Since this, I say, is every woman's fate,
Give me a mind to suit my slavish state.

RICHARD LELY (*floruit* 1727, ? *obiit* 1735)

An Ode

No longer preach, ye aged sires,
　　The power of reason over love ;
Nor blame in youth those tender fires
　　Your years deny you now to prove.

Love is a fever of the mind
　　By nature we must all expect :
A frenzy of so fond a kind
　　Enjoyment only can correct.

But reason checks its heat, you'll cry—
　　See ! see ! in Cloe's sparkling eyes
Reason her standard waves on high,
　　Her cogent rhetoric there employs.

Could Plato and the Stagyrite
　　More bulky volumes still compile,
Experience shows—howe'er they write—
　　The scale must turn at Cloe's smile.

* This poem, together with those attributed to Jabez Earle, and one of the Hervey's, comes from *A New Miscellany : Being a Collection of pieces of Poetry, from Bath, Tunbridge, Oxford, Epsom, and other places, in the year* 1725. *Written chiefly by Persons of quality* [? 1726]. I do not know who Mrs. B-ll M-rt-n was.

RICHARD LELY

Urge on then your philosophy ;
   This maxim all at length must own :
The way to conquer is to fly,
   The wretch who parleys is undone.

The Rev. MATTHEW PILKINGTON
(*floruit circa* 1730)

*An Ode to Lycidas**

Why, Lycidas, should man be vain
   If bounteous Heav'n hath made him great ?
Why look with insolent disdain
   On those undeck'd with wealth and state ?

Can splendid robes, or beds of down,
   Or costly gems to deck the hair,
Can all the glories of a crown,
   Give health, or smooth the brow of care ?

The scepter'd prince, the burden'd slave,
   The humble and the haughty, die,
The poor, the rich, the base, the brave,
   In dust without distinction lie.

Go, search the tombs where monarchs rest,
   Who once the richest glories wore,
Fled is that grandeur they possest,
   And all their greatness is no more.

So glides the meteor through the sky,
   And sweeps along a gilded train,
But, when its short-liv'd beauties die,
   Dissolves to common air again.

* A slightly different version of this poem is printed as anonymous by Locker Lampson in his *Lyra Elegantiarum*. Pilkington's
poems were touched up by Swift.

JAMES THOMSON (1700-1748)

On the Death of Mr. Aikman,
a particular friend of the author's

As those we love decay, we die in part,
String after string is sever'd from the heart ;
Till loosen'd life, at last but breathing clay,
Without one pang is glad to fall away.
Unhappy he, who latest feels the blow,
Whose eyes have wept o'er every friend laid low,
Dragg'd lingering on from partial death to death,
Till, dying, all he can resign is breath.

Ode

Tell me, thou soul of her I love,
 Ah ! tell me whither art thou fled ;
To what delightful world above,
 Appointed for the happy dead ?

Or dost thou, free, at pleasure roam,
 And sometimes share thy lover's woe ;
Where, void of thee, his cheerless home
 Can now, alas ! no comfort know ?

Oh ! if thou hover'st round my walk,
 While under every well-known tree,
I to thy fancied shadow talk,
 And every tear is full of thee ;

Should then the weary eye of grief,
 Beside some sympathetic stream,
In slumber find a short relief,
 Oh visit thou my soothing dream !

JAMES THOMSON

Song

For ever, Fortune, wilt thou prove
An unrelenting foe to Love,
And when we meet a mutual heart,
Come in between and bid us part ?

Bid us sigh on from day to day,
And wish, and wish the soul away ;
Till youth and genial years are flown,
And all the life of life is gone ?

But busy, busy still art thou,
To bind the loveless, joyless vow,
The heart from pleasure to delude,
To join the gentle to the rude.

For once O Fortune ! hear my prayer,
And I absolve thy future care ;
All other blessings I resign,
Make but the dear Amanda mine.

MATTHEW CONCANEN (1701-1749)

The Theft

Why are those charms by frowns disgrac'd,
  Too lovely, and too coy !
Since from your lips, with tim'rous haste,
  I snatch'd transporting joy ?

Too well I rue the hapless theft !
  Too fatal your disdain !
I lost—Ah, no ! my life is left,
  I feel it by the pain.

Sure, might I taste another such,
  So warm with keen desire,
My soul, exulting at the touch,
  Would, through my lips, expire.

Then, Julia, take my parting breath,
  In such another kiss ;
Glut your revenge, and let my death
  Atone the ravish'd bliss.

WILLIAM POPPLE (1701-1764)

A Lover's Reflection

How shall I shake off cold despair,
    And warm Amelia's breast ?
Be bold—Alas, what lover dare,
    Who trembles to be blest ?

A Song

Cupid and Venus jointly strove
    To warm Amintor's heart,
And give him all the joys of love,
    Unmix'd with any smart.

Venus advis'd, from every fair
    To steal the sweetest grace ;
No, no, says Cupid, ease your care,
    They meet in Mordaunt's face.

On Rosalinda

To Rosalinda's eyes, who not submit,
Fall the proud victims of her conquering wit;
And all, whose dullness dares her wit despise,
Bow to the piercing influence of her eyes.
Thou then, who wishest not her slave to be,
Become but deaf and blind—and thou art free.

A Song

Why should those eyes, Florella, wear
    A chilling scorn to me ;
Yet ardent gaze on one who ne'er
    Yet felt a sigh for thee ?

Or why, if you are not decreed,
    To ease another's pain,
Am I not of my passion freed ?
    Or you of your disdain ?

WILLIAM POPPLE

Forbear, fond youth, Florella said,
　　And blame not me, but Fate,
You're doom'd, alas ! by her betray'd,
　　To love, and I to hate.

The Rev. PHILIP DODDRIDGE, D.D. (1702-1751)

Dum Vivimus, Vivamus

" Live while you live," the Epicure would say,
" And seize the pleasures of the present day."
" Live while you live," the sacred Preacher cries,
" And give to God each moment as it flies."
Lord, in my views let both united be ;
I live in pleasure, when I live to Thee.

Mrs. JUDITH MADAN, *née* COWPER* (1702-1781)

Lines written in her Brother's " Coke upon Littleton "

O thou, who labour'st in this rugged mine,
May'st thou to gold th' unpolish'd ore refine !
May each dark page unfold its haggard brow!
Doubt not to reap, if thou canst bear to plough.
To tempt thy care, may, each revolving night,
Purses and maces swim before thy sight !
From hence in times to come, advent'rous deed !
May'st thou essay to look and speak like Mead.
When the black bag and rose no more shall shade
With martial air the honours of thy head ;
When the full wig thy visage shall enclose,
And only leave to view thy learned nose :
Safely may'st thou defy beaux, wits and scoffers ;
While tenants, in fee simple, stuff thy coffers.

* A friend of Pope and aunt to William Cowper.

ROBERT NUGENT, Earl NUGENT (1702-1788)

Epigrams

I

I lov'd thee beautiful and kind,
    And plighted an eternal vow.
So alter'd are thy face and mind,
    'Twere perjury to love thee now.

II

My heart still hovering round about you,
I thought I could not live without you ;
Now we have liv'd three months asunder,
How I liv'd with you is the wonder.

III

Lie on ! while my revenge shall be
To speak the very truth of thee.

IV

We thought you without titles great,
And wealthy with a small estate ;
While by your humble self alone,
You seem'd unrated and unknown.
But now on fortune's swelling tide
High-borne, in all the pomp of pride ;
Of grandeur vain, and fond of pelf—
'Tis plain, my lord, you knew yourself.

MOSES MENDEZ (-1758)

On the Death of a Lady's Owl

The Owl expires ! Death gave the dreadful word,
And lovely Anna weeps her fav'rite bird.
Ye feather'd choir, in willing throngs repair,
And soothe the sorrows of the melting fair ;
In sounds of woe the dear-departed greet,
With cypress strew, ye doves, the green retreat ;
The fateful raven tolls the passing bell,
The solemn dirge be sung by Philomel ;
Sir Chanticleer, a chief of hardy race,
Shall guard from kites and daws the sacred place.
With your just tears a bard shall mix his own,
And thus, in artless verse, inscribe the stone.

Epitaph

Interr'd within this little space
    The bird of wisdom lies ;
Learn hence, how vain is every grace,
    How fruitless to be wise.

Can mortal stop the arm of Death,
    Who ne'er compassion knew ?
He, Venus' lover robb'd of breath ;
    He, Anna's darling slew.

Ah, happy bird, to raise those sighs
    Which man could ne'er obtain !
Ah, happy bird, to cloud those eyes
    That fir'd each kneeling swain !

Thrice bless'd thy life, her joy, her bliss,
    Thrice bless'd thy happy doom ;
She gave thee many a melting kiss,
    She wept upon thy tomb.

THOMAS COOKE* (1703-1756)

To Phillis

Phillis from this hour adieu,
Fair no more, no longer true ;
I my wandering heart recall ;
Take thy vows, I quit them all ;
Henceforth thou no more shalt be
Than a vulgar maid to me.
Phillis from this hour adieu,
Fair no more, no longer true.
Why should I, presumptuous swain,
Dare to cherish hopes so vain,
That the heavens would hear my prayer
For a love as chaste as fair.
Phillis thou hast prov'd no more
Than a thousand belles before
Have to men who them believ'd,—
Plighted vows, and then deceiv'd !
Such was Delia to Tibullus,
Lesbia such to fond Catullus.
Horace, sacred bard, complains
Of the sex, and slighted pains.
Phillis thou art free to rove
As the natives of the grove :
From this moment, nymph, adieu,
Fair no more, no longer true.

To Phillis

While, Phillis, on thy charms I gaze,
    My soul is all desire ;
Who can oppose so bright a blaze,
    Secure his heart from fire ?

While thoughtful of the perjur'd maid,
    Fair Phillis I despise,
Nor longer fear, by her betray'd,
    The tyrants in her eyes.

* Best known as the translator of Hesiod.

But when I meet the faithless dame,
  My soul is all desire ;
So weak my vows, I catch the flame,
  And in a blaze expire.

ROBERT DODSLEY* (1703-1764)

Song

Man's a poor deluded bubble,
  Wandering in a mist of lies,
Seeing false, or seeing double,
  Who would trust to such weak eyes ?
Yet presuming on his senses,
  On he goes most wond'rous wise :
Doubts of truth, believes pretences ;
  Lost in error, lives and dies.

The Parting Kiss

One kind kiss before we part,
  Drop a tear, and bid adieu ;
Though we sever, my fond heart
  Till we meet shall pant for you.

Yet, yet weep not so, my love,
  Let me kiss that falling tear ;
Though my body must remove,
  All my soul will still be here.

All my soul, and all my heart,
  And every wish shall pant for you ;
One kind kiss then ere we part,
  Drop a tear, and bid adieu.

* The famous publisher or " book-seller." Started life as a footman.

ROBERT DODSLEY

An Epigram

Cries Sylvia to a reverend dean,
   " What reason can be given,
Since marriage is a holy thing,
   That there are none in heaven ? "

" There are no women," he replied ;
   She quick returns the jest—
" Women there are, but I'm afraid
   They cannot find a priest."

The Kings of Europe

A Jest

Why pray, of late, do Europe's kings
   No jester to their courts admit ?
They're grown such stately solemn things,
   To bear a joke they think not fit.

But though each court a jester lacks,
   To laugh at monarchs to their face ;
All mankind behind their backs
   Supply the honest jester's place.

An Epigram

*Occasioned by the words " one Prior " in the second volume
of Bishop Burnet's History*

One Prior—and is this, this all the fame
The poet from th' historian can claim !
No ; Prior's verse posterity shall quote,
When 'tis forgot ONE BURNET ever wrote.

The Rev. JOHN and the Rev. CHARLES WESLEY*

(1703-1791 and 1707-1788)

Jesu, Lover of My Soul

Jesu, lover of my soul,
    Let me to Thy bosom fly,
While the nearer waters roll,
    While the tempest still is high :
Hide me, O my Saviour, hide,
    Till the storm of life is past ;
Safe into the haven guide ;
    O, receive my soul at last.

Other refuge have I none,
    Hangs my helpless soul on Thee :
Leave, ah ! leave me not alone,
    Still support and comfort me.
All my trust on Thee is stay'd ;
    All my help from Thee I bring ;
Cover my defenceless head
    With the shadow of Thy wing.

Wilt Thou not regard my call ?
    Wilt Thou not accept my prayer ?
Lo ! I sink, I faint, I fall—
    Lo ! on Thee I cast my care :
Reach me out Thy gracious hand !
    While I of Thy strength receive,
Hoping against hope I stand,
    Dying, and behold I live !

Thou, O Christ, art all I want,
    More than all in Thee I find :
Raise the fallen, cheer the faint,
    Heal the sick, and lead the blind.

---

  * I believe the question of the exact parts played by the two brothers in writing the hymns has never been settled. It is generally supposed that Charles was mainly responsible for the original hymns, and John for the translations. These are probably by Charles.

Just and holy is Thy name,
  I am all unrighteousness ;
False and full of sin I am,
  Thou art full of truth and grace.

Plenteous grace with Thee is found,
  Grace to cover all my sin :
Let the healing streams abound,
  Make and keep me pure within.
Thou of life the fountain art :
  Freely let me drink of Thee,
Spring Thou up within my heart,
  Rise to all eternity !

Eternal Beam of Light Divine

Eternal beam of light divine,
  Fountain of unexhausted love,
In whom the Father's glories shine,
  Through earth beneath, and Heaven above !

Jesu ! the weary wanderer's rest ;
  Give me Thy easy yoke to bear,
With steadfast patience arm my breast,
  With spotless love and lowly fear.

Thankful I take the cup from Thee,
  Prepar'd and mingled by Thy skill ;
Though bitter to the taste it be,
  Powerful the wounded soul to heal.

Be Thou, O rock of ages, nigh :
  So shall each murmuring thought be gone,
And grief, and fear, and care shall fly,
  As clouds before the mid-day sun.

Speak to my warring passions, " Peace " ;
  Say to my trembling heart, " Be still " :
Thy power my strength and fortress is,
  For all things serve Thy sovereign will.

O death, where is thy sting ? where now
    Thy boasted victory, O grave ?
Who shall contend with God ? or who
    Can hurt whom God delights to save ?

Happy Soul, thy Days are ended

Happy soul, thy days are ended,
    All thy mourning days below :
Go, by angel guards attended,
    To the sight of Jesus, go !
Waiting to receive thy spirit,
    Lo ! the Saviour stands above,
Shows the purchase of His merit,
    Reaches out the crown of love.

Struggle through thy latest passion
    To thy dear Redeemer's breast,
To His uttermost salvation,
    To His everlasting rest :
For the joy He sets before thee,
    Bear a momentary pain,
Die, to live the life of glory,
    Suffer, with thy Lord to reign.

The fire shall be ever burning upon the altar

Leviticus vi, 13.

O Thou who camest from above,
    The pure, celestial fire t' impart,
Kindle a flame of sacred love
    On the mean altar of my heart ;
There let it for Thy glory burn
    With inextinguishable blaze,
And trembling to its source return,
    In humble prayer, and fervent praise.

Jesus, confirm my heart's desire
   To work, and speak, and think of Thee ;
Still let me guard the holy fire,
   And still stir up Thy gift in me :
Ready for all Thy perfect will,
   My acts of faith and love repeat,
Till death Thy endless mercies seal,
   And make my sacrifice complete.

GILBERT WEST* (1703-1756)

Father Francis's Prayer

Written in Lord Westmorland's Hermitage.

Ne gay attire, ne marble hall,
Ne arched roof, ne pictur'd wall ;
Ne cook of Fraunce, ne dainty board
Bestow'd with pyes of Perigord ;
Ne power, ne such like idle fancies,
Sweet Agnes, grant to Father Francis ;
Let me ne more myself deceive ;
Ne more regret the toys I leave ;
The world I quit, the proud, the vain ;
Corruption's and Ambition's train ;
But not the good, perdie, nor fair,
'Gainst them I make ne vow, ne prayer ;
But such aye welcome to my cell,
And oft, not always, with me dwell ;
Then cast, sweet Saint, a circle round,
And bless from fools this holy ground ;
From all the foes to worth and truth,
From wanton eld, and homely youth ;
The gravely dull, and pertly gay ;
Oh banish these ; and by my fay,
Right well I ween that in this age
Mine house shall prove an hermitage.

* West's most successful work was his translation of Pindar.

WILLIAM HAMILTON OF BANGOUR (1704-1754)

The Flower of Yarrow
To Lady Mary Montgomery

Go Yarrow flower, thou shalt be blest,
To lie on beauteous Mary's breast ;
Go Yarrow flower so sweetly smelling,
Is there on earth so soft a dwelling ?
    Go lovely flower, thou prettiest flower,
That ever smil'd in Yarrow bower,
Go daughter of the dewy morning,
With Alves' blush the fields adorning.
    Go lovely rose, what dost thou here ?
Lingering away thy short-liv'd year,
Vainly shining, idly blooming,
Thy unenjoyed sweets consuming.
    Vain is thy radiant Garlies hue,
No hand to pull, no eye to view ;
What are thy charms no heart desiring ?
What profits beauty none admiring ?
    Go Yarrow flower to Yarrow maid,
And on her panting bosom laid,
There all thy native form confessing,
The charm of beauty is possessing.
    Come Yarrow maid from Yarrow field,
What pleasure can the desert yield ?
Come to my breast, O all excelling,
Is there on earth so kind a dwelling ?
    Come my dear maid, thou prettiest maid,
That ever smil'd in Yarrow shade,
Come sister of the dewy morning,
With Alves' blush the dance adorning.
    Come lovely maid, love calls thee here,
Linger no more thy fleeting year,
Vainly shining, idly blooming,
Thy unenjoyed sweets consuming.
    Vain is thy radiant Garlies hue,
No hand to press, no eye to view ;
What are thy charms no heart desiring ?
What profits beauty none admiring ?

Come Yarrow maid with Yarrow rose,
Thy maiden graces all disclose ;
Come blest by all, to all a blessing,
The charm of beauty is possessing.

Song

Go plaintive sounds ! and to the fair
   My secret wounds impart,
Tell all I hope, tell all I fear,
   Each motion in my heart.

But she, methinks, is listening now
   To some enchanting strain,
The smile that triumphs o'er her brow,
   Seems not to heed my pain.

Yes, plaintive sounds, yet, yet delay,
   Howe'er my love repine,
Let that gay minute pass away,
   The next perhaps is thine.

Yes, plaintive sounds, no longer crost,
   Your griefs shall soon be o'er,
Her cheek, undimpled now, has lost
   The smile it lately wore.

Yes, plaintive sounds, she now is yours,
   'Tis now your time to move ;
Essay to soften all her powers,
   And be that softness, love.

Cease plaintive sounds, your task is done,
   That anxious tender air
Proves o'er her heart the conquest won,
   I see you melting there.

WILLIAM HAMILTON

Return ye smiles, return again,
  Return each sprightly grace,
I yield up to your charming reign
  All that enchanting face.

I take no outward show amiss,
  Rove where they will, her eyes,
Still let her smiles each shepherd bless,
  So she but hear my sighs.

SOAME JENYNS (1704-1787)

A Song

When first I sought fair Cœlia's love,
  And ev'ry charm was new,
I swore by all the gods above
  To be for ever true.

But long in vain did I adore,
  Long wept, and sigh'd in vain,
She still protested, vow'd and swore
  She ne'er would ease my pain.

At last o'ercome she made me blest,
  And yielded all her charms,
And I forsook her, when possest,
  And fled to other arms.

But let not this, dear Cœlia, now
  To rage thy breast incline,
For why, since you forgot your vow,
  Should I remember mine ?

Chloe Hunting

Whilst thousands court fair Chloe's love,
   She fears the dang'rous joy,
But, Cynthia-like, frequents the grove,
   As lovely, and as coy.

With the same speed she seeks the hind,
   Or hunts the flying hare,
She leaves pursuing swains behind,
   To languish and despair.

Oh strange caprice in thy dear breast !
   Whence first this whim began ;
To follow thus each worthless beast,
   And shun their sovereign man !

Consider, fair, what 'tis you do,
   How thus they both must die,
Not surer they, when you pursue,
   Than we, whene'er you fly.

Chloe to Strephon

A Song

Too plain, dear youth, these tell-tale eyes
   My heart your own declare,
But for Heav'n's sake let it suffice
   You reign triumphant there.

Forbear your utmost power to try,
   Nor farther urge your sway ;
Press not for what I must deny,
   For fear I should obey.

Could all your arts successful prove,
   Would you a maid undo,
Whose greatest failing is her love,
   And that her love for you ?

SOAME JENYNS

Say, would you use that very power
  You from her fondness claim,
To ruin, in one fatal hour,
  A life of spotless fame ?

Ah ! cease, my dear, to do an ill,
  Because perhaps you may ;
But rather try your utmost skill
  To save me, than betray.

Be you yourself my virtue's guard,
  Defend, and not pursue ;
Since 'tis a task for me too hard,
  To fight with love, and you.

ISAAC HAWKINS BROWNE, M.P. (1705-1760)

On the Author's Birthday

Now six and thirty rapid years are fled,
  Since I began, nor yet begin, to live ;
Painful reflection ! to look back I dread,
  What hope, alas ! can looking forward give !

Day urges day, and year succeeds to year,
  While hoary age steals unperceiv'd along ;
Summer is come, and yet no fruits appear,
  My joys a dream, my works an idle song.

Ah me ! I fondly thought, Apollo shone
  With beams propitious on my natal hour ;
Fair was my morn, but now at highest noon
  Shades gather round, and clouds begin to lour.

Yes, on thy natal hour, the God replies,
  I shone propitious, and the Muses smil'd ;
Blame not the Powers, they gave thee wings to rise,
  But earth thou lov'st, by low delights beguil'd.

Possessing wealth, beyond a Poet's lot,
  Thou the dull track of lucre hast prefer'd,
For contemplation form'd and lofty thought,
  Thou meanly minglest with the vulgar herd.

True bards select and sacred to the Nine
  Listen not thus to Pleasure's warbling lays ;
Nor on the downy couch of ease recline,
  Severe their lives, abstemious are their days.

Oh ! born for nobler ends, dare to be wise,
  'Tis not e'en now too late, assert thy claim ;
Rugged the path, that leads up to the skies,
  But the fair guerdon is immortal fame.

The Fire Side

A Pastoral Soliloquy

Hic secretum iter et fallentis semita vitae.—HORACE.

Thrice happy, who free from ambition and pride,
In a rural retreat, has a quiet fire side ;
I love my fire side, there I long to repair,
And to drink a delightful oblivion of care.
Oh ! when shall I 'scape to be truly my own,
From the noise, and the smoke, and the bustle of town.
Then I live, then I triumph, whene'er I retire
From the pomp and parade that the Many admire.
Hail ye woods and ye lawns, shady vales, sunny hills,
And the warble of birds, and the murmur of rills,
Ye flowers of all hues that embroider the ground,
Flocks feeding, or frisking in gambols around ;
Scene of joy to behold ! joy, that who would forego,
For the wealth and the power that a court can bestow ?
I have said it at home, I have said it abroad,
That the town is man's world, but that this is of God ;
Here my trees cannot flatter, plants nurs'd by my care
Pay with fruit or with fragrance, and incense the air ;

ISAAC HAWKINS BROWNE

Here contemplative solitude raises the mind,
(Least alone, when alone,) to ideas refin'd.
Methinks hid in groves, that no sound can invade,
Save when Philomel strikes up her sweet serenade,
I revolve on the changes and chances of things,
And pity the wretch that depends upon kings.

Now I pass with old authors an indolent hour,
And reclining at ease turn Demosthenes o'er.
Now facetious and vacant, I urge the gay flask
With a set of old friends—who have nothing to ask ;
Thus happy, I reck not of France nor of Spain,
Nor the *balance of power* what hand shall sustain.
The *balance of power ?* Ah ! till that is restor'd,
What solid delight can retirement afford ?
Some must be content to be drudges of state,
That the sage may securely enjoy his retreat.
In weather serene, when the ocean is calm,
It matters not much who presides at the helm ;
But as soon as clouds gather and tempests arise,
Then a pilot there needs, a man dauntless and wise.
If such can be found, sure he ought to come forth
And lend to the public his talents and worth.
Whate'er inclination or ease may suggest,
If the state wants his aid, he has no claim to rest ;
But who is the Man, a bad game to redeem ?
He whom Turin admires, who has Prussia's esteem,
Whom the Spaniard has felt ; and whose iron with dread
Haughty Lewis saw forging to fall on his head.
Holland loves him, nor less in the North all the powers
Court, honour, revere, and the Empress adores.
Hark ! what was that sound ? for it seem'd more sublime
Than befits the low genius of pastoral rhyme :
Was it Wisdom I heard ? or can fumes of the brain
Cheat my ears with a dream ? Ha ! repeat me that strain :
Yes, Wisdom, I hear thee ; Thou deign'st to declare
ME, ME, the sole Atlas to prop this whole sphere :
Thy voice says, or seems in sweet accents to say,
" Haste to save sinking Britain " ;—resign'd I obey ;

And O ! witness ye Powers, that ambition and pride
Have no share in this change—*for I love my fire side.*
Thus the Shepherd ; then throwing his crook away steals
Direct to St. James's and takes up the Seals.

NATHANIEL COTTON, M.D.* (1705-1788)

To a Child of Five Years Old

Fairest flower, all flowers excelling,
　　Which in Eden's garden grew ;
Flowers of Eve's embower'd dwelling
　　Are, my fair one, types of you.
Mark, my Polly, how the roses
　　Emulate thy damask cheek ;
How the bud its sweets discloses ;
　　Buds thy opening bloom bespeak.
Lilies are, by plain direction,
　　Emblems of a double kind ;
Emblems of thy fair complexion,
　　Emblems of thy fairer mind.
But, dear girl, both flowers and beauty
　　Blossom, fade, and die away ;
Then pursue good sense and duty,
　　Evergreens, that ne'er decay.

On Lord Cobham's Gardens

It puzzles much the sages' brains,
　　Where Eden stood of yore ;
Some place it in Arabia's plains ;
　　Some say it is no more.

But Cobham can these tales confute,
　　As all the curious know ;
For he has prov'd beyond dispute,
　　That Paradise is Stow.

---

* This good man kept the madhouse in which Cowper was confined. His kindness was largely responsible for restoring the greater
poet to his senses.

The Rev. STEPHEN DUCK* (1705-1756)

On Florella's Birthday

The Queen of Love and Pallas once, 'tis said,
Had both agreed to form a finish'd maid :
Upon a noted day they flew to earth,
A day still noted by Florella's birth :
Both Deities employ'd their utmost care,
To make their darling lady wise and fair :
This gave her beauty, that a sprightly wit,
Which render'd soul and body justly fit :
But Mercury, that nimble-winged thief,
Who loves his joke, as dearly as his life,
Down from Olympus to his sisters flew,
When just to life their little embryo grew,
And pour'd a little folly in her breast ;
A little folly leaven'd all the rest.
Hence 'tis, she's sometimes sprightly, sometimes dull,
And sometimes witty, sometimes quite a fool ;
Scarce foolish now, nor witty, sprightly neither ;
But sprightly, witty, foolish, all together.

On Mites : To a Lady

'Tis but by way of Simile.—PRIOR.

Dear madam, did you never gaze,
Through optic-glass, on rotten cheese ?
There, madam, did you ne'er perceive
A crowd of dwarfish creatures live ?
The little things, elate with pride,
Strut to and fro, from side to side :
In tiny pomp, and pertly vain,
Lords of their pleasing orb, they reign ;
And, fill'd with harden'd curds and cream,
Think the whole dairy made for *them*.

* Was originally a thresher-man. The first English peasant, I think, to become a poet. His earlier work (too long for insertion here) is much better than these two trifles.

So men, conceited lords of all,
Walk proudly o'er this pendent ball,
Fond of their little spot below,
Nor greater beings care to know ;
But think those worlds, which deck the skies,
Were only form'd to please *their* eyes.

DAVID MALLOCH, *alias* MALLET (1705 ?-1765)

William and Margaret

(*Founded on an old ballad*)

'Twas at the silent solemn hour
When night and morning meet,
In glided Marg'ret's grimly ghost,
And stood at William's feet.

Her face was like an April morn
Clad in a wintry cloud,
And clay-cold was her lily hand
That held her sable shroud.

So shall the fairest face appear,
When youth and years are flown ;
Such is the robe that kings must wear,
When Death has reft their crown.

Her bloom was like the springing flower
That sips the silver dew ;
The rose was budded in her cheek,
Just opening to the view.

But Love had, like the canker-worm,
Consum'd her early prime :
The rose grew pale, and left her cheek ;
She died before her time.

" Awake ! " she cried, " thy true love calls,
  Come from her midnight grave ;
Now let thy pity hear the maid
  Thy love refus'd to save.

" This is the dumb and dreary hour
  When injur'd ghosts complain,
When yawning graves give up their dead
  To haunt the faithless swain.

" Bethink thee, William ! of thy fault,
  Thy pledge and broken oath,
And give me back my maiden vow,
  And give me back my troth.

" Why did you promise love to me,
  And not that promise keep ?
Why did you swear my eyes were bright,
  Yet leave those eyes to weep ?

" How could you say my face was fair,
  And yet that face forsake ?
How could you win my virgin heart,
  Yet leave that heart to break ?

" Why did you say my lip was sweet,
  And made the scarlet pale ?
And why did I, young witless maid !
  Believe the flatt'ring tale ?

" That face, alas ! no more is fair,
  Those lips no longer red :
Dark are my eyes, now clos'd in death,
  And every charm is fled.

" The hungry worm my sister is ;
  This winding-sheet I wear ;
And cold and weary lasts our night,
  Till that last morn appear.

" But hark ! the cock has warn'd me hence ;
   A long and late adieu !
Come see, false man ! how low she lies,
   Who died for love of you."

The lark sung loud, the morning smil'd
   With beams of rosy red ;
Pale William quak'd in every limb,
   And raving left his bed.

He hied him to the fatal place
   Where Marg'ret's body lay,
And stretch'd him on the green-grass turf
   That wrapp'd her breathless clay.

And thrice he call'd on Marg'ret's name,
   And thrice he wept full sore,
Then laid his cheek to her cold grave,
   And word spoke never more.

Edwin and Emma

Far in the windings of a vale,
   Fast by a sheltering wood,
The safe retreat of health and peace,
   An humble cottage stood.

There beauteous Emma flourish'd fair,
   Beneath a mother's eye ;
Whose only wish on earth was now
   To see her blest, and die.

The softest blush that Nature spreads
   Gave colour to her cheek :
Such orient colour smiles through Heaven,
   When vernal mornings break.

Nor let the pride of great ones scorn
   This charmer of the plains :
That sun, who bids *their* diamond blaze,
   To paint *our* lily deigns.

Long had she fill'd each youth with love,
   Each maiden with despair ;
And though by all a wonder own'd,
   Yet knew not she was fair.

Till Edwin came, the pride of swains,
   A soul devoid of art ;
And from whose eye, serenely mild,
   Shone forth the feeling heart.

A mutual flame was quickly caught :
   Was quickly too reveal'd :
For neither bosom lodg'd a wish,
   That virtue keeps conceal'd.

What happy hours of home-felt bliss
   Did love on both bestow !
But bliss too mighty long to last,
   Where fortune proves a foe.

His sister, who, like Envy form'd,
   Like her in mischief joy'd,
To work them harm, with wicked skill,
   Each darker art employ'd.

The father, too, a sordid man,
   Who love nor pity knew,
Was all-unfeeling as the clod,
   From whence his riches grew.

Long had he seen their secret flame,
   And seen it long unmov'd :
Then with a father's frown at last
   Had sternly disapprov'd.

In Edwin's gentle heart a war
    Of differing passions strove :
His heart, that durst not disobey,
    Yet could not cease to love.

Denied her sight, he oft behind
    The spreading hawthorn crept,
To snatch a glance, to mark the spot
    Where Emma walk'd and wept.

Oft too on Stanemore's wintry waste,
    Beneath the moonlight-shade,
In sighs to pour his soften'd soul,
    The midnight-mourner stray'd.

His cheek, where health with beauty glow'd,
    A deadly pale o'ercast :
So fades the fresh rose in its prime,
    Before the northern blast.

The parents now, with late remorse,
    Hung o'er his dying bed ;
And wearied Heaven with fruitless vows,
    And fruitless sorrow shed.

" 'Tis past ! " he cried—" but if your souls
    Sweet mercy yet can move,
Let these dim eyes once more behold,
    What they must ever love ! "

She came ; his cold hand softly touch'd,
    And bath'd with many a tear :
Fast-falling o'er the primrose pale,
    So morning dews appear.

But oh ! his sister's jealous care,
    A cruel sister she !
Forbade what Emma came to say ;
    " My Edwin live for me."

Now homeward as she hopeless wept
  The church-yard path along,
The blast blew cold, the dark owl scream'd
  Her lover's funeral song.

Amid the falling gloom of night,
  Her startling fancy found
In every bush his hovering shade,
  His groan in every sound.

Alone, appall'd, thus had she pass'd
  The visionary vale—
When lo ! the death-bell smote her ear,
  Sad-sounding in the gale !

Just then she reach'd, with trembling step,
  Her aged mother's door—
" He's gone ! " she cried ; " and I shall see
  That angel-face no more !

" I feel, I feel this breaking heart
  Beat high against my side——"
From her white arm down sunk her head ;
  She shivering sigh'd, and died.

ANONYMOUS POEMS

From *Miscellaneous Poems* (1729), edited by
JAMES RALPH (1705 ?-1762)

Receipt to Make Love

Two or three Dears, and two or three Sweets,
Two or three balls, and two or three treats ;
Two or three serenades giv'n at the door,
Two or three vows how much you adore ;
Two or three messages sent in a day,
Two or three times leading out to the play,
Two or three soft things said by the way ;
Two or three tickets sent two or three times,
Two or three billets-doux all writ in rhymes ;
Two or three months keeping strict to these rules,
Can never fail making two or three fools.

ANONYMOUS

Song

Why, Celia, should you so much strive
    Your kindling passion to conceal ?
Your lips though they denial give,
    Yet all your actions love reveal.

In vain you strive, in vain, alas !
    The charming passion to disguise ;
It glows, it blushes, on your face,
    And sparkles in your swimming eyes.

Your eyes, those emblems of the heart,
    Still contradict whate'er you say ;
And though your lips deny the smart,
    Your eyes are more believ'd than they !

Song

Loud was the wind, and rough the main,
    But life was past my care ;
I thought of absence, and disdain,
    And felt no storm but there.

The seas their wonders might reveal,
    But Chloe's eyes have more ;
Nor all the treasure they conceal
    Can equal mine on shore.

From native Britain's temperate coast
    Remove me farther yet,
To shiver in eternal frost,
    Or melt with India's heat.

Her image shall my days beguile,
    And still my dream shall be
The tuneful voice, and tender smile,
    Though ne'er vouchsaf'd to me.

ANONYMOUS

The Rover Fix'd

Cloe ! your sovereign charms I own,
   I feel the fatal smart ;
The glory you can boast, alone,
   To fix my wand'ring heart.

Your beauteous sex, with various grace,
   My passions oft have mov'd ;
And now a shape, and then a face,
   As Fancy led, I lov'd.

So does the vagrant bee explore
   Each sweet that Nature yields,
Lightly she skims from flower to flower,
   And ranges all the fields.

But you have found the cruel art
   To cure my roving mind ;
Each female beauty you impart,
   Your sex, in one, combin'd !

My eyes disclose my secret pain ;
   My constant sighs discover,
Though in deep silence I remain,
   That I am Cloe's lover.

Irksome I pass the hours away,
   When banish'd from your sight ;
I languish all the livelong day,
   And all the wakeful night.

Tell me, ye learn'd, who study much
   The nature of Mankind,
Why, if I think, or look, or touch,
   If she be coy, or kind,

I feel my bosom strangely move,
   Quick throbbings seize my breast ?
All that I know is that I love ;
   Do you explain the rest.

BENJAMIN HOADLY, M.D. (1706-1757)

To Chloe
Written on the author's birthday, 1734

The minutes, the hours, the days, and the years,
  That fill up the current of Time,
Neither flowing with hopes, neither ebbing with fears,
  Unheeded roll'd on to my prime.

In infancy prattling, in youth full of play,
  Still pleas'd with whatever was new,
I bade the old cripple fly swifter away ;
  To o'ertake some gay trifle in view.

But when Chloe, with sweetness and sense in her look,
  First taught me the lesson of love ;
Then I counted each step the wing'd fugitive took,
  And bade him more leisurely move.

Stop, runaway, stop, nor thy journey pursue,
  For Chloe has giv'n me her heart :
To enjoy it thy years will prove many too few,
  If you make so much haste to depart.

Still, still he flies on—still, still let him fly,
  Till he's tir'd, and panting for breath ;
My love both his teeth and his scythe shall defy—
  That can only be conquer'd by death.

WILLIAM PATTISON (1706-1727)

Ad Cœlum

Good Heaven ! this mystery of life explain,
Nor let me think I bear the load in vain ;
Lest, with the tedious passage cheerless grown,
Urg'd by despair, I throw the burden down.

To Laura Weeping

If Laura weep for those her eyes have slain,
Then smile, my fair, and we'll revive again !

238

HENRY FIELDING (1707-1754)

To Sir Robert Walpole

Great Sir, as on each levée day
I still attend you—still you say
" I'm busy now, to-morrow come " ;
To-morrow, sir, you're not at home ;
So says your porter, and dare I
Give such a man as him the lie ?

In imitation, sir, of you,
I keep a mighty levée too :
Where my attendants, to their sorrow,
Are bid to come again to-morrow.
To-morrow they return, no doubt,
But then, like you sir, I'm gone out.
So says my maid ; but they less civil
Give maid and master to the devil ;
And then with menaces depart,
Which, could you hear, would pierce your heart.
Good sir, do make my levée fly me,
Or lend your porter to deny me.

Song

From " Don Quixote in England "

The dusky night rides down the sky,
    And ushers in the morn ;
The hounds all join in glorious cry ;
    The huntsman winds his horn.
        And a-hunting we will go !

The wife around her husband throws
    Her arms and begs his stay :
" My dear, it rains ! and hails ! and snows !
    You will not hunt to-day ! "
        But a-hunting we will go !

A brushing fox, in yonder wood,
    Secure to find we seek ;
For why ? I carried, sound and good,
    A cartload there last week !
        And a-hunting we will go !

Away he goes ! he flies the rout !
    Their steeds all spur and switch !
Some are thrown in, and some thrown out,
    And some thrown in the ditch !
        But a-hunting we will go !

At length, his strength to faintness worn,
    Poor Reynard ceases flight,
Then hungry homeward we return,
    To feast away the night.
        Then a-drinking we will go !

The Rev. THOMAS SEWARD* (1708-1790)

Song

When fair Serena first I knew,
    By friendship's happy union charm'd,
Incessant joys around her flew,
    And gentle smiles my bosom warm'd.

But when with fond officious care
    I press'd to breathe my amorous pain,
Her lips spoke nought but cold despair,
    Her eyes shot ice through every vein.

Thus in Italia's lovely vales
    The sun his genial vigour yields,
Reviving heat each sense regales,
    And plenty crowns the smiling fields.

* Father of the famous but unreadable *Swan of Litchfield.*

When nearer we approach his ray,
　　High on the Alps' stupendous brow,
Surpris'd we see pale sun-beams play
　　On everlasting hills of snow.

Sir CHARLES HANBURY WILLIAMS, K.B.
(1708-1759)

An Ode on Miss Harriet Hanbury
at six years old

Why should I thus employ my time
　　To paint those cheeks of rosy hue ?
Why should I search my brains for rhyme,
　　To sing those eyes of glossy blue ?

The power as yet is all in vain,
　　Thy numerous charms, and various graces :
They only serve to banish pain,
　　And light up joy, in parents' faces.

But soon those eyes their strength shall feel ;
　　Those charms their powerful sway shall find :
Youth shall in crowds before you kneel,
　　And own your empire o'er mankind.

Then when on Beauty's throne you sit,
　　And thousands court your wish'd-for arms ;
My Muse shall stretch her utmost wit,
　　To sing the victories of your charms.

Charms that in time shall ne'er be lost,
　　At least while verse like mine endures :
And future Hanburys shall boast,
　　Of verse like mine, of charms like yours.

A little vain we both may be,
　　Since scarce another house can show
A poet, that can sing like me ;
　　A beauty, that can charm like you.

Sir C. HANBURY WILLIAMS

Ode on the Death of Matzel
a favourite bull-finch,

*addressed to Mr. Stanhope, to whom the author had
given the reversion of it when he left Dresden*

Try not, my Stanhope, 'tis in vain,
To stop your tears, to hide your pain,
   Or check your honest rage ;
Give sorrow and revenge their scope,
My present joy, your future hope,
   Lies murder'd in his cage.

Matzel's no more ; ye Graces, Loves,
Ye linnets, nightingales, and doves,
   Attend th' untimely bier ;
Let every sorrow be exprest,
Beat with your wings each mournful breast,
   And drop each nat'ral tear.

In height of song, in beauty's pride,
By fell Grimalkin's claws he died—
   But vengeance shall have sway ;
On pains and tortures I'll refine ;
Yet, Matzel, that one death of thine,
   His nine will ill repay.

For thee, my bird, the sacred Nine,
Who lov'd thy tuneful notes, shall join
   In thy funereal verse :
My painful task shall be to write
Th' eternal dirge which they indite,
   And hang it on thy hearse.

In vain I lov'd, in vain I mourn
My bird, who never to return
   Is fled to happier shades,
Where Lesbia shall for him prepare
The place most charming, and most fair,
   Of all th' Elysian glades.

There shall thy notes in cypress grove
Soothe wretched ghosts that died for love ;
  There shall thy plaintive strain
Lull impious Phædra's endless grief,
To Procris yield some short relief,
  And soften Dido's pain.

Till Proserpine by chance shall hear
Thy notes, and make thee all her care,
  And love thee with my love ;
While each attendant soul shall praise
The matchless Matzel's tuneful lays,
  And all his songs approve.

An Ode,

Humbly inscribed to the Right Honourable William Earl of Bath

Great Earl of Bath, your reign is o'er ;
The Tories trust your word no more,
  The Whigs no longer fear you ;
Your gates are seldom now unbarr'd,
No crowds of coaches fill your yard,
  And scarce a soul comes near you.

Few now aspire at your good graces,
Scarce any sue to you for places,
  Or come with their petition,
To tell how well they have deserv'd,
How long, how steadily have starv'd
  For you in opposition.

Expect to see that tribe no more,
Since all mankind perceive that power
  Is lodg'd in other hands :
Sooner to Carteret now they'll go,
Or ev'n (though that's excessive low)
  To Wilmington or Sandys.

With your obedient wife retire,
And sitting silent by the fire,
   A sullen *Tête à tête*,
Think over all you've done or said,
And curse the hour that you were made
   Unprofitably great.

With vapours there, and spleen o'ercast,
Reflect on all your actions past,
   With sorrow and contrition ;
And there enjoy the thoughts that rise
From disappointed avarice,
   From frustrated ambition.

There soon you'll loudly, but in vain,
Of your deserting friends complain,
   That visit you no more ;
But in this country 'tis a truth,
As known as that love follows youth,
   That friendship follows power.

Such is the calm of your retreat !
You through the dregs of life must sweat
   Beneath this heavy load ;
And I'll attend you, as I've done,
Only to help reflection on,
   With now and then an ode.

Sir C. HANBURY WILLIAMS

The Statesman

*Quem virum, aut heroa, lyra, vel acri
Tibia sumes celebrare, Clio?
Quem deum?*

HORACE, Lib. I, Ode xii.

What statesman, what hero, what king,
  Whose name through the island is spread,
Will you choose, O my Clio, to sing,
  Of all the great living or dead?

Go, my Muse, from this place to Japan,
  In search of a topic for rhyme:
The great Earl of Bath is the man,
  Who deserves to employ your whole time.

But, howe'er, as the subject is nice,
  And perhaps you're unfurnish'd with matter,
May it please you to take my advice,
  That you mayn't be suspected to flatter.

When you touch on his Lordship's high birth,
  Speak Latin as if you were tipsy:
Say, we all are the sons of the earth,
  Et genus non fecimus ipsi.

Proclaim him as rich as a Jew;
  Yet attempt not to reckon his bounties.
You may say, he is married; that's true:
  Yet speak not a word of his Countess.

Leave a blank here and there in each page,
  To enroll the fair deeds of his youth!
When you mention the acts of his age,
  Leave a blank for his honour and truth!

Say, he made a great monarch change hands :
    He spake—and the minister fell.
Say, he made a great statesman of Sandys ;
    (Oh ! that he had taught him to spell !)

Then enlarge on his cunning and wit :
    Say, how he harangu'd at the fountain ;
Say, how the old patriots were bit,
    And a mouse was produc'd by a mountain.

Then say, how he mark'd the new year,
    By increasing our taxes, and stocks :
Then say, how he chang'd to a peer,
    Fit companion for Edgcumbe and Fox.

The Rev. WALTER HARTE, D.D. (1709-1774)

A Soliloquy,
Occasioned by the Chirping of a Grasshopper

Happy Insect ! ever blest
With a more than mortal rest,
Rosy dews the leaves among,
Humble joys, and gentle song !
Wretched Poet ! ever curst
With a life of lives the worst,
Sad despondence, restless fears,
Endless jealousies and tears.

In the burning summer, thou
Warblest on the verdant bough,
Meditating cheerful play,
Mindless of the piercing ray ;
Scorch'd in Cupid's fervours, I
Ever weep, and ever die.

Proud to gratify thy will,
Ready nature waits thee still :
Balmy wines to thee she pours,
Weeping through the dewy flowers ;
Rich as those by Hebe given
To the thirsty sons of Heaven.

Yet alas ! we both agree,
Miserable thou like me !
Each alike in youth rehearses
Gentle strains, and tender verses ;
Ever wandering far from home ;
Mindless of the days to come,
(Such as aged winter brings
Trembling on his icy wings)
Both alike at last we die ;
Thou art starv'd, and so am I !

*To a Young Lady**

with Mr. Fenton's Miscellany

These various strains, where every talent charms,
Where humour pleases, or where passion warms,
(Strains, where the tender and sublime conspire,
A Sappho's sweetness, and a Homer's fire)
Attend their doom, and wait with glad surprise
Th' impartial justice of Cleora's eyes.

'Tis hard to say, what mysteries of fate,
What turns of fortune, on good writers wait.
The party-slave will wound 'em as he can,
And damns the merit, if he hates the man.
Nay, even the bards with wit and laurels crown'd,
Bless'd in each strain, in every art renown'd,

* This beautifully written poem is printed rather for its manner
than for its matter.

Misled by pride, and taught to sin by power,
Still search around for those they may devour ;
Like savage monarchs on a guilty throne,
Who crush all might that can invade their own.

Others who hate, yet want the soul to dare,
So ruin bards—as beaus deceive the fair :
On the pleas'd ear their soft deceits employ ;
Smiling they wound, and praise but to destroy.
These are th' unhappy crimes of modern days,
And can the best of poets hope for praise ?

How small a part of human blessings share
The wise, the good, the noble, or the fair.
Short is the date unhappy wit can boast,
A blaze of glory in a moment lost.
Fortune still envious of the great man's praise,
Curses the coxcomb with a length of days.
So (Hector dead) amid the female choir,
Unmanly Paris tun'd the silver lyre.

Attend ye Britons ! in so just a cause
'Tis sure a scandal, to withhold applause ;
Nor let posterity reviling say,
Thus unregarded Fenton pass'd away !
Yet if the Muse may faith or merit claim,
(A Muse too just to bribe with venal fame)
Soon shalt thou shine " in majesty avow'd ;
As thy own goddess breaking through a cloud."
Fame, like a nation-debt, though long delay'd,
With mighty interest must at last be paid.

Like Vinci's strokes, thy verses we behold ;
Correctly graceful, and with labour bold.
At Sappho's woes we breathe a tender sigh,
And the soft sorrow steals from every eye ;
Here Spenser's thoughts in solemn numbers roll ;
Here lofty Milton seems to lift the soul ;
There sprightly Chaucer charms our hours away
With stories quaint, and gentle roundelay.

Muse ! at that name each thought of pride recall,
Ah ! think how soon the wise and glorious fall !
What though the Sisters every grace impart,
To smooth thy verse, and captivate the heart :
What though your charms, my fair Cleora ! shine
Bright as your eyes, and as your sex divine :
Yet shall the verses, and the charms decay,
The boast of youth, the blessing of a day !
Not Chaucer's beauties could survive the rage
Of wasting envy, and devouring age :
One mingled heap of ruin now we see ;
Thus Chaucer is, and Fenton thus shall be !

SAMUEL JOHNSON, LL.D. (1709-1784)

Prologue,

*Spoken by Mr. Garrick at the opening of the Theatre Royal,
Drury Lane,* 1747

When Learning's triumph o'er her barb'rous foes
First rear'd the stage, immortal Shakespeare rose ;
Each change of many-colour'd life he drew,
Exhausted worlds, and then imagin'd new :
Existence saw him spurn her bounded reign,
And panting Time toil'd after him in vain.
His pow'rful strokes presiding Truth impress'd,
And unresisted Passion storm'd the breast.

Then Jonson came, instructed from the school,
To please in method, and invent by rule ;
His studious patience and laborious art,
By regular approach essay'd the heart :
Cold Approbation gave the ling'ring bays,
For those who durst not censure, scarce could praise.
A mortal born, he met the gen'ral doom,
But left, like Egypt's kings, a lasting tomb.

SAMUEL JOHNSON

The wits of Charles found easier ways to fame,
Nor wish'd for Jonson's art, or Shakespeare's flame ;
Themselves they studied, as they felt they writ ;
Intrigue was plot, obscenity was wit.
Vice always found a sympathetic friend ;
They pleas'd their age, and did not aim to mend.
Yet bards like these aspir'd to lasting praise,
And proudly hop'd to pimp in future days.
Their cause was gen'ral, their supports were strong,
Their slaves were willing, and their reign was long :
Till Shame regain'd the post that Sense betray'd,
And Virtue call'd Oblivion to her aid.

Then, crush'd by rules, and weaken'd as refin'd,
For years the power of Tragedy declin'd :
From bard to bard the frigid caution crept,
Till Declamation roar'd, while Passion slept ;
Yet still did Virtue deign the stage to tread,
Philosophy remain'd, though Nature fled.
But forc'd at length her ancient reign to quit,
She saw great Faustus lay the ghost of Wit ;
Exulting Folly hail'd the joyful day,
And Pantomime and Song confirm'd her sway.

But who the coming changes can presage,
And mark the future periods of the Stage ?
Perhaps, if skill could distant times explore,
New Behns, new Durfeys, yet remain in store ;
Perhaps, where Lear has rav'd, and Hamlet died,
On flying cars new sorcerers may ride :
Perhaps (for who can guess th' effects of chance)
Here Hunt may box, and Mahomet may dance.

Hard is his lot that, here by Fortune plac'd,
Must watch the wild vicissitudes of taste ;
With every meteor of caprice must play,
And chase the new-blown bubbles of the day

Ah ! let not Censure term our fate our choice,
The stage but echoes back the public voice ;
The drama's laws, the drama's patrons give,
For we that live to please, must please to live.

Then prompt no more the follies you decry,
As tyrants doom their tools of guilt to die ;
'Tis yours, this night, to bid the reign commence
Of rescu'd Nature and reviving Sense ;
To chase the charms of Sound, the pomp of Show,
For useful Mirth, and salutary Woe ;
Bid scenic Virtue form the rising age,
And Truth diffuse her radiance from the stage.

On the Coming of Age of a Rich, Extravagant Young Man

Long-expected one-and-twenty,
  Ling'ring year, at length is flown ;
Pride and pleasure, pomp and plenty,
  Great Sir John, are now your own.

Loosen'd from the minor's tether,
  Free to mortgage or to sell,
Wild as wind, and light as feather,
  Bid the sons of thrift farewell.

Call the Betsies, Kates, and Jennies,
  All the names that banish care ;
Lavish of your grandsire's guineas,
  Shew the spirit of an heir.

All that prey on vice or folly
  Joy to see their quarry fly ;
There the gamester, light and jolly,
  There the lender, grave and sly.

Wealth, my lad, was made to wander,
   Let it wander as it will ;
Call the jockey, call the pander,
   Bid them come and take their fill.

When the bonny blade carouses,
   Pockets full, and spirits high—
What are acres ? what are houses ?
   Only dirt, or wet or dry.

Should the guardian friend or mother
   Tell the woes of wilful waste ;
Scorn their counsel, scorn their pother,—
   You can hang or drown at last.

To Stella

Not the soft sighs of vernal gales,
The fragrance of the flowery vales,
The murmurs of the crystal rill,
The vocal grove, the verdant hill ;
Not all their charms, though all unite,
Can touch my bosom with delight.

Not all the gems on India's shore,
Not all Peru's unbounded store,
Not all the power, nor all the fame,
That heroes, kings, or poets, claim ;
Nor knowledge, which the learn'd approve ;
To form one wish my soul can move.

Yet nature's charms allure my eyes,
And knowledge, wealth, and fame I prize ;
Fame, wealth, and knowledge I obtain,
Nor seek I nature's charms in vain ;
In lovely Stella all combine ;
And, lovely Stella ! thou art mine.

SAMUEL JOHNSON

Winter

An Ode

No more the morn, with tepid rays,
  Unfolds the flower of various hue ;
Noon spreads no more the genial blaze,
  Nor gentle eve distils the dew.
The ling'ring hours prolong the night,
  Usurping darkness shares the day ;
Her mists restrain the force of light,
  And Phœbus holds a doubtful sway.
By gloomy twilight half reveal'd,
  With sighs we view the hoary hill,
The leafless wood, the naked field,
  The snow-topt cot, the frozen rill.
No music warbles through the grove,
  No vivid colours paint the plain ;
No more with devious steps I rove
  Through verdant paths, now sought in vain.
Aloud the driving tempest roars,
  Congeal'd, impetuous showers descend ;
Haste, close the window, bar the doors,
  Fate leaves me Stella, and a friend.
In nature's aid, let art supply
  With light and heat my little sphere ;
Rouse, rouse the fire, and pile it high,
  Light up a constellation here.
Let music sound the voice of joy,
  Or mirth repeat the jocund tale ;
Let Love his wanton wiles employ,
  And o'er the season wine prevail.
Yet time life's dreary winter brings,
  When Mirth's gay tale shall please no more ;
Nor music charm—though Stella sings ;
  Nor love, nor wine, the spring restore.
Catch, then, oh ! catch the transient hour,
  Improve each moment as it flies ;
Life's a short summer—man a flower :
  He dies—alas ! how soon he dies !

SAMUEL JOHNSON

The Winter's Walk

Behold, my fair, where'er we rove,
  What dreary prospects round us rise ;
The naked hill, the leafless grove,
  The hoary ground, the frowning skies !
Nor only through the wasted plain,
  Stern Winter ! is thy force confess'd ;
Still wider spreads thy horrid reign,
  I feel thy power usurp my breast.
Enlivening hope, and fond desire,
  Resign the heart to spleen and care ;
Scarce frighted Love maintains her fire,
  And rapture saddens to despair.
In groundless hope, and causeless fear,
  Unhappy man ! behold thy doom ;
Still changing with the changeful year,
  The slave of sunshine and of gloom.
Tir'd with vain joys, and false alarms,
  With mental and corporeal strife,
Snatch me, my Stella, to thy arms,
  And hide me from the sight of life.

Epitaph on Claude Phillips,
an itinerant musician

Phillips ! whose touch harmonious could remove
The pangs of guilty pow'r, and hapless love,
Rest here, distrest by poverty no more,
Here find that calm thou gav'st so oft before ;
Sleep undisturb'd within this peaceful shrine,
Till angels wake thee with a note like thine.

SAMUEL JOHNSON

On the Death of Mr. Robert Levet,

a practiser in physic

Condemn'd to Hope's delusive mine,
  As on we toil from day to day,
By sudden blasts, or slow decline,
  Our social comforts drop away.

Well tried through many a varying year,
  See Levet to the grave descend,
Officious, innocent, sincere,
  Of every friendless name the friend.

Yet still he fills Affection's eye,
  Obscurely wise, and coarsely kind ;
Nor, letter'd Arrogance, deny
  Thy praise to merit unrefin'd.

When fainting Nature call'd for aid,
  And hov'ring Death prepar'd the blow,
His vig'rous remedy display'd
  The power of art without the show.

In Misery's darkest cavern known,
  His useful care was ever nigh,
Where hopeless Anguish pour'd his groan,
  And lonely Want retir'd to die.

No summons mock'd by chill delay,
  No petty gain disdain'd by pride,
The modest wants of every day
  The toil of every day supplied.

His virtues walk'd their narrow round,
  Nor made a pause, nor left a void ;
And sure th' Eternal Master found
  The single talent well employ'd.

The busy day—the peaceful night,
 Unfelt, uncounted, glided by ;
His frame was firm—his powers were bright,
 And now his eightieth year was nigh.

Then, with no fiery throbbing pain,
 No cold gradations of decay,
Death broke at once the vital chain,
 And freed his soul the nearest way.

The Rev. THOMAS LISLE, D.D. (1709-1767)

The Power of Music : * A Song*

*Imitated from the Spanish of Juan de Tassis, Conde de Villa-
mediana*

When Orpheus went down to the regions below,
 Which men are forbidden to see,
He tun'd up his lyre, as old histories show,
 To set his Eurydice free.

All hell was astonish'd a person so wise
 Should rashly endanger his life,
And venture so far,—but how vast their surprise
 When they heard that he came for his wife.

To find out a punishment due to his fault,
 Old Pluto had puzzled his brain ;
But hell had no torments sufficient, he thought,
 —So he gave him his wife back again.

But pity succeeding found place in his heart,
 And, pleas'd with his playing so well,
He took her again in reward of his art ;
 Such power had music in hell !

* These verses are said to have been Benjamin Franklin's favourite lines. A great man may be allowed some weaknesses.

GEORGE LYTTELTON, Baron LYTTELTON
(1709-1773)
Verses
*written at Mr. Pope's house at Twickenham, which he
had lent to Mrs. Greville*

Go, Thames ! and tell the busy town,
　　Not all its wealth or pride
Could tempt me from the charms that crown
　　Thy rural flowery side ;

Thy flowery side, where Pope has plac'd
　　The Muses' green retreat,
With every smile of nature grac'd,
　　With every art complete.

But now, sweet bard ! thy heavenly song
　　Enchants us here no more,
Their darling glory lost too long,
　　Thy once-lov'd shades deplore.

Yet still for beauteous Greville's sake
　　The Muses here remain ;
Greville ! whose eyes have power to make
　　A Pope of every swain.

Song

Say, Myra ! why is gentle love
　　A stranger to that mind,
Which pity and esteem can move,
　　Which can be just and kind ?

Is it because you fear to share
　　The ills that love molest,
The jealous doubt, the tender care,
　　That rack the amorous breast ?

Alas ! by some degree of woe
　　We every bliss must gain :
The heart can ne'er a transport know
　　That never feels a pain.

Song

The heavy hours are almost past
    That part my love and me ;
My longing eyes may hope at last
    Their only wish to see.

But how, my Delia ! will you meet
    The man you've lost so long ?
Will love in all your pulses beat,
    And tremble on your tongue ?

Will you in every look declare
    Your heart is still the same,
And heal each idly anxious care
    Our fears in absence frame ?

Thus, Delia ! thus I paint the scene
    When shortly we shall meet,
And try what yet remains between
    Of loitering time to cheat.

But if the dream that soothes my mind
    Shall false and groundless prove,
If I am doom'd at length to find
    You have forgot to love ?

All I of Venus ask is this,
    No more to let us join,
But grant me here the flattering bliss
    To die and think you mine.

Song

When Delia on the plain appears,
Aw'd by a thousand tender fears,
I would approach, but dare not move :
Tell me, my heart ! if this be love ?

Whene'er she speaks, my ravish'd ear
No other voice but hers can hear,
No other wit but hers approve :
Tell me, my heart ! if this be love ?

If she some other youth commend,
Though I was once his fondest friend,
His instant enemy I prove :
Tell me, my heart ! if this be love ?

When she is absent, I no more
Delight in all that pleas'd before,
The clearest spring or shadiest grove :
Tell me, my heart ! if this be love ?

When, fond of power, of beauty vain,
Her nets she spread for every swain,
I strove to hate, but vainly strove :
Tell me, my heart ! if this be love ?

JAMES HAMMOND (1710-1742)

To Delia

No second love shall e'er my heart surprise,
    This solemn league did first our passion bind :
Thou, only thou, canst please thy lover's eyes,
    Thy voice alone, can soothe his troubled mind.

Oh, that thy charms were only fair to me,
    Displease all others, and secure my rest,
No need of envy, let me happy be,
    I little care that others know me blest.

With thee in gloomy deserts let me dwell,
    Where never human footstep mark'd the ground ;
Thou, light of life, all darkness canst expel,
    And seem a world with solitude around.

I say too much—my heedless words restore,
  My tongue undoes me in this loving hour ;
Thou know'st thy strength, and thence insulting more,
  Wilt make me feel the weight of all thy power.

Whate'er I feel, thy slave I will remain,
  Nor fly the burden I am form'd to bear,
In chains I'll sit me down at Venus' fane,
  She knows my wrongs, and will regard my prayer.

The Rev. ROBERT LOWTH, D.D., Bishop of London
(1710-1787)

The Link

Ye ladies that live in the city or town,
  Fair Winton or Alresford so fine and so gay ;
And ye neat country lasses in clean linen gown,
  As neat and as blithe and as pretty as they :
Come away straight to Ovington, for you can't think
What a charming new walk there is made on the Link.

Look how lovely the prospect, the meadows how green,
  The fields and the woods, in the vale or the hill :
The trees, and the cottage that peeps out between,
  The clear stream that runs bubbling in many a rill,
That will show your fair face as you stand on the brink,
And murmurs most sweetly all under the Link.

How pleasant the morning, how clear the blue sky,
  How pure the fresh air, and how healthy the place !
Your heart goes a pit-a-pat light as a fly,
  And the blood circles briskly, and glows in your face :
Would you paint your fair cheeks with the rose and the
    pink ?
Throw your washes away, take a walk on the Link.

After dinner the squire, ere the ladies retreat,
 Marches off with some friends that will ply the brisk
  glass ;
" Give us liquor enough, and a good pleasant seat,
 And damn your fine taste, and your finical lass :
Al fresco, my lads, we'll carouse and we'll drink,
Take your bottle each man, and away to the Link."

Not so gentle Collin, whom Love holds in thrall,
 To Molly he steals all in silence away ;
And when naught can be heard but the rude water-fall,
 And the woodbine breathes sweetest at close of the day,
He takes her soft hand, and he tips her the wink,
" Come, my dear, let us take a cool walk on the Link."

But, O ye fair maidens, be sure have a care,
 Nor lay yourselves open to Love's cruel dart ;
Of the hour and the place and the season beware,
 And guard well each passage that leads to your heart ;
Sly Cupid will steal in at some little chink,
If you walk in the evening too late on the Link.

Ye poets so lofty, who love to retire
 From the noise of the town to the stream and the wood ;
Who in epics and tragics, with marvellous fire,
 Utter sounds by mere mortals not well understood :
Here mouth your loud strain, and here ply pen and ink,
Quit Parnassus and Pindus, and come to the Link.

And come you, who for thought are at little expense,
 Who indite gentle pastoral, ballad, or song ;
You see with smooth numbers, and not too much sense,
 How the verses run easy and glibly along ;
And the rhyme at the close how it falls with a clink,
So kind are the Muses that sport on the Link.

JOHN WHALEY* (1710-1745)

Song

Wanton gales that fondly play
   Round about my lovesick head ;
Quickly waft my sighs away
   To the nymph for whom I bleed.

Softly whisper in her ear
   All the pains for her I feel,
All the torments that I bear,
   Tell her, she alone can heal.

Then with unsuspected care
   Gently fan her lovely breast :
(Happy you may revel there,
   Where each god would wish to rest.)

If one spark of fond desire,
   Harbour'd there by chance you find,
Raise it to a lasting fire,
   Such as burns within my mind.

To Celia

The Amulet

From those bewildering charms which grace
Thy siren voice, thy angel face,
The only method to be free
Is not to hear, and not to see.

PAUL WHITEHEAD (1710-1774)

Death and the Doctor

'Twixt Death and Schomberg, t'other day,
   A contest did arise ;
Death swore his prize he'd bear away ;
   The Doctor, Death defies.

* Fellow of King's College, Cambridge.

Enrag'd to hear his power defied,
  Death drew his keenest dart ;
But wondering saw it glance aside,
  And miss the vital part.

To Dr. Schomberg, of Bath

To Schomberg quoth Death, " I your patient will have " ;
To Death replied Schomberg, " My patient I'll save."
Then Death seiz'd his arrow, the Doctor his pen,
And each wound the one gave, t'other heal'd it again ;
'Till Death swore he never had met such defiance,
Since he and the College had been in alliance.

Song

Sung by Mr. Beard in the entertainment of
" Apollo and Daphne "

The sun from the east tips the mountains with gold ;
The meadows all spangled with dew-drops behold !
Hear ! the lark's early matin proclaims the new day,
And the horn's cheerful summons rebukes our delay.

CHORUS
With the sports of the field there's no pleasure can vie,
While jocund we follow the hounds in full cry.

Let the drudge of the town make riches his sport ;
The slave of the state hunt the smiles of a court ;
No care and ambition our pastime annoy,
But innocence still gives a zest to our joy.

  With the sports, etc.

Mankind are all hunters in various degree ;
The priest hunts a living—the lawyer a fee,
The doctor a patient—the courtier a place,
Though often, like us, he's flung-out in the chase.

  With the sports, etc.

The cit hunts a plum—while the soldier hunts fame,
The poet a dinner—the patriot a name ;
And the practis'd coquette, though she seems to refuse,
In spite of her airs, still her lover pursues.

With the sports, etc.

Let the bold and the busy hunt glory and wealth ;
All the blessing we ask is the blessing of health,
With the hound and the horn through the woodlands to
    roam,
And, when tired abroad, find contentment at home.

With the sports, etc.

The Rev. JOHN HOADLY,* LL.D. (1711-1776)

Chloe Resolved

A Ballad

As Chloe on flowers reclin'd o'er the stream,
She sigh'd to the breeze, and made Colin her theme ;
Though pleasant the stream, and though cooling the breeze,
And the flowers though fragrant, she panted for ease.

The stream it was fickle, and hasted away,
It kiss'd the sweet banks, but no longer could stay ;
Though beauteous inconstant, and faithless though fair,
Ah ! Colin, look in, and behold thyself there.

The breeze that so sweet on its bosom did play,
Now rose to a tempest, and darken'd the day.
As sweet as the breeze, and as loud as the wind,
Such Colin when angry, and Colin when kind.

The flowers when gather'd, so beauteous and sweet,
Now fade on her bosom, and die at her feet ;
So fair in their bloom, and so foul in decay,
Such Colin when present, and Colin away.

* Chancellor of the Diocese of Winchester.

In rage and despair from the ground she arose,
And from her the flowers so faded she throws :
She weeps in the stream, and she sighs to the wind,
And resolves to drive Colin quite out of her mind.

But what her resolves when her Colin appear'd ?
The stream it stood still, and no tempest was heard ;
The flowers recover'd their beautiful hue :
She found he was kind, and believ'd he was true.

From " A Pipe of Tobacco "

*Imitation 2, Ambrose Philips (the rest of the series being
by I. H. Browne)*

Little tube of mighty pow'r,
Charmer of an idle hour,
Object of my warm desire,
Lip of wax, and eye of fire :
And thy snowy taper waist,
With my finger gently brac'd ;
And thy pretty swelling crest,
With my little stopper prest,
And the sweetest bliss of blisses,
Breathing from thy balmy kisses.
Happy thrice, and thrice agen,
Happiest he of mortal men ;
Who when agen the night returns,
When agen the taper burns ;
When agen the cricket's gay,
(Little cricket, full of play)
Can afford his tube to feed
With the fragrant Indian weed :
Pleasure for a nose divine,
Incense of the god of wine.
Happy thrice, and thrice agen,
Happiest he of happy men.

RICHARD GLOVER, M.P. (1712-1785)

Admiral Hosier's Ghost

As near Porto-Bello lying
  On the gently swelling flood,
At midnight, with streamers flying,
  Our triumphant navy rode ;
There while Vernon sat all-glorious
  From the Spaniards' late defeat,
And his crews, with shouts victorious,
  Drank success to England's fleet ;

On a sudden, shrilly sounding,
  Hideous yells and shrieks were heard ;
Then, each heart with fear confounding,
  A sad troop of ghosts appear'd,
All in dreary hammocks shrouded,
  Which for winding-sheets they wore,
And, with looks by sorrow clouded,
  Frowning on that hostile shore.

On them gleam'd the moon's wan lustre,
  When the shade of Hosier brave
His pale bands was seen to muster,
  Rising from their watery grave :
O'er the glimmering wave he hied him,
  Where the Burford rear'd her sail,
With three thousand ghosts beside him,
  And in groans did Vernon hail.

" Heed, O heed, our fatal story,
  I am Hosier's injur'd ghost ;
You, who now have purchas'd glory
  At this place where I was lost,
Though in Port-Bello's ruin
  You now triumph, free from fears,
When you think on our undoing,
  You will mix your joy with tears.

" See these mournful spectres, sweeping
    Ghastly o'er this hated wave,
Whose wan cheeks are stain'd with weeping ;
    These were English captains brave ;
Mark those numbers, pale and horrid,
    Those were once my sailors bold,
Lo, each hangs his drooping forehead,
    While his dismal tale is told.

" I, by twenty sail attended,
    Did this Spanish town affright ;
Nothing then its wealth defended
    But my orders not to fight ;
O ! that in this rolling ocean
    I had cast them with disdain,
And obey'd my heart's warm motion
    To have quell'd the pride of Spain.

" For resistance I could fear none,
    But with twenty ships had done
What thou, brave and happy Vernon,
    Hast achiev'd with six alone.
Then the Bastimentos never
    Had our foul dishonour seen,
Nor the sea the sad receiver
    Of this gallant train had been.

" Thus, like thee, proud Spain dismaying,
    And her galleons leading home,
Though, condemn'd for disobeying,
    I had met a traitor's doom.
To have fallen, my country crying
    ' He has play'd an English part,'
Had been better far than dying
    Of a griev'd and broken heart.

" Unrepining at thy glory,
    Thy successful arms we hail ;
But remember our sad story,
    And let Hosier's wrongs prevail.

Sent in this foul clime to languish,
  Think what thousands fell in vain,
Wasted with disease and anguish,
  Not in glorious battle slain.

" Hence with all my train attending
  From their oozy tombs below,
Through the hoary foam ascending,
  Here I feed my constant woe ;
Here, the Bastimentos viewing,
  We recall our shameful doom,
And, our plaintive cries renewing,
  Wander through the midnight gloom.

" O'er these waves, for ever mourning,
  Shall we roam depriv'd of rest,
If to Britain's shores returning
  You neglect my just request :
After this proud foe subduing,
  When your patriot friends you see,
Think on vengeance for my ruin,
  And for England sham'd in me."

EDWARD MOORE (1712-1757)

*The Poet and his Patron**

Why, Celia, is your spreading waist
So loose, so negligently lac'd ?
Why must the wrapping bed-gown hide
Your snowy bosom's swelling pride ?
How ill that dress adorns your head,
Distain'd, and rumpled from the bed !
Those clouds, that shade your blooming face,
A little water might displace,
As nature every morn bestows
The crystal dew, to cleanse the rose.

* From this author's *Fables for the Female Sex*.

Those tresses, as the raven black,
That wav'd in ringlets down your back,
Uncomb'd, and injur'd by neglect,
Destroy the face, which once they deck'd.

Whence this forgetfulness of dress ?
Pray, madam, are you married ? Yes.
Nay, then indeed the wonder ceases,
No matter now how loose your dress is ;
The end is won, your fortune's made,
Your sister now may take the trade.

Alas ! what pity 'tis to find
This fault in half the female kind !
From hence proceed aversion, strife,
And all that sours the wedded life.
Beauty can only point the dart,
'Tis neatness guides it to the heart ;
Let neatness then, and beauty strive
To keep a wavering flame alive.

'Tis harder far (you'll find it true)
To keep the conquest, than subdue ;
Admit us once behind the screen,
What is there farther to be seen ?
A newer face may raise the flame,
But every woman is the same.

Then study chiefly to improve
The charm, that fix'd your husband's love ;
Weigh well his humour. Was it dress,
That gave your beauty power to bless ?
Pursue it still ; be neater seen,
'Tis always frugal to be clean ;
So shall you keep alive desire,
And time's swift wing shall fan the fire.

In garret high (as stories say)
A Poet sung his tuneful lay ;
So soft, so smooth his verse, you'd swear
Apollo, and the Muses there ;
Through all the town his praises rung,
His sonnets at the playhouse sung ;

High waving o'er his lab'ring head,
The goddess Want her pinions spread,
And with poetic fury fir'd
What Phœbus faintly had inspir'd.
   A noble youth, of taste, and wit,
Approv'd the sprightly things he writ,
And sought him in his cobweb dome,
Discharg'd his rent, and brought him home.
   Behold him at the stately board,
Who, but the Poet, and my Lord !
Each day, deliciously he dines,
And greedy quaffs the gen'rous wines ;
His sides were plump, his skin was sleek,
And plenty wanton'd on his cheek ;
Astonish'd at the change so new,
Away th' inspiring goddess flew.
   Now, dropt for politics, and news,
Neglected lay the drooping muse,
Unmindful whence his fortune came,
He stifled the poetic flame ;
Nor tale, nor sonnet, for my lady,
Lampoon, nor epigram was ready.
   With just contempt his Patron saw,
Resolv'd his bounty to withdraw,
And thus, with anger in his look,
The late-repenting fool bespoke.
   " Blind to the good that courts thee grown,
Whence has the sun of favour shone ?
Delighted with thy tuneful art,
Esteem was growing in my heart,
But idly thou reject'st the charm,
That gave it birth, and kept it warm."
   Unthinking fools alone despise
The arts, that taught them first to rise.

EDWARD MOORE

Song

You tell me I'm handsome, I know not how true,
And easy, and chatty, and good-humour'd, too,
That my lips are as red as the rosebud in June,
And my voice like the nightingale's sweetly in tune :
All this has been told me by twenty before,
But he that would win me must flatter me more.

If beauty from virtue receive no supply,
Or prattle from prudence, how wanting am I !
My ease and good-humour short raptures will bring,
And my voice like the nightingale's know but a spring :
For charms such as these then your praises give o'er ;
To love me for life you must love me for more.

Then talk to me not of a shape or an air,
For Chloe the wanton can rival me there :
'Tis virtue alone that makes beauty look gay,
And brightens good-humour as sunshine the day ;
For that if you love me, your flame may be true,
And I in my turn may be taught to love too.

Mrs. LETITIA PILKINGTON, *née* Van LEWEN*

(1712-1750)

Written on her Death-bed

My Lord, my Saviour, and my God,
I bow to Thy correcting rod ;
Nor will I murmur or complain,
Though every limb be fill'd with pain ;
Though my weak tongue its aid denies,
And daylight wounds my wretched eyes.

* Dean Swift's friend, and wife of Matthew Pilkington.

LETITIA PILKINGTON

Memory

In what recesses of the brain
Does this amazing power remain,
By which all knowledge we attain ?

What art thou, Memory ? What tongue can tell,
What curious artist trace thy hidden cell,
Wherein ten thousand different objects dwell ?

Surprising store-house ! in whose narrow womb
All things, the past, the present, and to come,
Find ample space, and large and mighty room.

O falsely deem'd the foe of sacred wit !
Thou, who the nurse and guardian art of it,
Laying it up till season due and fit.

Then proud the wondrous treasure to produce,
As understanding points it, to conduce
Either to entertainment, or to use.

Nor love, nor holy friendship, without thee,
Could ever of the least duration be ;
Nor gratitude, nor truth, nor piety.

Where thou art not, the cheerless human mind
Is one vast void, all darksome, sad and blind ;
No trace of anything remains behind.

The sacred stores of learning all are thine ;
'Tis only thou record'st the faithful line ;
'Tis thou mak'st human-kind almost divine.

And when at length we quit this mortal scene,
Thou still shalt with our tender friends remain,
And Time and Death shall strike at thee in vain.

Lord, let me so this wondrous gift employ,
It may a fountain be of endless joy,
Which time, nor accident, may ne'er destroy.

Still let my faithful Memory impart,
And deep engrave it on my grateful heart,
How just, and good, and excellent Thou art.

The Rev. JOSIAH RELPH (1712-1743)

Song

All female charms, I own, my fair,
  In that accomplish'd form combine.
Yet why this proud, assuming air ?
  The praise is Nature's, none of thine.

Wouldst thou, with just pretensions, claim
  Of our applause an equal share ;
Be thy desert, my dear, the same,
  And prove as kind as thou art fair.

Tea

Let poets praise in rapt'rous dreams
Their pretty Naiads, purling streams ;
No stream purls half so sweet as ours,
No Naiad half so pretty pours.

Her powerful cups let Circe bless,
And men transform to savages ;
Of happier force our charmer's can
Polish the savage into man.

Medea's potions may bestow
On aged blood a youthful flow ;
Chloe's of power yet more uncouth
Quicken the very flow of youth.

And, Jove, though Hebe crown thy treat
With nectar and ambrosia sweet,
We envy not, while we can boast
Our as delicious tea and toast.

JOSIAH RELPH

Song

What charms has Chloe !
Her bosom how snowy !
  Each feature
  Is sweeter
Poor Venus than thine !
Her mind like her face is
Adorn'd with all graces,
Not Pallas possesses
  A wit so divine.

What crowds are bleeding,
While Chloe's ne'er heeding,
  All lying
  A-dying
Through cruel disdain :
Ye Gods deign to warm her,
Or quickly disarm her,
While Chloe's a charmer
  Your temples are vain.

The Rev. WILLIAM THOMPSON (1712 ?-1766 ?)

The Happy Life

A book, a friend, a song, a glass,
A chaste, yet laughter-loving lass,
To mortals various joys impart,
Inform the sense, and warm the heart.

Thrice happy they, who careless laid
Beneath a kind-embowering shade,
With rosy wreaths their temples crown,
In rosy wine their sorrow drown.

Meanwhile the Muses wake the lyre,
The Graces modest mirth inspire,
Good-natur'd humour, harmless wit ;
Well-temper'd joys, nor grave, nor light.

Let sacred Venus with her heir,
And dear Ianthe, too, be there.
Music and wine in concert move
With beauty, and refining love.

There Peace shall spread her dove-like wing,
And bid her olives round us spring.
There Truth shall reign, a sacred guest !
And Innocence, to crown the rest.

Begone, ambition, riches, toys,
And splendid cares, and guilty joys.—
Give me a book, a friend, a glass,
And a chaste, laughter-loving lass.

ANONYMOUS

(*From " Clio and Euterpe," 1759*)

The Lass of the Mill

Who has e'er been at Baldock, must needs know the Mill,
At the sign of the *Horse*, at the foot of the hill ;
Where the grave and the gay, the clown and the beau,
Without all distinction, promiscuously go.

The man of the Mill has a daughter so fair,
With so pleasing a shape, and so winning an air,
That once on the ever-green bank as I stood,
I'd swore she was Venus just sprung from the flood.

But, looking again, I perceive my mistake,
For Venus, though fair, has the look of a rake ;
While nothing but virtue and modesty fill
The more beautiful looks of the Lass of the Mill.

ANONYMOUS

Prometheus stole fire, as the poets all say,
To enliven that mass which he modell'd of clay.
Had Polly been with him, the beams of her eyes
Had sav'd him the trouble of robbing the skies !

Since first I beheld this dear Lass of the Mill,
I can ne'er be at quiet : but, do what I will,
All the day and all night I sigh, and think still,
I shall die, if I have not this Lass of the Mill !

ANONYMOUS

(From " The Laurel," circa 1750)

Song

No sooner peeps the rosy dawn,
　　Than Chloe leaves her rest :
So Phœbus opens to the morn
　　The glories of the east.

Yet this great odds I ever find
　　'Twixt Chloe and the sun :
The last to all is warm and kind,
　　But she, cross girl, to none.

ANONYMOUS

(From Dodsley's Collection, 1748-58)

The Plaything Changed

Kitty's charming voice and face,
　　Syren-like, first caught my fancy ;
Wit and humour next take place,
　　And now I doat on sprightly Nancy.

Kitty tunes her pipe in vain,
　　With airs most languishing and dying ;
Calls me false ungrateful swain,
　　And tries in vain to shoot me flying.

276

Nancy with resistless art,
  Always humorous, gay and witty,
Has talk'd herself into my heart,
  And quite excluded tuneful Kitty.

Ah, Kitty ! Love, a wanton boy,
  Now pleas'd with a song, and now with prattle,
Still longing for the newest toy,
  Has chang'd his whistle for a rattle.

On Wit

True wit is like the brilliant stone
  Dug from the Indian mine ;
Which boasts two various powers in one,
  To cut as well as shine.

Genius, like that, if polish'd right,
  With the same gifts abounds ;
Appears at once both keen and bright,
  And sparkles while it wounds.

ANONYMOUS
(*From Nichols's Collection*, 1780)

Epitaph on Albinia
From Marullus

Here fair Albinia lies, yet not alone ;
That was forbid by Cytherea's son :
His quiver, arrows, and his bow lie here,
And Beauty's self lay lifeless on her bier.
Strew roses then, and violets round her shower,
She, that's now dust, was yesterday a flower.

ANONYMOUS

(*From Ritson's Collection,* 1783)

What is Love ? *

Love's no irregular desire,
    No sudden start of raging pain,
Which in a moment grows a fire,
    And in a moment cools again.

Not found in the sad sonneteer,
    That sings of darts, despair, and chains,
And by whose dismal verse 'tis clear
    He wants not heart alone, but brains.

Nor does it centre in the beau,
    Who sighs by rule, by order dies ;
Whose all consists in outward show,
    And want of wit by dress supplies.

No, Love is something so divine,
    Description would but make it less :
'Tis what I feel, but can't define,
    'Tis what I know, but can't express.

ANONYMOUS

(*From Dalrymple's Collection,* 1796)

Song

Ah ! dear Belinda, hither fly,
    And such a light discover,
As may the absent sun supply,
    And cheer your drooping lover.

Arise ! my day ! with speed arise,
    And all my sorrows banish ;
Before the sun of thy bright eyes
    All gloomy terrors vanish.

* This poem is a variant text of one in Ralph's *Miscellany* of 1729.

ANONYMOUS

The petty powers of Hell destroy ;
  To save's the pride of Heaven ;
To you the first, if you prove coy,
  If kind, the last, is given.

The choice, then, sure's not hard to make,
  Betwixt the good and evil !
Which title had you rather take ?
  My Goddess ? or my Devil ?

The Fan

For various purpose serves the fan ;
  As thus—a decent blind,
Between the sticks to peep at man,
  Nor yet betray your mind.

Each action has a meaning plain,
  Resentment's in the snap ;
A flirt expresses strong disdain,
  Consent, a gentle tap.

All passions will the fan disclose,
  All modes of female art ;
And sweetly to advantage shows
  The hand—if not the heart.

'Tis Folly's sceptre, first design'd
  By Love's capricious Boy,
Who knows how lightly all mankind
  Are govern'd by a toy.

WILLIAM SHENSTONE (1714-1763)

The Landscape

How pleas'd within my native bowers
    Erewhile I pass'd the day !
Was ever scene so deck'd with flowers ?
    Were ever flowers so gay ?

How sweetly smil'd the hill, the vale,
    And all the landscape round !
The river gliding down the dale !
    The hill with beeches crown'd !

But now, when urg'd by tender woes
    I speed to meet my dear,
That hill and stream my zeal oppose,
    And check my fond career.

No more, since Daphne was my theme,
    Their wonted charms I see :
That verdant hill, and silver stream,
    Divide my love and me.

Song

Perhaps it is not love, said I,
That melts my soul when Flavia's nigh ;
Where wit and sense like hers agree,
One may be pleas'd, and yet be free.

The beauties of her polish'd mind,
It needs no lover's eye to find ;
The hermit freezing in his cell,
Might wish the gentle Flavia well.

It is not love—averse to bear
The servile chain that lovers wear,
Let, let me all my fears remove,
My doubts dispel—it is not love !

Oh ! when did wit so brightly shine
In any form less fair than thine ?
It is—it is love's subtle fire,
And under friendship lurks desire.

Written in a Collection of Bacchanalian Songs

Adieu, ye jovial youths, who join
To plunge old Care in floods of wine ;
And, as your dazzled eye-balls roll,
Discern him struggling in the bowl.

Not yet is hope so wholly flown,
Nor yet is thought so tedious grown,
But limpid stream and shady tree
Retain, as yet, some sweets for me.

And see, through yonder silent grove,
See yonder does my Daphne rove ;
With pride her footsteps I pursue,
And bid your frantic joys adieu.

The sole confusion I admire,
Is that my Daphne's eyes inspire :
I scorn the madness you approve,
And value reason next to love.

The Extent of Cookery

Aliusque et idem

When Tom to Cambridge first was sent,
    A plain brown bob he wore ;
Read much, and look'd as though he meant
    To be a fop no more.

See him to Lincoln's-Inn repair,
    His resolution flag ;
He cherishes a length of hair,
    And tucks it in a bag.

Nor Coke nor Salkeld he regards,
　　But gets into the house,
And soon a judge's rank rewards
　　His pliant votes and bows.

Adieu ye bobs ! ye bags give place !
　　Full-bottoms come instead !
Good Lord ! to see the various ways
　　Of dressing a calve's-head !

Written at an Inn at Henley

To thee, fair freedom ! I retire
　　From flattery, cards, and dice, and din ;
Nor art thou found in mansions higher
　　Than the low cot, or humble inn.

'Tis here with boundless power I reign ;
　　And every health which I begin,
Converts dull port to bright champagne ;
　　Such freedom crowns it, at an inn.

I fly from pomp, I fly from plate,
　　I fly from falsehood's specious grin !
Freedom I love, and form I hate,
　　And choose my lodgings at an inn.

Here, waiter ! take my sordid ore,
　　Which lackeys else might hope to win ;
It buys, what courts have not in store ;
　　It buys me freedom, at an inn.

Whoe'er has travell'd life's dull round,
　　Where'er his stages may have been,
May sigh to think he still has found
　　The warmest welcome at an inn.

WILLIAM SHENSTONE

Jemmy Dawson

A Ballad ; written about the Time of his Execution, in the Year 1745

Come listen to my mournful tale,
    Ye tender hearts and lovers dear ;
Nor will you scorn to heave a sigh,
    Nor need you blush to shed a tear.

And thou, dear Kitty, peerless maid,
    Do thou a pensive ear incline ;
For thou canst weep at every woe,
    And pity every plaint—but mine.

Young Dawson was a gallant boy,
    A brighter never trod the plain ;
And well he lov'd one charming maid,
    And dearly was he lov'd again.

One tender maid, she lov'd him dear,
    Of gentle blood the damsel came ;
And faultless was her beauteous form,
    And spotless was her virgin fame.

But curse on party's hateful strife,
    That led the favour'd youth astray ;
The day the rebel clans appear'd,
    O had he never seen that day !

Their colours and their sash he wore,
    And in that fatal dress was found ;
And now he must that death endure,
    Which gives the brave the keenest wound.

How pale was then his true-love's cheek,
    When Jemmy's sentence reach'd her ear,
For never yet did Alpine snows
    So pale, or yet so chill appear.

With faltering voice, she weeping said,
  " Oh Dawson, monarch of my heart ;
Think not thy death shall end our loves,
  For thou and I will never part.

" Yet might sweet mercy find a place,
  And bring relief to Jemmy's woes ;
O George, without a prayer for thee,
  My orisons should never close.

" The gracious prince that gave him life,
  Would crown a never-dying flame ;
And every tender babe I bore
  Should learn to lisp the giver's name.

" But though he should be dragg'd in scorn
  To yonder ignominious tree ;
He shall not want one constant friend
  To share the cruel fates' decree."

O then her mourning coach was call'd,
  The sledge mov'd slowly on before ;
Though borne in a triumphal car,
  She had not lov'd her fav'rite more.

She follow'd him, prepar'd to view
  The terrible behests of law ;
And the last scene of Jemmy's woes,
  With calm and steadfast eye she saw.

Distorted was that blooming face,
  Which she had fondly lov'd so long ;
And stifled was that tuneful breath,
  Which in her praise had sweetly sung :

And sever'd was that beauteous neck,
  Round which her arms had fondly clos'd ;
And mangled was that beauteous breast,
  On which her lovesick head repos'd :

WILLIAM SHENSTONE

And ravish'd was that constant heart,
  She did to every heart prefer ;
For though it could its king forget,
  'Twas true and loyal still to her.

Amid those unrelenting flames,
  She bore this constant heart to see ;
But when 'twas moulder'd into dust,
  " Yet, yet," she cried, " I follow thee.

" My death, my death alone can shew
  The pure, the lasting love I bore ;
Accept, O heaven ! of woes like ours,
  And let us, let us weep no more."

The dismal scene was o'er and past,
  The lover's mournful hearse retir'd ;
The maid drew back her languid head,
  And sighing forth his name, expir'd.

Though justice ever must prevail,
  The tear my Kitty sheds is due ;
For seldom shall she hear a tale
  So sad, so tender, yet so true.

ANTHONY WHISTLER* (1714-1754)

Song

Let wisdom boast her mighty power,
  With passion still at strife,
Yet love is sure the sovereign flower,
  The sweet perfume of life.

The happy breeze that swells the sail,
  When quite becalm'd we lie ;
The drop that will the heart regale,
  And sparkle in the eye ;

* A friend of Shenstone's.

The sun that wakes us to delight,
    And drives the shades away ;
The dream that cheers our dreary night,
    And makes a brighter day.

But if, alas ! it wrongly seize,
    The case is twice as bad ;
This flower, sun, drop, or dream, or breeze,
    Will drive a blockhead mad.

The Rev. RICHARD GRAVES* (1715-1804)

On Tully's Head, in Pall Mall

To Mr. Robert Dodsley, 1756

Where Tully's bust and honour'd name
    Point out the well-wrought page,
There Dodsley consecrates to fame
    The Classics of his age.

In vain the poets from their mine
    Extract the shining mass,
Till Dodsley's mint has stamp'd the coin
    And bid the sterling pass.

Yet he, I ween, in Cæsar's days
    A nobler fate had found :
Dodsley himself with verdant bays
    Had been by Cæsar crown'd.

His bust near Tully's had been plac'd,
    Himself a Classic bard ;
His works Apollo's temple grac'd,
    And met their just reward.

* Another friend of Shenstone's ; author of *The Spiritual Quixote*.

But still, my friend, be virtue, sense,
   And competence thy share !
And think each boon, that Courts dispense,
   Beneath a Poet's care.

Persist to grace this humbler post ;
   Be Tully's head the sign ;
Till future booksellers shall boast
   To vend their tomes at thine.

On the Death of a Fine Girl, at Nine Years Old

Joy of her friends ; her parents' only pride ;
When scarce she'd tasted life—Clarissa died.
She was—— but words are wanting to say what :
Say all that's good and pretty—she was that.

On an Urn to Mr. Shenstone
at Worville, Salop

Stranger ! if woods and lawns like these,
If rural scenes thy fancy please ;
Ah ! stop awhile, and pensive view
Poor Shenstone's Urn : who oft, like you,
These woods and lawns well-pleas'd has rov'd,
And oft these rural scenes approv'd.
Like him, be thou fair Virtue's friend,
And health and peace thy steps attend !

On the Death of an Epicure

At length, my friends, the feast of life is o'er :
I've eat sufficient—and I'll drink no more :
My night is come ; I've spent a jovial day ;
'Tis time to part : but oh ! what is to pay ?

RICHARD GRAVES

The Doctor's Arms

A Doctor, who, for want of skill,
Did seldom cure—but sometimes kill ;
Contriv'd at length, by many a puff,
And many a bottle fill'd with stuff,
To raise his fortune, and his pride,
And in a coach, forsooth ! must ride.
His family coat long since worn out,
What arms to take, was all the doubt.

A friend, consulted on the case,
Thus answer'd with a sly grimace :
" Take some device in your own way,
Neither too solemn nor too gay ;
Three Ducks, suppose, white, grey, or black ;
And let your motto be ' *Quack ! Quack !* ' "

JOHN HAWKESWORTH, LL.D.* (1715 ?-1773)

A Moral Thought

Through groves sequester'd, dark and still,
    Low vales, and mossy cells among,
In silent paths the careless rill,
    Which languid murmurs, steals along :

Awhile it plays with circling sweep,
    And ling'ring leaves its native plain,
Then pours impetuous down the steep,
    And mingles with the boundless main.

O let my years thus devious glide,
    Through silent scenes obscurely calm,
Nor wealth nor strife pollute the tide,
    Nor honour's sanguinary palm.

---

* Hawkesworth was possibly the author of some of the poems
(e.g., *A Winter's Walk*) which are usually included in Dr. Johnson's works.

When labour tires, and pleasure palls,
  Still let the stream untroubled be,
As down the steep of age it falls,
  And mingles with eternity.

The Rev. RICHARD JAGO* (1715-1781)

Absence

With leaden foot Time creeps along
  While Delia is away ;
With her, nor plaintive was the song,
  Nor tedious was the day.

Ah ! envious power ! reverse my doom,
  Now double thy career,
Strain every nerve, stretch every plume,
  And rest them when she's here.

To a Lady

When Nature joins a beauteous face
With shape, and air, and life, and grace,
To every imperfection blind,
I spy no blemish in the mind.

When wit flows pure from Stella's tongue,
Or animates the sprightly song,
Our hearts confess the power divine,
Nor lightly prize its mortal shrine.

Good-nature will a conquest gain,
Though wit, and beauty sigh in vain.

When generous thoughts the breast inspire,
I wish its rank and fortunes higher.

* Yet another of the Shenstone circle.

When Sidney's charms again unite
To win the soul, and bless the sight,
Fair, and learn'd, and good, and great !
An earthly goddess is compleat.

But when I see a sordid mind
With affluence and ill-nature join'd,
And pride without a grain of sense,
And without beauty insolence,
The creature with contempt I view,
And sure 'tis like Miss—— you know who.

The Blackbirds

An Elegy

The sun had chas'd the mountain snow,
  His beams had pierc'd the stubborn soil,
The melting streams began to flow,
  And ploughmen urg'd their annual toil.

'Twas then, amidst the vocal throng,
  Whom Nature wak'd to mirth and love,
A blackbird rais'd his am'rous song,
  And thus it echo'd through the grove.

" O fairest of the feather'd train !
  For whom I sing, for whom I burn,
Attend with pity to my strain,
  And grant my love a kind return.

" For see, the wintry storms are flown,
  And Zephyrs gently fan the air ;
Let us the genial influence own,
  Let us the vernal pastime share.

" The raven plumes his jetty wing,
  To please his croaking paramour,
The larks responsive carols sing,
  And tell their passion as they soar :

" But does the raven's sable wing
    Excel the glossy jet of mine ?
Or can the lark more sweetly sing,
    Than we, who strength with softness join ?

" O let me then thy steps attend !
    I'll point new treasures to thy sight :
Whether the grove thy wish befriend,
    Or hedge-rows green, or meadows bright.

" I'll guide thee to the clearest rill,
    Whose streams among the pebbles stray ;
There will we sip, and sip our fill,
    Or on the flowery margin play.

" I'll lead thee to the thickest brake,
    Impervious to the school-boy's eye ;
For thee the plaister'd nest I'll make,
    And to thy downy bosom fly.

" When, prompted by a mother's care,
    Thy warmth shall form th' imprison'd young,
The pleasing task I'll gladly share,
    Or cheer thy labours with a song.

" To bring thee food I'll range the fields,
    And cull the best of every kind,
Whatever Nature's bounty yields,
    And love's assiduous care can find.

" And when my lovely mate would stray,
    To taste the summer sweets at large,
I'll wait at home the live-long day,
    And fondly tend our little charge.

" Then prove with me the sweets of love,
    With me divide the cares of life,
No bush shall boast in all the grove
    A mate so fond, so blest a wife.''

RICHARD JAGO

He ceas'd his song—the plumy dame
  Heard with delight the love-sick strain,
Nor long conceal'd a mutual flame,
  Nor long repress'd his am'rous pain.

He led her to the nuptial bower,
  And perch'd with triumph by her side ;
What gilded roof could boast that hour
  A fonder mate, or happier bride ?

Next morn he wak'd her with a song,
  " Behold," he said, " the new-born day,
The lark his mattin-peal has rung,
  Arise, my love, and come away."

Together through the fields they stray'd,
  And to the murmuring riv'let's side,
Renew'd their vows, and hopp'd and play'd
  With artless joy, and decent pride.

When O ! with grief my Muse relates
  What dire misfortune clos'd the tale,
Sent by an order from the Fates,
  A gunner met them in the vale.

Alarm'd, the lover cried, " My dear,
  Haste, haste away, from danger fly ;
Here, gunner, point thy thunder here,
  O spare my love, and let me die ! "

At him the gunner took his aim,
  Too sure the volley'd thunder flew !
O had he chose some other game,
  Or shot—as he was wont to do !

Divided pair ! forgive the wrong,
  While I with tears your fate rehearse,
I'll join the widow's plaintive song,
  And save the lover in my verse.

WILLIAM WHITEHEAD, Poet Laureate (1715-1785)

The *Je ne sai quoi*

A Song

Yes, I'm in love, I feel it now,
  And Cœlia has undone me !
And yet I'll swear I can't tell how
  The pleasing plague stole on me.

'Tis not her face which love creates,
  For there no Graces revel ;
'Tis not her shape, for there the Fates
  Have rather been uncivil.

'Tis not her air, for sure in that
  There's nothing more than common ;
And all her sense is only chat,
  Like any other woman.

Her voice, her touch might give th' alarm—
  'Twas both perhaps, or neither ;
In short, 'twas that provoking charm
  Of Cœlia altogether.

Song for Ranelagh

Ye belles, and ye flirts, and ye pert little things,
  Who trip in this frolicsome round,
Pray tell me from whence this impertinence springs,
  The sexes at once to confound :
What means the cock'd hat, and the masculine air,
  With each motion design'd to perplex ?
Bright eyes were intended to languish, not stare,
  And softness the test of your sex.

The girl who on beauty depends for support,
  May call every art to her aid,
The bosom display'd, and the petticoat short,
  Are samples she gives of her trade.

But you, on whom Fortune indulgently smiles,
    And whom Pride has preserv'd from the snare,
Should slily attack us with coyness and wiles,
    Not with open and insolent air.

The Venus whose statue delights all mankind,
    Shrinks modestly back from the view,
And kindly should seem by the artist design'd
    To serve as a model for you.
Then learn, with her beauty, to copy her air,
    Nor venture too much to reveal ;
Our fancies will paint what you cover with care,
    And double each charm you conceal.

The blushes of morn, and the mildness of May,
    Are charms which no art can procure ;
O ! be but yourselves, and our homage we pay,
    And your empire is solid and sure.
But if Amazon-like you attack your gallants,
    And put us in fear of our lives,
You may do very well for sisters and aunts,
    But, believe me, you'll never be wives.

MARY JONES* (*fl. circa* 1750)

Stella's Epitaph

Which the author hopes will live as long as she does

Here rests poor Stella's restless part :
A riddle ! but I lov'd her heart.
Through life she rush'd a headlong wave,
And never slept, but in her grave.
Some wit, I think, and worth she had :
No saint indeed, nor yet quite mad ;
But laugh'd, built castles, rhym'd and sung,
" Was everything, but nothing long."
Some honest truths she would let fall ;
But much too wise to tell you all.

* This lady lived at Oxford. She knew Dr. Johnson.

From thought to thought incessant hurl'd,
Her scheme was but—to rule the world.
At morn she won it with her eyes,
At night, when beauty sick'ning sighs,
Like the mad Macedonian cried,
" What, no more worlds, ye Gods ! "—and died.

THOMAS GRAY (1716-1771)

Ode on the Spring

Lo ! where the rosy-bosom'd Hours,
Fair Venus' train appear,
Disclose the long-expecting flowers,
And wake the purple year !
The Attic warbler pours her throat,
Responsive to the cuckoo's note,
The untaught harmony of spring :
While whispering pleasure as they fly,
Cool Zephyrs through the clear blue sky
Their gather'd fragrance fling.

Where'er the oak's thick branches stretch
A broader browner shade ;
Where'er the rude and moss-grown beech
O'er-canopies the glade,
Beside some water's rushy brink
With me the Muse shall sit, and think
(At ease reclin'd in rustic state)
How vain the ardour of the Crowd,
How low, how little are the Proud,
How indigent the Great !

Still is the toiling hand of Care :
The panting herds repose :
Yet hark, how through the peopled air
The busy murmur glows !

The insect youth are on the wing,
Eager to taste the honey'd spring,
And float amid the liquid noon :
Some lightly o'er the current skim,
Some shew their gaily-gilded trim
Quick-glancing to the sun.

To Contemplation's sober eye
Such is the race of Man :
And they that creep, and they that fly,
Shall end where they began.
Alike the Busy and the Gay
But flutter through life's little day,
In fortune's varying colours drest :
Brush'd by the hand of rough Mischance,
Or chill'd by age, their airy dance
They leave, in dust to rest.

Methinks I hear in accents low
The sportive kind reply :
Poor moralist ! and what art thou ?
A solitary fly !
Thy joys no glittering female meets,
No hive hast thou of hoarded sweets,
No painted plumage to display :
On hasty wings thy youth is flown ;
Thy sun is set, thy spring is gone—
We frolic, while 'tis May.

Ode

on the Death of a Favourite Cat, Drowned in a Tub of Gold Fishes

'Twas on a lofty vase's side,
Where China's gayest art had dy'd
  The azure flowers, that blow ;
Demurest of the tabby kind,
The pensive Selima reclin'd,
  Gaz'd on the lake below.

Her conscious tail her joy declar'd ;
The fair round face, the snowy beard,
 The velvet of her paws,
Her coat, that with the tortoise vies,
Her ears of jet, and emerald eyes,
 She saw ; and purr'd applause.

Still had she gaz'd ; but midst the tide
Two angel forms were seen to glide,
 The Genii of the stream :
Their scaly armour's Tyrian hue
Through richest purple to the view
 Betray'd a golden gleam.

The hapless Nymph with wonder saw :
A whisker first and then a claw,
 With many an ardent wish,
She stretch'd in vain to reach the prize.
What female heart can gold despise ?
 What cat's averse to fish ?

Presumptuous Maid ! with looks intent
Again she stretch'd, again she bent,
 Nor knew the gulf between.
(Malignant Fate sat by, and smil'd)
The slipp'ry verge her feet beguil'd,
 She tumbled headlong in.

Eight times emerging from the flood
She mew'd to every wat'ry God,
 Some speedy aid to send.
No Dolphin came, no Nereid stirr'd :
Nor cruel Tom, nor Susan heard.
 A Fav'rite has no friend !

From hence, ye Beauties, undeceiv'd,
Know, one false step is ne'er retriev'd,
 And be with caution bold.
Not all that tempts your wandering eyes
And heedless hearts, is lawful prize ;
 Nor all, that glisters, gold.

THOMAS GRAY

Ode

on a distant prospect of Eton College.

Ye distant spires, ye antique towers,
That crown the wat'ry glade,
Where grateful Science still adores
Her Henry's holy Shade ;
And ye, that from the stately brow
Of Windsor's heights th' expanse below
Of grove, of lawn, of mead survey,
Whose turf, whose shade, whose flowers among
Wanders the hoary Thames along
His silver-winding way.

Ah happy hills, ah pleasing shade,
Ah fields belov'd in vain,
Where once my careless childhood stray'd,
A stranger yet to pain !
I feel the gales, that from ye blow,
A momentary bliss bestow,
As waving fresh their gladsome wing,
My weary soul they seem to soothe,
And, redolent of joy and youth,
To breathe a second spring.

Say, Father Thames, for thou hast seen
Full many a sprightly race
Disporting on thy margent green
The paths of pleasure trace,
Who foremost now delight to cleave
With pliant arm thy glassy wave ?
The captive linnet which enthrall ?
What idle progeny succeed
To chase the rolling circle's speed,
Or urge the flying ball ?

While some on earnest business bent
Their murm'ring labours ply
'Gainst graver hours, that bring constraint
To sweeten liberty :

Some bold adventurers disdain
The limits of their little reign,
And unknown regions dare descry :
Still as they run they look behind,
They hear a voice in every wind,
And snatch a fearful joy.

Gay hope is theirs by fancy fed,
Less pleasing when possest ;
The tear forgot as soon as shed,
The sunshine of the breast :
Theirs buxom health of rosy hue,
Wild wit, invention ever-new,
And lively cheer of vigour born ;
The thoughtless day, the easy night,
The spirits pure, the slumbers light,
That fly th' approach of morn.

Alas, regardless of their doom,
The little victims play !
No sense have they of ills to come,
Nor care beyond to-day :
Yet see how all around 'em wait
The Ministers of human fate,
And black Misfortune's baleful train !
Ah, shew them where in ambush stand
To seize their prey the murth'rous band !
Ah, tell them, they are men !

These shall the fury Passions tear,
The vultures of the mind,
Disdainful Anger, pallid Fear,
And Shame that skulks behind ;
Or pining Love shall waste their youth,
Or Jealousy with rankling tooth,
That inly gnaws the secret heart,
And Envy wan, and faded Care,
Grim-visag'd comfortless Despair,
And Sorrow's piercing dart.

Ambition this shall tempt to rise,
Then whirl the wretch from high,
To bitter Scorn a sacrifice,
And grinning Infamy.
The stings of Falsehood those shall try,
And hard Unkindness' alter'd eye,
That mocks the tear it forc'd to flow ;
And keen Remorse with blood defil'd,
And moody Madness laughing wild
Amid severest woe.

Lo, in the vale of years beneath
A grisly troop are seen,
The painful family of Death,
More hideous than their Queen :
This racks the joints, this fires the veins,
That every labouring sinew strains,
Those in the deeper vitals rage :
Lo, Poverty, to fill the band,
That numbs the soul with icy hand,
And slow-consuming Age.

To each his suff'rings : all are men,
Condemn'd alike to groan ;
The tender for another's pain,
Th' unfeeling for his own.
Yet ah ! why should they know their fate ?
Since sorrow never comes too late,
And happiness too swiftly flies.
Thought would destroy their paradise.
No more ; where ignorance is bliss,
'Tis folly to be wise.

THOMAS GRAY

Sonnet on the Death of Richard West

In vain to me the smiling mornings shine,
   And redd'ning Phœbus lifts his golden fire :
The birds in vain their amorous descant join ;
   Or cheerful fields resume their green attire :
These ears, alas ! for other notes repine,
   A different object do these eyes require.
My lonely anguish melts no heart, but mine ;
   And in my breast the imperfect joys expire.
Yet morning smiles the busy race to cheer,
   And new-born pleasure brings to happy men :
The fields to all their wonted tribute bear :
   To warm their little loves the birds complain :
I fruitless mourn to him, who cannot hear,
   And weep the more because I weep in vain.

Elegy

written in a Country Churchyard

The Curfew tolls the knell of parting day,
The lowing herd wind slowly o'er the lea,
The plowman homeward plods his weary way,
And leaves the world to darkness and to me.

Now fades the glimmering landscape on the sight,
And all the air a solemn stillness holds,
Save where the beetle wheels his droning flight,
And drowsy tinklings lull the distant folds ;

Save that from yonder ivy-mantled tower
The moping owl does to the moon complain
Of such, as wand'ring near her secret bower,
Molest her ancient solitary reign.

Beneath those rugged elms, that yew-tree's shade,
Where heaves the turf in many a mould'ring heap
Each in his narrow cell for ever laid,
The rude Forefathers of the hamlet sleep.

The breezy call of incense-breathing Morn,
The swallow twitt'ring from the straw-built shed,
The cock's shrill clarion, or the echoing horn,
No more shall rouse them from their lowly bed.

For them no more the blazing hearth shall burn,
Or busy housewife ply her evening care :
No children run to lisp their sire's return,
Or climb his knees the envied kiss to share.

Oft did the harvest to their sickle yield,
Their furrow oft the stubborn glebe has broke ;
How jocund did they drive their team afield !
How bow'd the woods beneath their sturdy stroke !

Let not Ambition mock their useful toil,
Their homely joys, and destiny obscure ;
Nor Grandeur hear with a disdainful smile,
The short and simple annals of the poor.

The boast of heraldry, the pomp of power,
And all that beauty, all that wealth e'er gave,
Awaits alike th' inevitable hour.
The paths of glory lead but to the grave.

Nor you, ye proud, impute to these the fault,
If Mem'ry o'er their Tomb no Trophies raise,
Where through the long-drawn aisle and fretted vault
The pealing anthem swells the note of praise.

Can storied urn or animated bust
Back to its mansion call the fleeting breath ?
Can Honour's voice provoke the silent dust,
Or Flatt'ry soothe the dull cold ear of Death ?

Perhaps in this neglected spot is laid
Some heart once pregnant with celestial fire ;
Hands, that the rod of empire might have sway'd,
Or wak'd to ecstasy the living lyre.

But Knowledge to their eyes her ample page
Rich with the spoils of time did ne'er unroll ;
Chill Penury repress'd their noble rage,
And froze the genial current of the soul.

Full many a gem of purest ray serene,
The dark unfathom'd caves of ocean bear :
Full many a flower is born to blush unseen,
And waste its sweetness on the desert air.

Some village-Hampden, that with dauntless breast
The little Tyrant of his fields withstood ;
Some mute inglorious Milton here may rest,
Some Cromwell guiltless of his country's blood.

Th' applause of listening senates to command,
The threats of pain and ruin to despise,
To scatter plenty o'er a smiling land,
And read their hist'ry in a nation's eyes,

Their lot forbad : nor circumscrib'd alone
Their growing virtues, but their crimes confin'd ;
Forbad to wade through slaughter to a throne,
And shut the gates of mercy on mankind,

The struggling pangs of conscious truth to hide,
To quench the blushes of ingenuous shame,
Or heap the shrine of Luxury and Pride
With incense kindled at the Muse's flame.

Far from the madding crowd's ignoble strife,
Their sober wishes never learnt to stray ;
Along the cool sequester'd vale of life
They kept the noiseless tenor of their way.

Yet ev'n these bones from insult to protect
Some frail memorial still erected nigh,
With uncouth rhymes and shapeless sculpture deck'd,
Implores the passing tribute of a sigh.

Their names, their years, spelt by th' unletter'd Muse,
The place of fame and elegy supply :
And many a holy text around she strews,
That teach the rustic moralist to die.

For who to dumb Forgetfulness a prey,
This pleasing anxious being e'er resign'd,
Left the warm precincts of the cheerful day,
Nor cast one longing ling'ring look behind ?

On some fond breast the parting soul relies,
Some pious drops the closing eye requires ;
Ev'n from the tomb the voice of Nature cries,
Ev'n in our ashes live their wonted fires.

For thee, who mindful of th' unhonour'd Dead
Dost in these lines their artless tale relate ;
If chance, by lonely contemplation led,
Some kindred Spirit shall enquire thy fate,

Haply some hoary-headed Swain may say,
" Oft have we seen him at the peep of dawn
Brushing with hasty steps the dews away
To meet the sun upon the upland lawn.

"There at the foot of yonder nodding beech
That wreathes its old fantastic roots so high,
His listless length at noontide would he stretch,
And pore upon the brook that babbles by.

"Hard by yon wood, now smiling as in scorn,
Mutt'ring his wayward fancies he would rove,
Now drooping, woeful wan, like one forlorn,
Or craz'd with care, or cross'd in hopeless love.

"One morn I miss'd him on the custom'd hill,
Along the heath and near his fav'rite tree ;
Another came ; nor yet beside the rill,
Nor up the lawn, nor at the wood was he ;

" The next with dirges due in sad array
Slow through the church-way path we saw him borne.
Approach and read (for thou canst read) the lay,
Grav'd on the stone beneath yon aged thorn.''

The Epitaph

Here rests his head upon the lap of Earth
A Youth to Fortune and to Fame unknown.
Fair Science frown'd not on his humble birth,
And Melancholy mark'd him for her own.

Large was his bounty, and his soul sincere,
Heav'n did a recompense as largely send :
He gave to Mis'ry all he had, a tear,
He gain'd from Heav'n ('twas all he wish'd) a friend.

No farther seek his merits to disclose,
Or draw his frailties from their dread abode,
(There they alike in trembling hope repose,)
The bosom of his Father and his God.

RICHARD WEST* (1716-1742)

Ode to May

Dear Gray ! that always in my heart
Possessest far the better part,
What mean these sudden blasts that rise,
And drive the zephyrs from the skies ?
O join with mine thy tuneful lay,
And invocate the tardy May.

Come, fairest nymph ! resume thy reign,
Bring all the Graces in thy train :
With balmy breath and flowery tread
Rise from thy soft ambrosial bed,
Where in elysian slumber bound
Embowering myrtles veil thee round.

* At Eton with Gray and Horace Walpole.

Awake, in all thy glories drest,
Recall the zephyrs from the west ;
Restore the sun, revive the skies,
At mine and Nature's call arise !
Great Nature's self upbraids thy stay,
And misses her accustom'd May.

See ! all her works demand thy aid,
The labours of Pomona fade ;
A plaint is heard from every tree,
Each budding floweret calls for thee ;
The birds forget to love and sing,
With storms alone the forests ring.

Come then, with pleasure at thy side,
Diffuse thy vernal spirit wide ;
Create where'er thou turn'st thy eye
Peace, plenty, love and harmony,
Till every being share its part,
And heaven and earth be glad at heart.

ELIZABETH CARTER* (1717-1806)

A Dialogue

Says *Body* to *Mind*, 'Tis amazing to see,
We're so nearly related yet never agree,
But lead a most wrangling strange sort of a life,
As great plagues to each other as husband and wife.
The fault's all your own, who with flagrant oppression,
Encroach every day on my lawful possession.
The best room in my house you have seiz'd for your own,
And turn'd the whole tenement quite upside down,
While you hourly call in a disorderly crew
Of vagabond rogues, who have nothing to do

* " My old friend, Mrs. Carter, could make a pudding as well as
translate Epictetus from the Greek, and work a handkerchief as
well as compose a poem."—Dr. Johnson.

But to run in and out, hurry scurry, and keep
Such a horrible uproar, I can't get to sleep.
There's my kitchen sometimes is as empty as sound,
I call for my servants, not one's to be found :
They all are sent out on your ladyship's errand,
To fetch some more riotous guests in, I warrant !
And since things are growing, I see, worse and worse,
I'm determin'd to force you to alter your course.
   Poor *Mind*, who heard all with extreme moderation,
Thought it now time to speak, and make her allegation.
   'Tis I, that, methinks, have most cause to complain,
Who am crampt and confin'd like a slave in a chain.
I did but step out, on some weighty affairs,
To visit, last night, my good friends in the stars,
When, before I was got half as high as the moon,
You dispatch'd *Pain* and *Languor* to hurry me down ;
Vi & Armis they seiz'd me, in midst of my flight,
And shut me in caverns as dark as the night.
   'Twas no more, replied *Body*, than what you deserv'd,
While you rambled abroad, I at home was half starv'd :
And, unless I had closely confin'd you in hold,
You had left me to perish with hunger and cold.
   I've a friend, answers *Mind*, who, though slow, is yet
      sure,
And will rid me at last of your insolent power :
Will knock down your walls, the whole fabric demolish,
And at once your strong holds and my slavery abolish :
And while in the dust your dull ruins decay,
I'll snap off my chains and fly freely away.

DAVID GARRICK (1717-1779)

Advice to the Marquis of Rockingham,
upon a late occasion. Written in 1765.

Well may they, Wentworth, call thee young :
What, hear and feel ! sift right from wrong,
   And to a wretch be kind !
Old statesmen would reverse your plan,
Sink, in the minister, the man,
   And be both deaf and blind.

If thus, my lord, your heart o'erflows,
Know you how many mighty foes
   Such weakness will create you ?
Regard not what Fitzherbert says,
For though you gain each good man's praise,
   We older folks shall hate you.

You should have sent, the other day,
Garrick, the player, with frowns away ;
   Your smiles but made him bolder :
Why would you hear his strange appeal,
Which dar'd to make a statesman feel ?
   I would that you were older.

You should be proud, and seem displeas'd,
Or you for ever will be teas'd,
   Your house with beggars haunted :
What, every suitor kindly us'd ?
If wrong, their folly is excus'd,
   If right, their suit is granted.

From pressing crowds of great and small
To free yourself, give hopes to all,
   And fail nineteen in twenty :
" What, wound my honour, break my word ? "
You're young again.—You may, my lord,
   Have precedents in plenty !

Indeed, young statesman, 'twill not do—
Some other ways and means pursue,
   More fitted to your station :
What from your boyish freaks can spring ?
Mere toys ! The favour of your King,
   And love of all the Nation.

Sylvia

If truth can fix thy wav'ring heart,
   Let Damon urge his claim ;
He feels the passion void of art,
   The pure, the constant flame.

Though sighing swains their torments tell,
   Their sensual love contemn :
They only prize the beauteous shell,
   But slight the inward gem.

Possession cures the wounded heart,
   Destroys the transient fire ;
But when the mind receives the dart,
   Enjoyment whets desire.

By age your beauty will decay,
   Your mind improves with years ;
As when the blossoms fade away,
   The rip'ning fruit appears.

May Heav'n and Sylvia grant my suit,
   And bless the future hour,
That Damon, who can taste the fruit,
   May gather every flower !

Written in a copy of " Fables for the Female Sex,"
by Edward Moore

While here the poet paints the charms
Which bless the perfect dame,
How unaffected beauty warms,
And wit preserves the flame :

How prudence, virtue, sense agree
To form the happy wife :
In Lucy, and her book, I see
The picture, and the life.

Death and the Doctor
Occasioned by a physician's lampooning a friend of the author

As Doctor —— musing sat,
Death saw, and came without delay :
Enters the room, begins the chat
With, " Doctor, why so thoughtful, pray ? "

The Doctor started from his place,
But soon they more familiar grew :
And then he told his piteous case,
How trade was low, and friends were few.

" Away with fear," the phantom said,
As soon as he had heard his tale :
" Take my advice, and mend your trade ;
We both are losers if you fail.

" Go write, your wit in satire show,
No matter, whether smart or true ;
Call —— names, the greatest foe
To dullness, folly, pride and you.

" Then copies spread, there lies the trick,
Among your friends be sure you send 'em ;
   For all who read will soon grow sick,
And when you're call'd upon, attend 'em.

" Thus trade increasing by degrees,
Doctor, we both shall have our ends :
   For you are sure to have your fees,
And I am sure to have your friends."

Epitaph on William Hogarth
in Chiswick Church-yard

Farewell, great painter of mankind,
   Who reach'd the noblest point of art ;
Whose pictur'd morals charm the mind,
   And through the eye correct the heart !

If Genius fire thee, reader stay ;
   If Nature touch thee, drop a tear :—
If neither move thee, turn away,
   For Hogarth's honour'd dust lies here.

Epitaph on James Quin,
in Bath Cathedral

That tongue, which set the table on a roar,
And charm'd the public ear, is heard no more !
Clos'd are those eyes, the harbingers of wit,
Which spoke, before the tongue, what Shakespeare writ.
Cold are those hands, which, living, were stretch'd forth,
At friendship's call to succour modest worth.
Here lies James Quin ! Deign, reader, to be taught
(Whate'er thy strength of body, force of thought,
In nature's happiest mould however cast)
To this complexion thou must come at last.

HORATIO (HORACE) WALPOLE, Earl of Orford

(1717-1797)

Anna Grenville, Countess Temple, appointed Poet Laureate to the King of the Fairies

Written, at the desire of Lady Suffolk, January 3, 1763

By these presents, be it known
To all who bend before our throne,
Fays and Fairies, Elves and Sprites,
Beauteous Dames and gallant Knights,
That We, OBERON the Grand,
Emperor of Fairy-Land,
King of Moonshine, Prince of Dreams,
Lord of Aganippe's streams,
Baron of the Dimpled Isles
That lie in pretty maiden's smiles,
Arch-Treasurer of all the Graces
Dispers'd through fifty lovely faces,
Sovereign of the Slipper's Order
With all the rites thereon that border,
Defender of the Sylphic Faith,
Declare—and thus your Monarch saith :

Whereas there is a noble Dame,
Whom mortals Countess Temple name,
To whom Ourself did erst impart
The choicest secrets of our art,
Taught her to tune th' harmonious line
To our own melody divine,
Taught her the graceful negligence
Which, scorning art and veiling sense,
Achieves that conquest o'er the heart
Sense seldom gains, and never art !

This lady, 'tis Our Royal Will
Our Laureate's vacant seat should fill ;
A chaplet of immortal bays
Shall crown her brows, and guard her lays ;

Of nectar-sack an acorn-cup
Be, at her board, each year fill'd up ;
And as each quarter feast comes round,
A silver penny shall be found
Within the compass of her shoe !
And so we bid you all adieu.

Given at our Palace of Cowslip Castle, the shortest night
of the year.   OBERON.

To Lady ——, when about Five Years Old,
with a Present of Shells, 1772

O Nymph, compar'd with whose young bloom
  Hebe's herself an ancient fright ;
May these gay shells find grace and room
  Both in your baby-house and sight !
Shells ! What are shells ? you ask, admiring
  With stare half pleasure, half surprise ;
And sly with nature's art, enquiring
  In dear mamma's all-speaking eyes.
Shells, fairest Anne, are playthings, made
  By a brave god call'd Father Ocean,
Whose frown from pole to pole's obey'd,
  Commands the waves, and stills their motion.
From that old sire a daughter came,
  As like mamma, as blue to blue,
And, like mamma, the sea-born dame
  An urchin bore, not unlike you.
For him fond grand-papa compels
  The floods to furnish such a state
Of corals and of cockleshells,
  Would turn a little lady's pate.
The chit has tons of baubles more ;
  His nurs'ry's stuff'd with doves and sparrows ;
And litter'd is its azure floor
  With painted quivers, bows and arrows.

313

Spread, spread your frock, you must be friends ;
   His toys shall fill your lap and breast :
To-day the boy this sample sends,
   —And some years hence he'll send the rest.

Epigrams

I

On the New Archbishop of Canterbury, March 1758

The Bench hath oft pos'd us, and set us a scoffing,
By signing Will. London, John Sarum, John Roffen. ;
But *this* head of the Church no expounder will want,
For His Grace signs his own proper name, Thomas *Cant.*

II

Left on the Duchess of Queensberry's Toilet, the Author finding her from home

To many a Kitty, Love his car
   Would for a day engage ;
But Prior's Kitty, ever fair,
   Retains it for an age.

The Rev. FRANCIS FAWKES (1720-1777)

The Brown Jug

A Song

Imitated from the Latin of Hieronymus Amaltheus

Dear Tom, this brown jug that now foams with mild ale,
(In which I will drink to sweet Nan of the Vale)
Was once Toby Fillpot, a thirsty old soul
As e'er drank a bottle, or fathom'd a bowl ;
In boosing about 'twas his praise to excel,
And among jolly topers he bore off the bell.

It chanc'd as in dog-days he sat at his ease
In his flow'r-woven arbour as gay as you please,
With a friend and a pipe puffing sorrows away,
And with honest old stingo was soaking his clay,
His breath-doors of life on a sudden were shut,
And he died full as big as a Dorchester butt.

His body, when long in the ground it had lain,
And time into clay had resolv'd it again,
A potter found out in its covert so snug,
And with part of fat Toby he form'd this brown jug,
Now sacred to friendship, and mirth, and mild ale,
So here's to my lovely sweet Nan of the Vale.

On a Lady's Singing, and Playing upon the Harpsichord

" Say, Zephyr, what music enchants the gay plains,
As soft and as sweet as the nightingale's strains?
My heart it goes pitapatee, with a bound,
And gently transported beats time to the sound.

" O say, is it Sappho that touches the strings?
Or some of the Syrens you bear on your wings? "
Said Zephyr, and whisper'd distinctly the lays,
" 'Tis Belinda that sings, and Belinda that plays."

Ah! swains, if you value your freedom, beware,
You hear her sweet voice, and I know that she's fair;
She's fair and inconstant; and thus with her art,
She will ravish your ears to inveigle your heart.

FRANCIS FAWKES

A Nosegay for Laura
July 1745

Come, ye fair, ambrosial flowers,
Leave your beds, and leave your bowers,
Blooming, beautiful, and rare,
Form a posy for my fair ;
Fair, and bright, and blooming be,
Meet for such a nymph as she.
Let the young vermilion rose
A becoming blush disclose ;
Such as Laura's cheeks display,
When she steals my heart away.
Add carnation's varied hue,
Moisten'd with the morning dew :
To the woodbine's fragrance join
Sprigs of snow-white jessamine.

Add no more ; already I
Shall, alas ! with envy die,
Thus to see my rival blest,
Sweetly dying on her breast.

The Stage-Coach
From the Latin of Vincent Bourne

To pay my duty to sweet Mrs. Page,
A place was taken in the Stamford stage.
Our coachman Dick, the shades of night to shun,
Had yok'd his horses long before the sun :
Disturb'd I start ; and drowsy all the while,
Rise to be jolted many a weary mile ;
On both sides squeez'd, how highly was I bless'd !
Between two plump old women to be press'd !
A corporal fierce, a nurse and child that cried,
And a fat landlord fill'd the other side.
Scarce dawns the morning, ere the cumbrous load
Rolls roughly rumbling o'er the rugged road.

One old wife coughs, and wheezes in my ears,
Loud scolds the other, and the corporal swears ;
Sour, unconcocted breath escapes my host,
The squalling child returns his milk and toast :
Ye Gods ! if such the pleasures of the stage,
I choose to walk and visit Mrs. Page.

Two Epigrams from Menander

I

Sorrow familiar to all men

Sure sorrows are to human-kind allied :
They reign where Fortune pours her golden tide ;
Besiege the son of glory's splendid door,
Grow gray and old together with the poor.

II

Man blind to future events

Say not, O man ! for it becomes thee not,
" This evil shall not happen to my lot."

The Rev. JAMES FORDYCE, D.D. (1720-1796)

Virtue and Ornament
To the Ladies

The diamond's and the ruby's rays
    Shine with a milder, finer flame,
And more attract our love and praise,
    Than Beauty's self, if lost to fame.

But the sweet tear in Pity's eye
    Transcends the diamond's brightest beams ;
And the soft blush of Modesty
    More precious than the ruby seems.

317

The glowing gem, the sparkling stone,
  May strike the sight with quick surprise;
But Truth and Innocence alone
  Can still engage the good and wise.

No glittering ornament or show
  Will aught avail in grief or pain:
Only from inward worth can flow
  Delight that ever shall remain.

Behold, ye fair, your lovely queen!
  'Tis not her jewels, but her mind—
A meeker, purer, ne'er was seen—
  It is her virtue charms mankind!

Mrs. FRANCES GREVILLE, *née* MACARTNEY
(*? born* 1720)

Prayer for Indifference

Oft I've implor'd the gods in vain,
  And pray'd till I've been weary:
For once I'll seek my wish to gain
  Of Oberon the fairy.

Sweet airy being, wanton spright,
  Who liv'st in woods unseen;
And oft by Cynthia's silver light
  Tripp'st gaily o'er the green;

If e'er thy pitying heart was mov'd
  As ancient stories tell;
And for th' Athenian maid who lov'd,
  Thou sought'st a wondrous spell.

Oh! deign once more t' exert thy power!
  Haply some herb or tree,
Sovereign as juice from western flower,
  Conceals a balm for me.

Mrs. GREVILLE

I ask no kind return in love,
   No tempting charm to please ;
Far from the heart such gifts remove,
   That sighs for peace and ease !

Nor ease nor peace that heart can know,
   That, like the needle true,
Turns at the touch of joy or woe ;
   But, turning, trembles too.

Far as distress the soul can wound,
   'Tis pain in each degree :
'Tis bliss but to a certain bound—
   Beyond is agony.

Then take this treacherous sense of mine,
   Which dooms me still to smart ;
Which pleasure can to pain refine ;
   To pain new pangs impart.

Oh ! haste to shed the sovereign balm,
   My shatter'd nerves new-string :
And for my guest, serenely calm,
   The nymph Indifference bring.

At her approach see hope, see fear,
   See expectation fly !
And disappointment in the rear,
   That blasts the purpos'd joy.

The tears, which pity taught to flow,
   My eyes shall then disown ;
The heart, that throbb'd at others' woe,
   Shall then scarce feel its own.

The wounds which now each moment bleed,
   Each moment then shall close ;
And tranquil days shall still succeed
   To nights of sweet repose.

Oh ! fairy elf, but grant me this,
    This one kind comfort send !
And so may never-fading bliss
    Thy flowery paths attend !

So may the glow-worm's glimmering light
    Thy tiny footsteps lead
To some new region of delight,
    Unknown to mortal tread !

And be thy acorn goblet fill'd
    With heaven's ambrosial dew,
From sweetest, freshest flowers distill'd,
    That shed fresh sweets for you !

And what of life remains for me,
    I'll pass in sober ease ;
Half-pleas'd, contented will I be,
    Content but half to please.

The Rev. JAMES MERRICK (1720-1769)

The Ignorance of Man

Behold yon new-born infant, griev'd
    With hunger, thirst, and pain ;
That asks to have the wants reliev'd,
    It knows not to explain.

Aloud the speechless suppliant cries,
    And utters, as it can,
The woes that in its bosom rise,
    And speaks its nature man.

That infant, whose advancing hour
    Life's various sorrows try,
(Sad proof of sin's transmissive power)
    That infant, Lord, am I.

A childhood yet my thoughts confess,
　　Though long in years mature ;
Unknowing whence I feel distress,
　　And where, or what its cure.

Author of good ! to Thee I turn ;
　　Thy ever-wakeful eye
Alone can all my wants discern,
　　Thy hand alone supply.

O let Thy fear within me dwell,
　　Thy love my footsteps guide :
That love shall vainer loves expel,
　　That fear all fears beside.

And O, by error's force subdu'd,
　　Since oft my stubborn will,
Preposterous, shuns the latent good,
　　And grasps the specious ill ;

Not to my wish, but to my want,
　　Do Thou Thy gifts apply :
Unask'd, what good Thou knowest, grant ;
　　What ill, though ask'd, deny.

An Epitaph

(*From the Latin of Dr. John Jortin*)

Thee, Pæta, Death's relentless hand
　　Cut off in earliest bloom :
Oh ! had the Fates for me ordain'd
　　To share an equal doom ;

With joy this busy world I'd leave,
　　This hated light resign,
To lay me in the peaceful grave,
　　And be for ever thine.

Do thou, if Lethe court thy lip,
    To taste its stream forbear :
Still in thy soul his image keep,
    Who hastes to meet thee there.

Safe o'er the dark and dreary shore,
    In quest of thee I'll roam ;
Love with his lamp shall run before,
    And break the circling gloom.

MARK AKENSIDE, M.D. (1721-1770)

Ode to the Cuckoo

O rustic herald of the spring,
At length in yonder woody vale
Fast by the brook I hear thee sing ;
And, studious of thy homely tale,
Amid the vespers of the grove,
Amid the chanting choir of love,
    Thy sage responses hail.

The time has been when I have frown'd
To hear thy voice the woods invade ;
And while thy solemn accent drown'd
Some sweeter poet of the shade,
Thus, thought I, thus the sons of care
Some constant youth or generous fair
    With dull advice upbraid.

I said, " While Philomela's song
Proclaims the passion of the grove,
It ill beseems a cuckoo's tongue
Her charming language to reprove "—
Alas, how much a lover's ear
Hates all the sober truth to hear,
    The sober truth of love !

When hearts are in each other bless'd,
When nought but lofty faith can rule
The nymph's and swain's consenting breast,
How cuckoo-like in Cupid's school,
With store of grave prudential saws
On fortune's power and custom's laws,
   Appears each friendly fool !

Yet think betimes, ye gentle train
Whom love and hope and fancy sway,
Who every harsher care disdain,
Who by the morning judge the day,
Think that, in April's fairest hours,
To warbling shades and painted flowers
   The cuckoo joins his lay.

Ode at Study

Whither did my fancy stray ?
By what magic drawn away
   Have I left my studious theme ?
From this philosophic page,
From the problems of the sage,
   Wandering through a pleasing dream ?

'Tis in vain, alas ! I find,
Much in vain, my zealous mind
   Would to learned wisdom's throne
Dedicate each thoughtful hour :
Nature bids a softer power
   Claim some minutes for his own.

Let the busy or the wise
View him with contemptuous eyes ;
   Love is native to the heart :
Guide its wishes as you will ;
Without Love you'll find it still
   Void in one essential part.

Me though no peculiar fair
Touches with a lover's care ;
　　Though the pride of my desire
Asks immortal friendship's name,
Asks the palm of honest fame,
　　And the old heroic lyre ;

Though the day have smoothly gone,
Or to letter'd leisure known,
　　Or in social duty spent ;
Yet at eve my lonely breast
Seeks in vain for perfect rest ;
　　Languishes for true content.

The Complaint

　　　Away ! Away !
Tempt me no more, insidious love :
　　　Thy soothing sway
Long did my youthful bosom prove :
At length thy treason is discern'd,
At length some dear-bought caution earn'd :
Away ! nor hope my riper age to move.

　　　I know, I see
Her merit. Needs it now be shown,
　　　Alas, to me ?
How often, to myself unknown,
The graceful, gentle, virtuous maid
Have I admir'd ! How often said,
" What joy to call a heart like hers one's own ! "

　　　But, flattering god,
O squanderer of content and ease,
　　　In thy abode
Will Care's rude lesson learn to please ?
O say, deceiver, hast thou won
Proud Fortune to attend thy throne,
Or plac'd thy friends above her stern decrees ?

Ode on a Sermon against Glory

Come then, tell me, sage divine,
Is it an offence to own
That our bosoms e'er incline
Toward immortal Glory's throne?
For with me nor pomp, nor pleasure,
Bourbon's might, Braganza's treasure,
So can Fancy's dream rejoice,
So conciliate Reason's choice,
As one approving word of her impartial voice.

If to spurn at noble praise
Be the passport to thy heaven,
Follow thou those gloomy ways;
No such law to me was given,
Nor, I trust, shall I deplore me
Faring like my friends before me:
Nor an holier place desire
Than Timoleon's arms acquire,
And Tully's curule chair, and Milton's golden lyre.

Ode to the Evening Star

To-night retir'd the Queen of Heaven
    With young Endymion stays:
And now to Hesper is it given
Awhile to rule the vacant sky,
Till she shall to her lamp supply
    A stream of brighter rays.

O Hesper, while the starry throng
    With awe thy path surrounds,
Oh listen to my suppliant song,
If haply now the vocal sphere
Can suffer thy delighted ear
    To stoop to mortal sounds.

So may the bridegroom's genial strain
   Thee still invoke to shine :
So may the bride's unmarried train
To Hymen chant their flattering vow,
Still that his lucky torch may glow
   With lustre pure as thine.

Far other vows must I prefer
   To thy indulgent power.
Alas, but now I paid my tear
On fair Olympia's virgin tomb :
And lo, from thence, in quest I roam
   Of Philomela's bower.

Propitious send thy golden ray,
   Thou purest light above :
Nor let false flame seduce to stray
Where gulf or steep lie hid for harm :
But lead where music's healing charm
   May soothe afflicted love.

To them, by many a grateful song
   In happier seasons vow'd,
These lawns, Olympia's haunt, belong :
Oft by yon silver stream we walk'd,
Or fix'd, while Philomela talk'd,
   Beneath yon copses stood.

Nor seldom, where the beachen boughs
   That roofless tower invade,
We came while her enchanting Muse
The radiant moon above us held :
Till by a clamorous owl compell'd
   She fled the solemn shade.

But hark ; I hear her liquid tone.
   Now, Hesper, guide my feet
Down the red marl with moss o'ergrown,
Through yon wild thicket next the plain,
Whose hawthorns choke the winding lane
   Which leads to her retreat.

MARK AKENSIDE

See the green space : on either hand
   Enlarg'd it spreads around :
See, in the midst she takes her stand,
Where one old oak his awful shade
Extends o'er half the level mead
   Enclos'd in woods profound.

Hark, how through many a melting note
   She now prolongs her lays :
How sweetly down the void they float !
The breeze their magic path attends :
The stars shine out : the forest bends :
   The wakeful heifers gaze.

Whoe'er thou art whom chance may bring
   To this sequester'd spot,
If then the plaintive Syren sing,
Oh softly tread beneath her bower,
And think of Heaven's disposing power,
   And man's uncertain lot.

Oh think, o'er all this mortal stage,
   What mournful scenes arise :
What ruin waits on kingly rage :
How often virtue dwells with woe :
How many griefs from knowledge flow :
   How swiftly pleasure flies.

O sacred bird, let me at eve,
   Thus wandering all alone,
Thy tender counsel oft receive,
Bear witness to thy pensive airs,
And pity nature's common cares
   Till I forget my own.

MARK AKENSIDE

Ode to Sleep

Thou silent power, whose welcome sway
Charms every anxious thought away ;
In whose divine oblivion drown'd,
Sore pain and weary toil grow mild,
Love is with kinder looks beguil'd,
And Grief forgets her fondly cherish'd wound ;
Oh whither hast thou flown, indulgent god ?
God of kind shadows and of healing dews,
Whom dost thou touch with thy Lethean rod ?
Around whose temples now thy opiate airs diffuse ?

Lo, midnight from her starry reign
Looks awful down on earth and main.
The tuneful birds lie hush'd in sleep,
With all that crop the verdant food,
With all that skim the crystal flood,
Or haunt the caverns of the rocky steep.
No rushing winds disturb the tufted bowers ;
No wakeful sound the moon-light valley knows,
Save where the brook its liquid murmur pours,
And lulls the waving scene to more profound repose.

Oh let me not alone complain,
Alone invoke thy power in vain !
Descend, propitious, on my eyes ;
Not from the couch that bears a crown,
Not from the courtly statesman's down,
Nor where the miser and his treasure lies :
Bring not the shapes that break the murderer's rest,
Nor those the hireling soldier loves to see,
Nor those which haunt the bigot's gloomy breast :
Far be their guilty nights, and far their dreams from me !

Nor yet those awful forms present,
For chiefs and heroes only meant :
The figur'd brass, the choral song,
The rescu'd people's glad applause,
The listening senate, and the laws

MARK AKENSIDE

Fix'd by the counsels of Timoleon's tongue,
Are scenes too grand for Fortune's private ways ;
And though they shine in youth's ingenuous view,
The sober gainful arts of modern days
To such romantic thoughts have bid a long adieu.

I ask not, god of dreams, thy care
To banish Love's presentments fair :
Nor rosy cheek nor radiant eye
Can arm him with such strong command
That the young sorcerer's fatal hand
Should round my soul his pleasing fetters tie.
Nor yet the courtier's hope, the giving smile,
(A lighter phantom, and a baser chain)
Did e'er in slumber my proud lyre beguile
To lend the pomp of thrones her ill-according strain.

But, Morpheus, on thy balmy wing
Such honourable visions bring,
As sooth'd great Milton's injur'd age,
When in prophetic dreams he saw
The race unborn with pious awe
Imbibe each virtue from his heavenly page :
Or such as Mead's benignant fancy knows
When health's deep treasures, by his art explor'd,
Have sav'd the infant from an orphan's woes,
Or to the trembling sire his age's hope restor'd.

WILLIAM COLLINS (1721-1759)

Hassan; or, The Camel Driver
Scene, the desert.   Time, mid-day

In silent horror o'er the desert waste
The driver Hassan with his camels pass'd.
One cruse of water on his back he bore,
And his light scrip contain'd a scanty store :
A fan of painted feathers in his hand,
To guard his shaded face from scorching sand.
The sultry sun had gain'd the middle sky,
And not a tree, and not an herb was nigh.
The beasts, with pain, their dusty way pursue,
Shrill roar'd the winds, and dreary was the view !
With desperate sorrow wild th' affrighted man
Thrice sigh'd, thrice strook his breast, and thus began :

Sad was the hour, and luckless was the day,
When first from Schiraz' *walls I bent my way.*

Ah ! little thought I of the blasting wind,
The thirst or pinching hunger that I find !
Bethink thee, Hassan, where shall thirst assuage,
When fails this cruse, his unrelenting rage ?
Soon shall this scrip its precious load resign,
Then what but tears and hunger shall be thine ?

Ye mute companions of my toils, that bear
In all my griefs a more than equal share !
Here, where no springs in murmurs break away,
Or moss-crown'd fountains mitigate the day,
In vain ye hope the green delights to know,
Which plains more bless'd, or verdant vales bestow.
Here rocks alone, and tasteless sands are found,
And faint and sickly winds for ever howl around.

Sad was the hour, and luckless was the day,
When first from Schiraz' *walls I bent my way.*

330

Curs'd be the gold and silver which persuade
Weak men to follow far-fatiguing trade.
The lily-peace outshines the silver store,
And life is dearer than the golden ore.
Yet money tempts us o'er the desert brown,
To every distant mart, and wealthy town :
Full oft we tempt the land, and oft the sea,
And are we only yet repaid by thee ?
Ah ! why was ruin so attractive made,
Or why fond man so easily betray'd ?
Why heed we not, whilst mad we haste along,
The gentle voice of Peace, or Pleasure's song ?
Or wherefore think the flowery mountain's side,
The fountain's murmurs, and the valley's pride,
Why think we these less pleasing to behold,
Than dreary deserts, if they lead to gold ?

Sad was the hour, and luckless was the day,
When first from Schiraz' *walls I bent my way.*

O cease, my fears ! all frantic as I go,
When thought creates unnumber'd scenes of woe,
What if the lion in his rage I meet !
Oft in the dust I view his printed feet :
And fearful ! oft, when day's declining light
Yields her pale empire to the mourner night,
By hunger rous'd, he scours the groaning plain,
Gaunt wolves and sullen tigers in his train :
Before them Death with shrieks directs their way,
Fills the wild yell, and leads them to their prey.

Sad was the hour, and luckless was the day,
When first from Schiraz' *walls I bent my way.*

At that dead hour the silent asp shall creep,
If ought of rest I find, upon my sleep :
Or some swoln serpent twist his scales around,
And wake to anguish with a burning wound.
Thrice happy they, the wise contented poor,
From lust of wealth, and dread of death secure ;

They tempt no deserts, and no griefs they find ;
Peace rules the day, where reason rules the mind.

Sad was the hour, and luckless was the day,
When first from Schiraz' walls I bent my way.

O hapless youth ! for she thy love hath won,
Thy tender Zara, will be most undone !
Big swell'd my heart, and own'd the powerful maid,
When fast she dropp'd her tears, as thus she said :
" Farewell the youth whom sighs could not detain,
Whom Zara's breaking heart implor'd in vain ;
Yet as thou go'st, may every blast arise,
Weak and unfelt as these rejected sighs !
Safe o'er the wild, no perils mayst thou see,
No griefs endure, nor weep, false youth, like me."
O let me safely to the fair return,
Say with a kiss, she must not, shall not mourn.
Go teach my heart, to lose its painful fears,
Recall'd by wisdom's voice, and Zara's tears.

He said, and call'd on Heaven to bless the day,
When back to Schiraz' walls he bent his way.

Ode,

written in the beginning of the year 1746

How sleep the brave, who sink to rest,
By all their country's wishes blest !
When Spring, with dewy fingers cold,
Returns to deck their hallow'd mould,
She there shall dress a sweeter sod,
Than Fancy's feet have ever trod.

By fairy hands their knell is rung,
By forms unseen their dirge is sung ;
There Honour comes, a pilgrim grey,
To bless the turf that wraps their clay,
And Freedom shall awhile repair,
To dwell a weeping hermit there !

WILLIAM COLLINS

Ode to Evening

If ought of oaten stop, or pastoral song,
May hope, O pensive Eve, to soothe thine ear,
    Like thy own brawling springs,
    Thy springs, and dying gales,
O nymph reserv'd, while now the bright-hair'd sun
Sits in yon western tent, whose cloudy skirts,
    With brede ethereal wove,
    O'erhang his wavy bed :
Now air is hush'd, save where the weak-ey'd bat,
With short shrill shriek flits by on leathern wing,
    Or where the beetle winds
    His small but sullen horn,
As oft he rises 'midst the twilight path,
Against the pilgrim borne in heedless hum :
    Now teach me, maid compos'd,
    To breathe some soften'd strain,
Whose numbers stealing through thy darkening vale,
May not unseemly with its stillness suit,
    As musing slow, I hail
    Thy genial lov'd return !
For when thy folding star arising shews
His paly circlet, at his warning lamp
    The fragrant Hours, and Elves
    Who slept in buds the day,
And many a Nymph who wreaths her brows with sedge,
And sheds the freshening dew, and lovelier still,
    The pensive Pleasures sweet
    Prepare thy shadowy car.
Then let me rove some wild and heathy scene,
Or find some ruin 'midst its dreary dells,
    Whose walls more awful nod
    By thy religious gleams.
Or if chill blustering winds, or driving rain,
Prevent my willing feet, be mine the hut,
    That from the mountain's side
    Views wilds, and swelling floods,

And hamlets brown, and dim-discover'd spires,
And hears their simple bell, and marks o'er all
    Thy dewy fingers draw
    The gradual dusky veil.
While Spring shall pour his showers, as oft he wont,
And bathe thy breathing tresses, meekest Eve !
    While Summer loves to sport,
    Beneath thy lingering light :
While sallow Autumn fills thy lap with leaves,
Or Winter yelling through the troublous air,
    Affrights thy shrinking train,
    And rudely rends thy robes,
So long regardful of thy quiet rule,
Shall Fancy, Friendship, Science, smiling Peace,
    Thy gentlest influence own,
    And love thy fav'rite name !

Ode on the Death of Thomson

In yonder grave a druid lies,
    Where slowly winds the stealing wave !
The year's best sweets shall duteous rise
    To deck its Poet's sylvan grave !

In yon deep bed of whispering reeds
    His airy harp shall now be laid,
That he, whose heart in sorrow bleeds,
    May love through life the soothing shade.

Then maids and youths shall linger here,
    And while its sounds at distance swell,
Shall sadly seem in Pity's ear
    To hear the woodland pilgrim's knell.

Remembrance oft shall haunt the shore
    When Thames in summer wreaths is drest,
And oft suspend the dashing oar
    To bid his gentle spirit rest !

And oft as ease and health retire
　To breezy lawn, or forest deep,
The friend shall view yon whitening spire,
　And 'mid the varied landscape weep.

But thou, who own'st that earthy bed,
　Ah ! what will every dirge avail ?
Or tears, which love and pity shed,
　That mourn beneath the gliding sail ?

Yet lives there one, whose heedless eye
　Shall scorn thy pale shrine glimmering near ?
With him, sweet bard, may fancy die,
　And joy desert the blooming year.

But thou, lorn stream, whose sullen tide
　No sedge-crown'd sisters now attend,
Now waft me from the green hill's side,
　Whose cold turf hides the buried friend !

And see, the fairy valleys fade,
　Dun night has veil'd the solemn view !
Yet once again, dear parted shade,
　Meek Nature's child, again adieu !

The genial meads assign'd to bless
　Thy life, shall mourn thy early doom ;
Their hinds, and shepherd girls shall dress
　With simple hands thy rural tomb.

Long, long, thy stone, and pointed clay
　Shall melt the musing Briton's eyes,
O ! vales, and wild woods, shall he say,
　In yonder grave your Druid lies !

Dirge in Cymbeline

*Sung by Guiderius and Arviragus over Fidele, supposed
to be dead.*

To fair Fidele's grassy tomb
    Soft maids and village hinds shall bring
Each opening sweet of earliest bloom,
    And rifle all the breathing spring.

No wailing ghost shall dare appear
    To vex with shrieks this quiet grove :
But shepherd lads assemble here,
    And melting virgins own their love.

No wither'd witch shall here be seen,
    No goblins lead their nightly crew ;
The female fays shall haunt the green,
    And dress thy grave with pearly dew !

The red-breast oft at evening hours
    Shall kindly lend his little aid :
With hoary moss, and gather'd flowers,
    To deck the ground where thou art laid.

When howling winds, and beating rain,
    In tempests shake the sylvan cell,
Or 'midst the chase on every plain,
    The tender thought on thee shall dwell.

Each lonely scene shall thee restore,
    For thee the tear be duly shed :
Belov'd till life can charm no more,
    And mourn'd, till pity's self be dead.

On a Fine Crop of Peas being Spoil'd by a Storm

When Morrice views his prostrate peas,
　By raging whirlwinds spread,
He wrings his hands, and in amaze
　He sadly shakes his head.

" Is this the fruit of my fond toil,
　My joy, my pride, my cheer !
Shall one tempestuous hour thus spoil
　The labours of a year !

" Oh ! what avails, that day by day
　I nurs'd the thriving crop,
And settl'd with my foot the clay,
　And rear'd the social prop !

" Ambition's pride had spurr'd me on
　All gard'ners to excel ;
I often call'd them one by one,
　And boastingly would tell,

" How I prepar'd the furrow'd ground,
　And how the grain did sow,
Then challeng'd all the country round
　For such an early blow.

" How did their bloom my wishes raise !
　What hopes did they afford,
To earn my honour'd master's praise,
　And crown his cheerful board ! "

Poor Morrice, wrapt in sad surprise,
　Demands in sober mood,
Should storms molest a man so wise,
　A man so just and good ?

Ah ! Morrice, cease thy fruitless moan,
    Nor at misfortunes spurn,
Misfortune's not thy lot alone ;
    Each neighbour has his turn.

Thy prostrate peas, which low recline
    Beneath the frowns of Fate,
May teach much wiser heads than thine
    Their own uncertain state.

The sprightly youth in beauty's prime,
    The lovely nymph so gay,
Oft victims fall to early time,
    And in their bloom decay.

In vain th' indulgent father's care,
    In vain wise precepts form :
They droop, like peas, in tainted air,
    Or perish in a storm.

TOBIAS GEORGE SMOLLETT, M.D. (1721-1771)

Ode to Leven-Water

On Leven's banks, while free to rove,
And tune the rural pipe to love ;
I envied not the happiest swain
That ever trod the Arcadian plain.

Pure stream ! in whose transparent wave
My youthful limbs I wont to lave ;
No torrents stain thy limpid source ;
No rocks impede thy dimpling course,
That sweetly warbles o'er its bed,
With white, round, polish'd pebbles spread ;
While, lightly pois'd, the scaly brood
In myriads cleave thy crystal flood ;
The springing trout in speckled pride ;
The salmon, monarch of the tide ;

The ruthless pike, intent on war ;
The silver eel, and mottled par.
Devolving from thy parent lake,
A charming maze thy waters make,
By bowers of birch, and groves of pine,
And edges flower'd with eglantine.

Still on thy banks so gaily green,
May numerous herds and flocks be seen,
And lasses chanting o'er the pail,
And shepherds piping in the dale,
And ancient faith that knows no guile,
And industry embrown'd with toil,
And hearts resolv'd, and hands prepar'd,
The blessings they enjoy to guard.

Song

To fix her—'twere a task as vain
To count the April drops of rain,
To sow in Afric's barren soil,
Or tempests hold within a toil.

I know it, friend, she's light as air,
False as the fowler's artful snare ;
Inconstant as the passing wind,
As winter's dreary frost unkind.

She's such a miser too in love,
Its joys she'll neither share nor prove ;
Though hundreds of gallants await
From her victorious eyes their fate.

Blushing at such inglorious reign,
I sometimes strive to break her chain ;
My reason summon to my aid,
Resolv'd no more to be betray'd.

Ah ! friend ! 'tis but a short-liv'd trance,
Dispell'd by one enchanting glance ;
She need but look, and, I confess,
Those looks completely curse or bless.

So soft, so elegant, so fair,
Sure something more than human's there ;
I must submit, for strife is vain,
'Twas destiny that forg'd the chain.

The Rev. WILLIAM WILKIE, D.D.* (1721-1772)

The Fable of the Boy and the Rainbow

Declare, ye sages, if ye find
'Mongst animals of every kind,
Of each condition sort and size,
From whales and elephants to flies,
A creature that mistakes his plan,
And errs so constantly as man.
Each kind pursues his proper good,
And seeks for pleasure, rest and food,
As nature points, and never errs
In what it chooses and prefers ;
Man only blunders, though possest
Of talents far above the rest.

Descend to instances and try ;
An ox will scarce attempt to fly,
Or leave his pasture in the wood
With fishes to explore the flood.
Man only acts, of every creature,
In opposition to his nature.
The happiness of human-kind
Consists in rectitude of mind,

* " The Scottish Homer " !

340

WILLIAM WILKIE

A will subdu'd to reason's sway,
And passions practis'd to obey ;
An open and a gen'rous heart,
Refin'd from selfishness and art ;
Patience which mocks at fortune's power,
And wisdom never sad nor sour :
In these consist our proper bliss ;
Else Plato reasons much amiss :
But foolish mortals still pursue
False happiness instead of true ;
Ambition serves us for a guide,
Or Lust, or Avarice, or Pride ;
While Reason no assent can gain,
And Revelation warns in vain.
Hence through our lives in every stage,
From infancy itself to age,
A happiness we toil to find,
Which still avoids us like the wind ;
Ev'n when we think the prize our own,
At once 'tis vanish'd, lost and gone.
You'll ask me why I thus rehearse
All Epictetus in my verse,
And if I fondly hope to please
With dry reflections, such as these,
So trite, so hackneyed, and so stale ?
I'll take the hint and tell a tale.

One ev'ning as a simple swain
His flock attended on the plain,
The shining bow he chanc'd to spy,
Which warns us when a show'r is nigh ;
With brightest rays it seem'd to glow,
Its distance eighty yards or so.
This bumpkin had, it seems, been told
The story of the cup of gold,
Which Fame reports is to be found
Just where the rainbow meets the ground ;
He therefore felt a sudden itch
To seize the goblet and be rich ;

Hoping, yet hopes are oft but vain,
No more to toil through wind and rain,
But sit indulging by the fire,
'Midst ease and plenty, like a squire :
He mark'd the very spot of land
On which the rainbow seem'd to stand,
And stepping forward at his leisure
Expected to have found the treasure.
But as he mov'd, the colour'd ray
Still chang'd its place and slipt away,
As seeming his approach to shun ;
From walking he began to run,
But all in vain, it still withdrew
As nimbly as he could pursue ;
At last through many a bog and lake,
Rough craggy road and thorny brake,
It led the easy fool, till night
Approach'd, then vanish'd in his sight,
And left him to compute his gains,
With nought but labour for his pains.

MARY LEAPOR* (1722-1746)

The Month of August

Sylvanus, a Courtier, Phillis, a Country Maid.

SYLVANUS

Hail, Phillis, brighter than a morning sky,
Joy of my heart, and darling of my eye ;
See the kind year her grateful tribute yields,
And round-fac'd plenty triumphs o'er the fields.
But to yon gardens let me lead thy charms,
Where the curl'd vine extends her willing arms :
Whose purple clusters lure the longing eye,
And the ripe cherries show their scarlet dye.

* This girl was a cook-maid, and the daughter of a gardener.

MARY LEAPOR

PHILLIS

Not all the sights your boasted gardens yield,
Are half so lovely as my father's field,
Where large increase has bless'd the fruitful plain,
And we with joy behold the swelling grain,
Whose heavy ears toward the earth reclin'd,
Wave, nod, and tremble to the whisking wind.

SYLVANUS

But see, to emulate those cheeks of thine,
On yon fair tree the blushing nect'rines shine :
Beneath their leaves the ruddy peaches glow,
And the plump figs compose a gallant show.
With gaudy plums see yonder boughs recline,
And ruddy pears in yon *espalier* twine.
There humble dwarfs in pleasing order stand,
Whose golden product seems to court thy hand.

PHILLIS

In vain you tempt me, while our orchard bears
Long-keeping russets, lovely Cath'rine pears,
Pearmains and codlings, wheaten plums cnow,
And the black damsons load the bending bough.
No pruning-knives our fertile branches tease,
While yours must grow but as their masters please.
The grateful trees our mercy well repay,
And rain us bushels at the rising day.

SYLVANUS

Fair are my gardens, yet you slight them all ;
Then let us haste to yon majestic hall,
Where the glad roofs shall to thy voice resound,
Thy voice more sweet than music's melting sound ;
Now Orion's beam infests the sultry sky,
And scorching fevers through the welkin fly ;
But art shall teach us to evade his ray,
And the forc'd fountains near the windows play ;

There choice perfumes shall give a pleasing gale,
And orange-flowers their od'rous breath exhale,
While on the walls the well-wrought paintings glow,
And dazzling carpets deck the floors below :
O tell me, thou whose careless beauties charm,
Are these not fairer than a thresher's barn ?

PHILLIS

Believe me, I can find no charms at all
In your fine carpets and your painted hall.
'Tis true our parlour has an earthen floor,
The sides of plaster and of elm the door :
Yet the rubb'd chest and table sweetly shines,
And the spread mint along the window climbs :
An aged laurel keeps away the sun,
And two cool streams across the garden run.

SYLVANUS

Can feasts or music win my lovely maid ?
In both those pleasures be her taste obey'd.
The ransack'd earth shall all its dainties send,
Till with its load her plenteous table bend.
Then to the roofs the swelling notes shall rise,
Pierce the glad air and gain upon the skies,
While ease and rapture spreads itself around,
And distant hills roll back the charming sound.

PHILLIS

Not this will lure me, for I'd have you know
This night to feast with Corydon I go :
To-night his reapers bring the gather'd grain
Home to his barns, and leave the naked plain :
Then beef and coleworts, beans and bacon too,
And the plum-pudding of delicious hue,
Sweet-spiced cake, and apple-pies good store,
Deck the brown board ; who can desire more ?
His flute and tabor too Amyntor brings,
And while he plays soft Amaryllis sings.

MARY LEAPOR

Then strive no more to win a simple maid,
From her lov'd cottage and her silent shade.
Let Phillis ne'er, ah! never let her rove
From her first virtue and her humble grove.
Go seek some nymph that equals your degree,
And leave content and Corydon for me.

CHRISTOPHER SMART (1722-1771)

Ode on the Fifth of December,
being the Birthday of a beautiful young Lady

Hail, eldest of the monthly train,
   Sire of the winter drear,
December, in whose iron reign
   Expires the checker'd year.
Hush all the blustering blasts that blow,
And proudly plum'd in silver snow,
   Smile gladly on this blest of days.
The liveried clouds shall on thee wait,
And Phœbus shine in all his state
   With more than summer rays.

Though jocund June may justly boast
   Long days and happy hours,
Though August be Pomona's host,
   And May be crown'd with flowers;
Tell June, his fire and crimson dies,
By Harriot's blush and Harriot's eyes,
   Eclips'd and vanquish'd, fade away;
Tell August, thou canst let him see
A richer, riper fruit than he,
   A sweeter flower than May.

CHRISTOPHER SMART

Ode on an Eagle
confined in a College Court

Imperial bird, who wont to soar
   High o'er the rolling cloud,
Where Hyperborean mountains hoar
   Their heads in ether shroud ;
Thou servant of almighty Jove,
Who, free and swift as thought, couldst rove
   To the bleak North's extremest goal ;
Thou, who magnanimous couldst bear
The sovereign Thunderer's arms in air,
   And shake thy native pole !

Oh cruel fate ! what barbarous hand,
   What more than Gothic ire,
At some fierce tyrant's dread command,
   To check thy daring fire,
Has plac'd thee in this servile cell,
Where Discipline and Dullness dwell,
   Where Genius ne'er was seen to roam ;
Where every selfish soul's at rest,
Nor ever quits the carnal breast,
   But lurks and sneaks at home !

Though dimm'd thine eye, and clipt thy wing,
   So grovelling ! once so great !
The grief-inspired Muse shall sing
   In tenderest lays thy fate.
What time by thee scholastic Pride
Takes his precise, pedantic stride,
   Nor on thy misery casts a care,
The stream of love ne'er from his heart
Flows out, to act fair pity's part ;
   But stinks, and stagnates there.

Yet useful still, hold to the throng,
   Hold the reflecting glass ;
That not untutor'd at thy wrong
   The passenger may pass :

CHRISTOPHER SMART

Thou type of wit and sense confin'd,
Cramp'd by the oppressors of the mind,
    Who study downward on the ground ;
Type of the fall of Greece and Rome ;
While more than mathematic gloom
    Envelops all around !

The Lass with the Golden Locks

No more of my Harriot, of Polly no more,
Nor all the bright beauties that charm'd me before ;
My heart for a slave to gay Venus I've sold,
And barter'd my freedom for ringlets of gold :
I'll throw down my pipe, and neglect all my flocks,
And will sing to my lass with the golden locks.

Though o'er her white forehead the gilt tresses flow,
Like the rays of the sun on a hillock of snow ;
Such painters of old drew the Queen of the Fair,
'Tis the taste of the Ancients, 'tis Classical Hair !
And though witlings may scoff, and though raillery mocks,
Yet I'll sing to my lass with the golden locks.

To live and to love, to converse and be free,
Is loving, my charmer, and living with thee :
Away go the hours in kisses and rhyme,
Spite of all the grave lectures of old Father Time ;
A fig for his dials, his watches and clocks,
He's best spent with the lass of the golden locks.

Than the swan in the brook she's more dear to my sight,
Her mien is more stately, her breast is more white,
Her sweet lips are rubies, all rubies above,
Which are fit for the language or labour of love ;
At the park in the mall, at the play in the box,
My lass bears the bell with her golden locks.

Her beautiful eyes, as they roll or they flow,
Shall be glad for my joy, or shall weep for my woe ;
She shall ease my fond heart, and shall soothe my soft pain,
While thousands of rivals are sighing in vain ;
Let them rail at the fruit they can't reach, like the fox,
While I have the lass with the golden locks.

Ode to Idleness

Goddess of ease, leave Lethe's brink,
  Obsequious to the Muse and me ;
For once endure the pain to think,
  Oh ! sweet Insensibility !

Sister of Peace and Indolence,
  Bring, Muse, bring numbers soft and slow ;
Elaborately void of sense,
  And sweetly thoughtless let them flow.

Near some cowslip-painted mead,
  There let me doze out the dull hours,
And under me let Flora spread
  A sofa of her softest flow'rs ;

Where, Philomel, your notes you breathe
  Forth from behind the neighbouring pine,
And murmurs of the stream beneath
  Still flow in unison with thine.

For thee, O Idleness, the woes
  Of life we patiently endure,
Thou art the source whence labour flows,
  We shun thee but to make thee sure.

For who'd sustain war's toil and waste,
  Or who th' hoarse thund'ring of the sea,
But to be idle at the last,
  And find a pleasing end in thee ?

The Rev. JOSEPH WARTON, D.D. (1722-1800)

Address of an Indian Girl to an Adder
Written while the author was a scholar at Winchester

Stay, stay, thou lovely fearful snake !
Nor hide thee in yon darksome brake ;
But let me oft thy form review,
Thy sparkling eyes, and golden hue :
From thence a chaplet shall be wove
To grace the youth I dearest love.

Then, ages hence, when thou no more
Shalt glide along the sunny shore,
Thy copied beauties shall be seen :
Thy vermeil red and living green
In mimic folds thou shalt display :
Stay lovely, fearful adder, stay !

Ode to a Lady who hates the Country

Now summer, daughter of the sun,
O'er the gay fields comes dancing on
   And earth o'erflows with joys ;
Too long in routs and drawing-rooms
The tasteless hours my fair consumes,
   'Midst folly, flattery, noise.

Come hear mild Zephyr bid the rose
Her balmy-breathing buds disclose,
   Come hear the falling rill ;
Observe the honey-loaded bee,
The beech-embower'd cottage see,
   Beside yon sloping hill.

By health awoke at early morn,
We'll brush sweet dews from every thorn,
   And help unpen the fold ;
Hence to yon hollow oak we'll stray,
Where dwelt, as village fables say,
   An holy Druid old.

349

Come wildly rove through desert dales
To listen how lone nightingales
    In liquid lays complain ;
Adieu the tender, thrilling note,
That pants in Monticelli's throat,
    And Handel's stronger strain.

" Insipid pleasures these ! " you cry,
" Must I from dear assemblies fly,
    To see rude peasants toil ?
For operas listen to a bird ?
Shall Sidney's fables* be prefer'd
    To my sagacious Hoyle† ? "

O falsely fond of what seems great,
Of purple pomp and robes of state,
    And all life's tinsel glare !
Rather with humble violets bind,
Or give to wanton in the wind,
    Your length of sable hair.

Soon as you reach the rural shade,
Will Mirth, the sprightly mountain-maid,
    Your days and nights attend,
She'll bring fantastic Sport and Song,
Nor Cupid will be absent long,
    Your true ally and friend.

* *i.e.,* the *Arcadia.*
† Author of a book on Whist.

Sir WILLIAM BLACKSTONE, Knight, D.C.L.
(1723-1780)

The Lawyer's Farewell to his Muse
Written in the year 1744

As, by some tyrant's stern command,
A wretch forsakes his native land,
In foreign climes condemn'd to roam
An endless exile from his home ;
Pensive he treads the destin'd way,
And dreads to go, nor dares to stay ;
'Till on some neighb'ring mountain's brow
He stops, and turns his eyes below ;
There, melting at the well-known view,
Drops a last tear, and bids adieu :
So I, thus doom'd from thee to part,
Gay queen of fancy and of art,
Reluctant move, with doubtful mind,
Oft stop, and often look behind.

Companion of my tender age,
Serenely gay, and sweetly sage,
How blithesome were we wont to rove
By verdant hill or shady grove,
Where fervent bees, with humming voice,
Around the honey'd oak rejoice,
And aged elms with awful bend
In long cathedral walks extend !
Lull'd by the lapse of gliding floods,
Cheer'd by the warbling of the woods,
How blest my days, my thoughts how free,
In sweet society with thee !
Then all was joyous, all was young,
And years unheeded roll'd along :
But now the pleasing dream is o'er,
These scenes must charm me now no more :
Lost to the field, and torn from you,—
Farewell !—a long, a last adieu.

Sir WILLIAM BLACKSTONE

Me wrangling courts, and stubborn law,
To smoke, and crowds, and cities draw ;
There selfish Faction rules the day,
And Pride and Av'rice throng the way :
Diseases taint the murky air,
And midnight conflagrations glare ;
Loose Revelry and Riot bold
In frighted streets their orgies hold ;
Or, when in silence all is drown'd,
Fell Murder walks her lonely round :
No room for Peace, no room for you,
Adieu, celestial nymph, adieu !

Shakespeare, no more thy sylvan son,
Nor all the art of Addison,
Pope's heav'n-strung lyre, nor Waller's ease,
Nor Milton's mighty self must please :
Instead of these, a formal band
In furs and coifs around me stand ;
With sounds uncouth, and accents dry,
That grate the soul of harmony,
Each pedant sage unlocks his store
Of mystic, dark, discordant lore ;
And points with tottering hand the ways,
That lead me to the thorny maze.

There, in a winding, close retreat,
Is Justice doom'd to fix her seat,
There, fenc'd by bulwarks of the law,
She keeps the wondering world in awe,
And there, from vulgar sight retir'd,
Like eastern queens, is more admir'd.

O let me pierce the secret shade
Where dwells the venerable maid !
There humbly mark, with reverent awe,
The guardian of Britannia's law,
Unfold with joy her sacred page,
(Th' united boast of many an age,

352

Sir WILLIAM BLACKSTONE

Where mix'd, yet uniform, appears
The wisdom of a thousand years)
In that pure spring the bottom view,
Clear, deep, and regularly true,
And other doctrines thence imbibe
Than lurk within the sordid scribe ;
Observe how parts with parts unite
In one harmonious rule of right ;
See countless wheels distinctly tend
By various laws to one great end ;
While mighty Alfred's piercing soul
Pervades, and regulates the whole.

Then welcome business, welcome strife,
Welcome the cares, the thorns of life,
The visage wan, the pore-blind sight,
The toil by day, the lamp at night,
The tedious forms, the solemn prate,
The pert dispute, the dull debate,
The drowsy bench, the babbling hall,
For thee, fair Justice, welcome all !

Thus though my noon of life be past,
Yet let my setting sun, at last,
Find out the still, the rural cell,
Where sage retirement loves to dwell !
There let me taste the home-felt bliss
Of innocence, and inward peace ;
Untainted by the guilty bribe ;
Uncurs'd amid the harpy tribe ;
No orphan's cry to wound my ear ;
My honour and my conscience clear ;
Thus may I calmly meet my end,
Thus to the grave in peace descend.

CHRISTOPHER ANSTEY (1724-1805)

From " The New Bath Guide "

Letter VII

Mr. Simkin Blunderhead to Lady Blunderhead, at ――― Hall, North.

A Panegyric on Bath, and a Moravian Hymn

Of all the gay places the world can afford,
By gentle and simple for pastime ador'd,
Fine balls, and fine concerts, fine buildings, and springs,
Fine walks, and fine views, and a thousand fine things,
(Not to mention the sweet situation and air)
What place, my dear mother, with Bath can compare ?
Let Bristol for commerce and dirt be renown'd,
At Sal'sbury pen-knives and scissors be ground ;
The towns of Devizes, of Bradford, and Frome,
May boast that they better can manage the loom ;
I believe that they may ;—but the world to refine,
In manners, in dress, in politeness to shine,
O Bath ! let the art, let the glory be thine.
I'm sure I have travell'd our country all o'er,
And ne'er was so civilly treated before ;
Would you think, my dear mother, (without the least hint
That we all should be glad of appearing in print)
The news-writers here were so kind as to give all
The world an account of our happy arrival ?—
You scarce can imagine what numbers I've met,
(Though to me they are perfectly strangers as yet)
Who all with address and civility came,
And seem'd vastly proud of *subscribing* our name.
Young Timothy Canvass is charm'd with the place,
Who, I hear, is come hither, his fibres to brace ;
Poor man ! at th' election he threw, t'other day,
All his victuals, and liquor, and money away ;
And some people think with such haste he began,
That soon he the constable greatly outran,
And is qualified now for a parliament-man :

CHRISTOPHER ANSTEY

Goes every day to the coffee-house, where
The wits and the great politicians repair ;
Harangues on the funds, and the state of the nation,
And plans a good speech for an administration,
In hopes of a place, which he thinks he deserves,
As the love of his country has ruin'd his nerves.—
Our neighbour, Sir Easterlin Widgeon, has swore
He ne'er will return to his bogs any more ;
The Thicksculls are settled ;   we've had invitations
With a great many more on the score of relations ;
The Loungers are come too.—Old Stucco has just sent
His plan for a house to be built in the Crescent ;
'Twill soon be complete, and they say all their work
Is as strong as St. Paul's, or the minster at York.
Don't you think 'twould be better to lease our estate,
And buy a good house here before 'tis too late ?
You never can go, my dear mother, where you
So much have to see, and so little to do.

I write this in haste, for the Captain is come,
And so kind as to go with us all to the room ;
But be sure by the very next post you shall hear
Of all I've the pleasure of meeting with there :
For I scribble my verse with a great deal of ease,
And can send you a letter whenever I please ;
And while at this place I've the honour to stay,
I think I can never want something to say.
But now, my dear mother, &c. &c. &c.

                              SIMKIN BLUNDERHEAD.

Postscript.
I'm sorry to find at the city of Bath,
Many folks are uneasy concerning their faith :
Nicodemus, the preacher, strives all he can do
To quiet the conscience of good sister Prue ;
But Tabby from scruples of mind is releas'd
Since she met with a learned Moravian priest,

Who says, *There is neither transgression nor sin ;*
A doctrine that brings many customers in.
She thinks this the prettiest ode upon earth,
Which he made on his infant that died in the birth.

Ode

Chicken blessed
And caressed,
Little bee on Jesu's breast !
From the hurry
And the flurry
Of the earth thou'rt now at rest.

SAMUEL DERRICK* (1724-1769)

Air

From " The Enchantress," a Cantata

Love, tenacious of his right,
Shuts his ears to amorous tales ;
With scorn rejects each fond delight,
Where sympathising nature fails :
For freedom sits on Cupid's throne ;
And love depends on choice alone.

Riches may the blooming maid
To a loath'd embrace allure ;
But, by motives false betray'd,
The heart is restless, unsecure :
For freedom sits on Cupid's throne ;
And love depends on choice alone.

* " ' Pray, sir, . . . whether do you reckon Derrick or Smart the best poet ? ' . . . ' Sir, there is no settling the point of precedency between a louse and a flea.' "—Boswell's *Johnson.*
" ' Derrick may do very well, as long as he can outrun his character ; but the moment his character gets up with him, it is all over.' It is, however, but just to record, that some years afterwards, when I reminded him of this sarcasm, he said, ' Well, but Derrick has now got a character that he need not run away from.' "
—The same.
Derrick succeeded Nash as Master of the Ceremonies at Bath.

Beauty would you then subdue,
   Would you win the hand and heart ;
With gentle arts the fair pursue ;
   Let soft persuasion play its part ;
By tender usage fairly won,
Her heart is yours, and yours alone.

Cupid Gone Astray

A Song, imitated from Johannes Secundus

Tell me, lasses, have ye seen
Lately wandering o'er the green,
Beauty's son, a little boy,
Full of frolic, mirth, and joy ?
If you know his shelter, say ;
He's from Venus gone astray.
   Tell me, lasses, have ye seen
   Such a one trip o'er the green ?

By his marks the god you'll know :
O'er his shoulder hangs a bow,
And a quiver fraught with darts,
Poison sure to human hearts ;
Though he's naked, little, blind,
He can triumph o'er the mind.
   Tell me, lasses, have ye seen
   Such a one trip o'er the green ?

Subtle as the light'ning's wound
Is his piercing arrow found ;
While the bosom'd heart it pains,
No external mark remains ;
Reason's shield itself is broke
By the unsuspected stroke.
   Tell me, lasses, have ye seen
   Such a one trip o'er the green ?

357

SAMUEL DERRICK

Oft the urchin's seen to lie
Basking in the sunny eye ;
Or his destin'd prey he seeks
On the maiden's rosy cheeks ;
Snowy breasts, or curling hair,
Oft conceal his pleasing snare.
   Tell me, lasses, have ye seen
   Such a one trip o'er the green ?

She that the recess reveals
Where the god himself conceals,
Shall a kiss receive this night
From him who is her heart's delight ;
To Venus let her bring the boy,
She shall taste love's sweetest joy.
   Tell me, lasses, have ye seen
   Such a one trip o'er the green ?

EDWARD LOVIBOND (1724-1775)

Song to ——

What ! bid me seek another fair
   In untried paths of female wiles ?
And posies wreathe of other hair,
   And bask secure in other smiles ?
Thy friendly stars no longer prize,
And light my course by other eyes ?

Ah no !—My dying lips shall close,
   Unalter'd love, as faith, professing ;
Nor, praising Him who life bestows,
   Forget who makes that gift a blessing.
My last address to Heaven is due ;
The last-but-one is all—to you.

EDWARD LOVIBOND

Inscription for a Fountain

O you, who mark what flowerets gay,
    What gales, what odours breathing near,
What sheltering shades from summer's ray
    Allure my spring to linger here :

Yet see me quit this margin green,
    Yet see me, deaf to pleasure's call,
Explore the thirsty haunts of men,
    Yet see my bounty flow for all.

O learn from me—no partial rill,
    No slumbering, selfish pool be you ;
But social laws alike fulfil ;
    O flow for all creation too !

The Rev. WILLIAM MASON* (1724-1797)

Epitaph on Mrs. Mason
In Bristol Cathedral

Take, holy earth ! all that my soul holds dear :
    Take that best gift which Heaven so lately gave :
To Bristol's fount I bore with trembling care
    Her faded form : she bow'd to taste the wave
And died. Does Youth, does Beauty, read the line ?
    Does sympathetic fear their breasts alarm ?
Speak, dead Maria ! breathe a strain divine :
    Ev'n from the grave thou shalt have power to charm.
Bid them be chaste, be innocent, like thee ;
    Bid them in duty's sphere as meekly move ;
And if so fair, from vanity as free ;
    As firm in friendship, and as fond in love.
†Tell them, though 'tis an awful thing to die,
    ('Twas ev'n to thee) yet the dread path once trod,
Heav'n lifts its everlasting portals high,
    And bids the pure in heart behold their God.

* Gray's biographer and friend.
† The last four lines (almost the only tolerable ones) of this epitaph are by Thomas Gray.

WILLIAM MASON

Epitaph

on the Honourable Miss Drummond, in the Church of Brodsworth, Yorkshire

Here sleeps what once was beauty, once was grace ;
    Grace, that with tenderness and sense combin'd
To form that harmony of soul and face,
    Where beauty shines the mirror of the mind.
Such was the maid, that in the morn of youth,
    In virgin innocence, in nature's pride,
Blest with each art that owes its charm to truth,
    Sunk in her father's fond embrace, and died.
He weeps : O venerate the holy tear :
    Faith lends her aid to ease Affliction's load ;
The parent mourns his child upon her bier,
    The Christian yields an Angel to his God.

The Rev. JOHN NEWTON, D.D.* (1725-1807)

The Name of Jesus

How sweet the name of Jesus sounds
    In a believer's ear !
It soothes his sorrows, heals his wounds,
    And drives away his fear.

It makes the wounded spirit whole,
    And calms the troubled breast ;
'Tis Manna to the hungry soul,
    And to the weary rest.

Dear name ! the rock on which I build,
    My shield and hiding-place ;
My never-failing treas'ry fill'd
    With boundless stores of grace.

* Cowper's collaborator in the *Olney Hymns*.

By Thee my prayers acceptance gain,
   Although with sin defil'd ;
Satan accuses me in vain,
   And I am own'd a child.

Jesus ! my Shepherd, Husband, Friend,
   My Prophet, Priest, and King ;
My Lord, my Life, my Way, my End,
   Accept the praise I bring.

Weak is the effort of my heart,
   And cold my warmest thought ;
But when I see Thee as Thou art,
   I'll praise Thee as I ought.

Till then I would Thy love proclaim
   With ev'ry fleeting breath ;
And may the music of Thy name
   Refresh my soul in death.

SAMUEL BOYCE (——1775)

Daphne

Young Daphne was the prettiest maid
   The eyes of love could see ;
And but one fault the charmer had,
   'Twas cruelty to me.
No swain that e'er the nymph ador'd
   Was fonder, or was younger ;
Yet when her pity I implor'd,
   'Twas " Stay a little longer."

It chanc'd I met the blooming fair
   One May-morn in the grove ;
When Cupid whisper'd in my ear,
   " Now, now's the time for love."
I clasp'd the maid, it wak'd her pride,
   " What, did I mean to wrong her ? "
" Not so, my gentle dear ! " I cried,
   " But love will stay no longer."

Then kneeling at her feet I swore,
   How much I lov'd, how well ;
And that my heart, which beat for her,
   With her should ever dwell.
Consent stood speaking in the eye
   Of all my care's prolonger ;
Yet soft she utter'd, with a sigh,
   " Oh, stay a little longer."

The conflict in her soul I saw,
   'Twixt virtue and desire ;
" Oh, come," I cried, " let Hymen's law
   Give sanction to love's fire."
Ye lovers, guess how great my joys ;
   Could rapture well prove stronger ?
When Virtue spoke, in Daphne's voice,
   " You now shall stay no longer."

Sally

No nymph that trips the verdant plains
   With Sally can compare ;
She wins the hearts of all the swains,
   And rivals all the fair.
The beams of Sol delight and cheer,
   While summer seasons roll ;
But Sally's smiles can all the year
   Give summer to the soul.

When from the east the morning ray
   Illumes the world below,
Her presence bids the god of day
   With emulation glow :
Fresh beauties deck the painted ground ;
   Birds sweeter notes prepare ;
The playful lambkins skip around,
   And hail the sister fair.

The lark but strains his liquid throat
   To bid the maid rejoice ;
And mimics, while he swells the note,
   The sweetness of her voice :
The fanning Zephyrs round her play,
   While Flora sheds perfume ;
And every floweret seems to say,
   " I but for Sally bloom."

The am'rous youths her charms proclaim ;
   From morn to eve their tale ;
Her beauty and unspotted fame
   Make vocal every vale.
The stream, meandering through the mead,
   Her echo'd name conveys ;
And every voice, and every reed,
   Is tun'd to Sally's praise.

No more shall blithesome lass and swain
   To mirthful wake resort ;
Nor every May-morn on the plain
   Advance in rural sport :
No more shall gush the gurgling rill,
   Nor music wake the grove ;
Nor flocks look snow-like on the hill,
   When I forget to love.

The Confession

Oh, Sephalissa ! dearest maid !
   So blooming, kind, and free,
The goddess of Cythera's shade
   Is not so fair as thee !
Thy image always fills my mind ;
   The theme of every song :
I'm fix'd to thee alone, I find,
   But ask not for how long.
The fair in general I've admir'd ;
   Have oft been false and true ;

And when the last my fancy tir'd,
   It wander'd round to you.
Then while I can I'll be sincere,
   As turtles to their mates :
This moment's yours and mine, my dear !
   The next, you know, is Fate's.

To the Muse

I poetry and mirth admire ;
   Sink sorrow in the sea !
I care not who to thrones aspire,
   For what are Kings to me ?
Celestial Muse ! delightful maid !
   Pluck each poetic flower ;
And weave a crown, the brows to shade
   Of her whom I adore.
Attune the harp, the pipe inspire,
   The voice of music raise ;
'Tis Celia fans your sacred fire,
   And Celia's be the praise.

Epigram

Quoth his heir to Sir John,
   " I'd to travel begone,
Like others, the world for to see."
   Quoth Sir John to his heir,
   " Prithee, novice, forbear,
For I'd not have the world to see thee."

LADY DOROTHEA DU BOIS, *née* ANNESLEY
(1728-1774)

Song

A scholar first my love implor'd,
And then an empty, titled lord ;
The pedant talk'd in lofty strains ;
Alas ! his Lordship wanted brains :
I listen'd not to one or t'other,
But straight referr'd them to my mother.

LADY DOROTHEA DU BOIS

A poet next my love assail'd,
A lawyer hop'd to have prevail'd ;
The bard too much approv'd himself ;
The lawyer thirsted after pelf :
I listen'd not to one or t'other,
But still referr'd them to my mother.

An officer my heart would storm,
A miser sought me too, in form ;
But Mars was over-free and bold ;
The miser's heart was in his gold :
I listen'd not to one or t'other,
Referring still unto my mother.

And after them some twenty more
Successless were, as those before ;
When Damon, lovely Damon, came !
Our hearts straight felt a mutual flame ;
I vow'd I'd have him, and no other,
Without referring to my mother.

OLIVER GOLDSMITH, M.B. (1728-1774)

Song

From " The Vicar of Wakefield "

When lovely woman stoops to folly,
  And finds too late that men betray,
What charm can soothe her melancholy,
  What art can wash her guilt away ?

The only art her guilt to cover,
  To hide her shame from every eye,
To give repentance to her lover,
  And wring his bosom, is—to die.

OLIVER GOLDSMITH

Song

From " The Captivity,"

O Memory, thou fond deceiver,
  Still importunate and vain ;
To former joys recurring ever,
  And turning all the past to pain ;

Hence, intruder, most distressing,
  Seek the happy and the free :
The wretch who wants each other blessing,
  Ever wants a friend in thee.

Another Song

From the same

To the last moment of his breath
  On hope the wretch relies ;
And e'en the pang preceding death
  Bids expectation rise.

Hope, like the gleaming taper's light,
  Adorns and cheers our way ;
And still, as darker grows the night,
  Emits a brighter ray.

On a Beautiful Youth Struck Blind with Lightning

(Imitated from the Spanish)

Sure 'twas by Providence design'd,
  Rather in pity, than in hate,
That he should be, like Cupid, blind,
  To save him from Narcissus' fate.

OLIVER GOLDSMITH

The Gift

To Iris, in Bow Street, Covent Garden

Say, cruel Iris, pretty rake,
    Dear mercenary beauty,
What annual offering shall I make,
    Expressive of my duty ?

My heart, a victim to thine eyes,
    Should I at once deliver,
Say, would the angry fair one prize
    The gift, who slights the giver ?

A bill, a jewel, watch, or toy,
    My rivals give—and let 'em ;
If gems, or gold, impart a joy,
    I'll give them—when I get 'em.

I'll give—but not the full-blown rose,
    Or rose-bud more in fashion ;
Such short-liv'd offerings but disclose
    A transitory passion.

I'll give thee something yet unpaid,
    Not less sincere, than civil :
I'll give thee— Ah ! too charming maid,
    I'll give thee—to the devil.

The Clown's Reply

John Trott was desired by two witty peers
To tell them the reason why asses had ears ?
" An't please you," quoth John, " I'm not given to letters,
Nor dare I pretend to know more than my betters ;
Howe'er, from this time I shall ne'er see your graces,
As I hope to be sav'd ! without thinking on asses."

OLIVER GOLDSMITH

An Elegy on that Glory of her Sex, Mrs. Mary Blaize

Good people all, with one accord,
    Lament for Madame Blaize,
Who never wanted a good word—
    From those who spoke her praise.

The needy seldom pass'd her door,
    And always found her kind ;
She freely lent to all the poor,—
    Who left a pledge behind.

She strove the neighbourhood to please,
    With manners wondrous winning,
And never follow'd wicked ways,—
    Unless when she was sinning.

At Church, in silks and satins new,
    With hoop of monstrous size,
She never slumber'd in her pew,—
    But when she shut her eyes.

Her love was sought, I do aver,
    By twenty beaux and more ;
The king himself has follow'd her,—
    When she has walk'd before.

But now her wealth and finery fled,
    Her hangers-on cut short all ;
The doctors found, when she was dead,—
    Her last disorder mortal.

Let us lament, in sorrow sore,
    For Kent-Street well may say,
That had she liv'd a twelve-month more,—
    She had not died to-day.

OLIVER GOLDSMITH

Elegy on the Death of a Mad Dog

Good people all, of every sort,
  Give ear unto my song ;
And if you find it wond'rous short,
  It cannot hold you long.

In Islington there was a man,
  Of whom the world might say,
That still a godly race he ran,
  Whene'er he went to pray.

A kind and gentle heart he had,
  To comfort friends and foes ;
The naked every day he clad,
  When he put on his clothes.

And in that town a dog was found,
  As many dogs there be,
Both mongrel, puppy, whelp, and hound,
  And curs of low degree.

This dog and man at first were friends ;
  But, when a pique began,
The dog, to gain some private ends,
  Went mad and bit the man.

Around from all the neighbouring streets
  The wond'ring neighbours ran,
And swore the dog had lost his wits,
  To bite so good a man.

The wound it seem'd both sore and sad
  To every Christian eye ;
And while they swore the dog was mad,
  They swore the man would die.

But soon a wonder came to light,
  That show'd the rogues they lied :
The man recover'd of the bite,
  The dog it was that died.

The Rev. THOMAS WARTON,* Poet Laureate
(1728-1790)

Ode to Sleep

On this my pensive pillow, gentle Sleep !
Descend, in all thy downy plumage drest :
Wipe with thy wings these eyes that wake to weep,
And place thy crown of poppies on my breast.

O steep my senses in oblivion's balm,
And soothe my throbbing pulse with lenient hand ;
This tempest of my boiling blood becalm !—
Despair grows mild at thy supreme command.

Yet ah ! in vain, familiar with the gloom,
And sadly toiling through the tedious night,
I seek sweet slumber, while that virgin bloom,
For ever hovering, haunts my wretched sight.

Nor would the dawning day my sorrows charm :
Black midnight, and the blaze of noon, alike
To me appear, while with uplifted arm
Death stands prepar'd, but still delays, to strike.

Sonnet

written in Dugdale's " Monasticon "

Deem not devoid of elegance the Sage,
By Fancy's genuine feelings unbeguil'd,
Of painful Pedantry the poring child,
Who turns, of these proud domes, th' historic page,
Now sunk by Time, and Henry's fiercer rage.
Think'st thou the warbling Muses never smil'd
On his lone hours ? Ingenuous views engage
His thoughts, on themes, unclassic falsely styl'd,
Intent. While cloister'd Piety displays
Her mouldering roll, the piercing eye explores
New manners, and the pomp of elder days,
Whence culls the pensive bard his pictur'd stores.
Nor rough, nor barren, are the winding ways
Of hoar Antiquity, but strewn with flowers.

* Also Professor of Poetry at Oxford. Author of the famous
History of English Poetry.

JOHN CUNNINGHAM (1729-1773)

Morning

In the barn the tenant cock,
　　Close to partlet perch'd on high,
Briskly crows, (the shepherd's clock !)
　　Jocund that the morning's nigh.

Swiftly from the mountain's brow
　　Shadows, nurs'd by night, retire :
And the peeping sunbeam now
　　Paints with gold the village spire.

Philomel forsakes the thorn,
　　Plaintive where she prates at night ;
And the lark, to meet the morn,
　　Soars beyond the shepherd's sight.

From the low-roof'd cottage ridge
　　See the chattering swallow spring ;
Darting through the one-arch'd bridge
　　Quick she dips her dappled wing.

Now the pine-tree's waving top
　　Gently greets the morning gale :
Kidlings, now, begin to crop
　　Daisies on the dewy dale.

From the balmy sweets uncloy'd,
　　(Restless till her task be done)
Now the busy bee's employ'd
　　Sipping dew before the sun.

Trickling through the crevic'd rock,
　　Where the limpid stream distils,
Sweet refreshment waits the flock,
　　When 'tis sun-drove from the hills.

JOHN CUNNINGHAM

Colin's for the promis'd corn
   (Ere the harvest hopes are ripe)
Anxious ; whilst the huntsman's horn,
   Boldly sounding, drowns his pipe.

Sweet, O sweet, the warbling throng,
   On the white emblossom'd spray !
Nature's universal song
   Echoes to the rising day.

The Narcissus

As pendent o'er the limpid stream
   I bow'd my snowy pride,
And languish'd in a fruitless flame
   For what the Fates denied ;
The fair Pastora chanc'd to pass,
   With such an angel air,
I saw her in the wat'ry glass,
   And lov'd the rival fair.

Ye Fates, no longer let me pine
   A self-admiring sweet,
Permit me by your grace divine
   To kiss the fair one's feet :
That if by chance the gentle maid
   My fragrance should admire,
I may, upon her bosom laid,
   In sister sweets expire.

Fancy

A song in a Pantomime Entertainment

Fancy leads the fetter'd senses
   Captives to her fond control ;
Merit may have rich pretences,
   But 'tis Fancy fires the soul.

Far beyond the bounds of meaning
  Fancy flies, a fairy queen !
Fancy, wit and worth disdaining,
  Gives the prize to Harlequin.

If the virgin's false, forgive her,
  Fancy was your only foe :
Cupid claims the dart and quiver,
  But 'tis Fancy twangs the bow.

Delia : a Pastoral

The gentle swan with graceful pride
  Her glossy plumage laves,
And sailing down the silver tide
  Divides the whispering waves.
The silver tide, that wandering flows,
  Sweet to the bird must be !
But not so sweet, blithe Cupid knows,
  As Delia is to me.

A parent bird in plaintive mood
  On yonder fruit-tree sung,
And still the pendent nest she view'd,
  That held her callow young :
Dear to the mother's fluttering heart,
  The genial brood must be :
But not so dear (the thousandth part !)
  As Delia is to me.

The roses that my brow surround,
  Were natives of the dale :
Scarce pluck'd, and in a garland bound,
  Before their sweets grew pale !
My vital bloom would thus be froze,
  If luckless torn from thee ;
For what the root is to the rose,
  My Delia is to me.

373

Two doves I found like new-fall'n snow,
    So white the beauteous pair !
The birds to Delia I'll bestow,
    They're like her bosom fair !
When, in their chaste connubial love,
    My secret wish she'll see ;
Such mutual bliss as turtles prove
    May Delia share with me.

An Epigram

A member of the modern great
    Pass'd Sawney with his budget ;
The peer was in his car of state,
    The tinker forc'd to trudge it.

But Sawney shall receive the praise
    His lordship would parade for ;
One's debtor for his dapple greys,
    And t'other's shoes are paid for.

On Alderman W——

The History of his Life

That he was born, it cannot be denied,
He eat, drank, slept, talk'd politics, and died.

Newcastle Beer

When Fame brought the news of Great Britain's success,
    And told at Olympus each Gallic defeat ;
Glad Mars sent by Mercury orders express,
    To summon the deities all to a treat :
        Blithe Comus was plac'd
        To guide the gay feast,
And freely declar'd there was choice of good cheer ;
        Yet vow'd to his thinking,
        For exquisite drinking,
Their nectar was nothing to Newcastle beer.

The great god of war, to encourage the fun,
  And humour the taste of his whimsical guest,
Sent a message that moment to Moor's for a tun
  Of stingo, the stoutest, the brightest and best :
      No gods, they all swore,
      Regal'd so before,
With liquor so lively, so potent and clear :
      And each deified fellow
      Got jovially mellow,
In honour, brave boys, of our Newcastle beer.

Apollo, perceiving his talents refine,
  Repents he drank Helicon water so long :
He bow'd, being ask'd by the musical Nine,
  And gave the gay board an extempore song ;
      But ere he began
      He toss'd off his can ;
There's nought like good liquor the fancy to clear :
      Then sang with great merit
      The flavour and spirit
His godship had found in the Newcastle beer.

'Twas stingo like this made Alcides so bold ;
  It brac'd up his nerves, and enliven'd his powers :
And his mystical club, that did wonders of old,
  Was nothing, my lads, but such liquor as ours.
      That horrible crew
      That Hercules slew,
Were Poverty, Calumny, Trouble and Fear :
      Such a club would you borrow,
      To drive away sorrow,
Apply for a *quantum* of Newcastle beer.

Ye youngsters, so diffident, languid, and pale !
  Whom love, like the cholic, so rudely infests ;
Take a cordial of this, 'twill *probatum* prevail,
  And drive the cur Cupid away from your breasts :
      Dull whining despise,
      Grow rosy and wise,

No longer the jest of good fellows appear ;
    Bid adieu to your folly,
    Get drunk and be jolly,
And smoke o'er a tankard of Newcastle beer.

Ye fanciful folk, for whom physic prescribes,
   Whom bolus and potion have harass'd to death !
Ye wretches, whom law and her ill-looking tribes,
   Have hunted about 'till you're quite out of breath !
    Here's shelter and ease,
    No craving for fees,
No danger, no doctor, no bailiff is near !
    Your spirits this raises,
    It cures your diseases,
There's freedom and health in our Newcastle beer.

The Rt. Rev. THOMAS PERCY,* D.D.
Bishop of Dromore (1729-1811)

Song

  O Nancy, wilt thou go with me,
    Nor sigh to leave the flaunting town :
  Can silent glens have charms for thee,
    The lowly cot and russet gown ?
  No longer dress'd in silken sheen,
    No longer deck'd with jewels rare,
  Say, canst thou quit each courtly scene,
    Where thou wert fairest of the fair ?

  O Nancy ! when thou'rt far away,
    Wilt thou not cast a wish behind ?
  Say, canst thou face the parching ray,
    Nor shrink before the wintry wind ?
  O can that soft and gentle mien
    Extremes of hardship learn to bear,
  Nor, sad, regret each courtly scene,
    Where thou wert fairest of the fair ?

* Editor of the *Reliques of Ancient English Poetry*.

THOMAS PERCY

O Nancy ! canst thou love so true,
  Through perils keen with me to go,
Or, when thy swain mishap shall rue,
  To share with him the pang of woe ?
Say, should disease or pain befall,
  Wilt thou assume the nurse's care,
Nor, wistful, those gay scenes recall,
  Where thou wert fairest of the fair ?

And when at last thy love shall die,
  Wilt thou receive his parting breath ?
Wilt thou repress each struggling sigh,
  And cheer with smiles the bed of death ?
And wilt thou o'er his breathless clay
  Strew flowers, and drop each tender tear,
Nor *then* regret those scenes so gay,
  Where thou wert fairest of the fair ?

JOHN WEST, Earl DE LA WARR (1729-1777)

Farewell to the Maids of Honour

*on his being promoted to his late father's troop, and resigning
the place of Vice-Chamberlain to the Queen*

Ye maids, who Britain's court bedeck,
Miss Wrottesly, Beauclerk, Tryon, Keck,
  Miss Meadows, and Boscawen !
A dismal tale I have to tell ;
This is to bid you all farewell :
  Farewell ! for I am going.

I leave you, girls ; indeed 'tis true,
Although to be esteem'd by you
  Has ever been my pride :
'Tis often done at court, you know ;
I leave my dearest friends, and go
  Over to t'other side.

No longer shall we laugh and chat
In th' outer room on this and that,
    Until the Queen shall call :
Our gracious King has call'd me now ;
Nay, holds a stick up too, I vow,
    And so God bless you all !

They tell me that one word a day
From him is worth the whole you say,
    Fair ladies, in a year :
A word from him I highly prize—
But who can leave your beauteous eyes
    Without one tender tear ?

No longer shall I now be seen
Handing along our matchless Queen,
    So generous, good, and kind ;
While one by one each smiling lass
First drops a curtsey as we pass,
    Then trips along behind.

Adieu, my much-lov'd golden key !
No longer to be worn by me,
    Adorn'd with ribband blue ;
Which late I heard look'd ill and pale—
I thought it but an idle tale,
    But now believe 'twas true.

Farewell, my good Lord Harcourt, too !
What can, alas ! your Lordship do
    Alone among the maids ?
You soon must some assistance ask ;
You'll have a very arduous task,
    Unless you call for aids.

Great is the charge you have in care ;
Indeed, my pretty maidens fair,
    His situation's nice :
As Chamberlain, we shall expect
That he, sole guardian, shall protect
    Six maids, without a vice.

Sir JAMES MARRIOTT, Knight, LL.D., Judge of the
High Court of Admiralty (1730 ?-1803)

Arion : an Ode

Queen of each sacred sound, sweet child of air,
Who sitting thron'd upon the vaulted sky,
Dost catch the notes which undulating fly,
Oft wafted up to thy exalted sphere,
On the soft bosom of each rolling cloud,
    Charming thy list'ning ear
With strains that bid the panting lover die :
Or laughing mirth, or tender grief inspire,
    Or with full chorus loud
Which lift our holy hope, or fan the hero's fire :
  Enchanting Harmony, 'tis thine to cheer
    The soul by woe which sinks opprest,
    From sorrow's eye to wipe the tear,
And on the bleeding wound to pour the balmy rest.

  'Twas when the winds were roaring loud,
  And Ocean swell'd his billows high,
  By savage hands condemn'd to die,
Rais'd on the stern the trembling Lesbian stood ;
  All pale he heard the tempest blow,
  As on the wat'ry grave below
    He fix'd his weeping eye.
  Ah ! hateful lust of impious gold,
  What can thy mighty rage withhold,
Deaf to the melting powers of Harmony !
  But ere the bard unpitied dies,
  Again his soothing art he tries,
    Again he sweeps the strings ;
    Slowly sad the notes arise,
While thus in plaintive sounds the sweet musician sings.

    " From beneath the coral cave
    Circled with the silver wave,
  Where with wreaths of emerald crown'd
  Ye lead the festive dance around,
  Daughters of Nereus, hear and save !

Ye Tritons, hear, whose blast can swell
    With mighty sounds the twisted shell ;
And you, ye sister Syrens, hear,
        Ever beauteous, ever sweet,
    Who lull the list'ning pilot's ear
With magic song, and softly breath'd deceit.
    By all the gods who subject roll
From gushing urns their tribute to the main,
    By him who bids the winds to roar,
    By him whose trident shakes the shore,
If e'er for you I raise the sacred strain
When pious mariners your power adore,
    Daughters of Nereus, hear and save."

He sung, and from the coral cave,
    Circled with the silver wave,
        With pitying ear
        The Nereids hear.
    Gently the waters flowing,
    The winds now ceas'd their blowing,
In silence listening to his tuneful lay.
    Around the barque's sea-beaten side
        The sacred dolphin play'd,
    And sportive dash'd the briny tide :
The joyous omen soon the bard survey'd,
And sprung with bolder leap to try the watery way.
    On his scaly back now riding,
    O'er the curling billow gliding,
    Again with bold triumphant hand
        He bade the notes aspire,
        Again to joy attun'd the lyre,
Forgot each danger past, and reach'd secure the land.

JOHN SCOTT of Amwell* (1730-1783)

The Drum

I hate that drum's discordant sound,
Parading round and round and round :
To thoughtless youth it pleasure yields,
And lures from cities and from fields,
To sell their liberty for charms
Of tawdry lace, and glittering arms ;
And when Ambition's voice commands,
To march, and fight, and fall in foreign lands.

I hate that drum's discordant sound,
Parading round and round and round :
To me it talks of ravag'd plains,
And burning towns, and ruin'd swains,
And mangled limbs, and dying groans,
And widows' tears, and orphans' moans ;
And all that Misery's hand bestows,
To fill the catalogue of human woes.

MARY WHATELY, later Mrs. DARWALL (*circa* 1764)

Song

Ye verdant woods, ye crystal streams,
    On whose enamell'd side
I shar'd the sun's refreshing beams,
    When Damon was my guide ;
No more your shades, or murmurs, please
    Poor Sylvia's love-sick mind ;
No rural scenes can give me ease,
    Since Damon proves unkind.

Come, gloomy eve, and veil the sky
    With clouds of darkest hue ;
Wither, ye plants, ye flowerets die,
    Uncheer'd with balmy dew :

* A Quaker poet.

381

Ye wildly-warbling birds, no more
  Your songs can soothe my mind ;
My hours of joy, alas ! are o'er,
  Since Damon proves unkind.

I 'll hie me to some dreary grove,
  For sighing sorrow made ;
Where nought but plaintive strains of love
  Resound through every shade ;
Where the sad turtle's melting grief,
  With Philomela's join'd,
Alone shall yield my heart relief,
  Since Damon proves unkind.

Be warn'd by Sylvia's fate, ye maids,
  And shun the soft deceit ;
Though Love's own eloquence persuades,
  'Tis all a dangerous cheat ;
Fly, quickly fly the faithless swain,
  His baffled arts despise ;
So shall you live exempt from pain,
  While hapless Sylvia dies.

THOMAS JOEL (*floruit circa* 1766)

Aspiration

An Ode

Why, my soft am'rous passions, do you glow
At earthly scenes ? Why cleave to things below ?
Away from Folly's paths, from Pleasure's seat ;
  Away from Pow'r's domain, from Beauty's throne !
My thoughts now venture from your low retreat,
  And soar to reach the Infinite Unknown !

THOMAS JOEL

Where shall I find Him ? How direct the eye
Through boundless scenes of vast immensity ?
I reason ; yet in vain : my doubtful guide
    Leads me to mazes dark and intricate,
Only to mortify my daring pride ;
    And points the mysteries of the present state.

Come good, almighty, glorious Excellence,
Dispel the gloom, and nearer strike my sense ;
A *Shechinah* divine I would behold ;
    Or let me, silent, listening, trembling, hear
That still instructive voice, which spoke of old
    And utter'd wisdom in a Samuel's ear.

By eagle's pinions borne, plac'd let me be
On Sinai's mount, and there Thy Glory see :
Oh ! for an angel's wing to quit this sphere !
    Roll'd up in clouds, fain would my longing soul
Something about Thy matchless Greatness hear,
    While sovereign Grace should all my fears control.

It cannot be : the soul immur'd must lie
Within the prison of mortality ;
She, only through the avenues of sense,
    Can view, like fleeting shadows of the night,
Faint glimm'rings of divine intelligence,
    And hears from faith what is denied to sight.

Yet one important moment shall remove
The gloomy veil, and show me Him I love :
Yes, Death will lead me from my dread abode ;
    Then, through thick clouds and darkness, shall I rise
Up to the secret dwelling of my God,
    And see His splendour with immortal eyes.

The Rev. SAMUEL BISHOP (1731-1795)

To his Wife, with a Knife

A knife, dear girl, cuts love, they say—
Mere modish love perhaps it may ;
For any tool of any kind
Can sep'rate what was never join'd.
The knife that cuts our love in two
Will have much tougher work to do :
Must cut your softness, truth, and spirit
Down to the vulgar size of merit ;
To level yours with modern taste,
Must cut a world of sense to waste ;
And from your single beauty's store,
Clip what would dizen out a score.
That self-same blade from me must sever
Sensation, judgment, sight—for ever !
All memory of endearments past,
All hope of comforts long to last,
All that makes fourteen years with you
A summer—and a short one too :
All that affection feels and fears,
When hours, without you, seem like years.
Till that be done,—and I'd as soon
Believe this knife will chip the moon,—
Accept my present undeterr'd,
And leave their proverbs to the herd.
If in a kiss—delicious treat !
Your lips acknowledge the receipt ;
Love, fond of such substantial fare,
And proud to play the glutton there,
All thoughts of cutting will disdain,
Save only—" cut and come again."

SAMUEL BISHOP

To his Wife

*on the fourteenth anniversary of her Wedding-day,
with a Ring*

" Thee, Mary, with this ring I wed,"
So fourteen years ago I said—
Behold another ring ! " For what ? "
To wed thee o'er again—why not ?

With the first ring I married youth,
Grace, beauty, innocence, and truth ;
Taste long admir'd, sense long rever'd,
And all my Molly then appear'd.

If she, by merit since disclos'd,
Prove twice the woman I suppos'c,
I plead that double merit now,
To justify a double vow.

Here then, to-day, with faith as sure,
With ardour as intense and pure,
As when amidst the rites divine
I took thy troth, and plighted mine,
To thee, sweet girl, my second ring,
A token and a pledge I bring ;
With this I wed, till death us part,
Thy riper virtues to my heart ;
Those virtues which, before untried,
The wife has added to the bride—
Those virtues, whose progressive claim,
Endearing wedlock's very name,
My soul enjoys, my song approves,
For conscience' sake as well as love's.

For why ? They show me every hour
Honour's high thought, affection's power,
Discretion's deed, sound judgment's sentence,
And teach me all things—but repentance.

WILLIAM COWPER (1731-1800)

Olney Hymns

I

Lovest thou Me ?—JOHN xxi. 16

Hark, my soul ! it is the Lord ;
'Tis thy Saviour, hear His word ;
Jesus speaks, and speaks to thee ;
" Say, poor sinner, lov'st thou me ?

" I deliver'd thee when bound,
And, when wounded, heal'd thy wound ;
Sought thee wandering, set thee right,
Turn'd thy darkness into light.

" Can a woman's tender care
Cease, towards the child she bare ?
Yes, she may forgetful be,
Yet will I remember thee.

" Mine is an unchanging love,
Higher than the heights above ;
Deeper than the depths beneath,
Free and faithful, strong as death.

" Thou shalt see my glory soon,
When the work of grace is done ;
Partner of my throne shalt be ;
Say, poor sinner, lov'st thou me ? "

Lord, it is my chief complaint,
That my love is weak and faint ;
Yet I love Thee and adore,
Oh for grace to love Thee more.

WILLIAM COWPER

II

On opening a place for Social Prayer

Jesus, where'er Thy people meet,
There they behold Thy mercy-seat ;
Where'er they seek Thee Thou art found,
And every place is hallow'd ground.

For Thou, within no walls confin'd,
Inhabitest the humble mind ;
Such ever bring Thee, where they come,
And going, take Thee to their home.

Dear Shepherd of Thy chosen few !
Thy former mercies here renew ;
Here, to our waiting hearts, proclaim
The sweetness of Thy saving name.

Here may we prove the power of prayer,
To strengthen faith, and sweeten care ;
To teach our faint desires to rise,
And bring all Heaven before our eyes.

Behold ! at Thy commanding word,
We stretch the curtain and the cord ;
Come Thou, and fill this wider space,
And help us with a large increase.

Lord, we are few, but Thou art near ;
Nor short Thine arm, nor deaf Thine ear ;
Oh rend the heavens, come quickly down,
And make a thousand hearts Thine own.

WILLIAM COWPER

III

Light Shining out of Darkness

God moves in a mysterious way,
   His wonders to perform ;
He plants His footsteps in the sea,
   And rides upon the storm.

Deep in unfathomable mines
   Of never failing skill ;
He treasures up His bright designs,
   And works His sovereign will.

Ye fearful saints fresh courage take,
   The clouds ye so much dread
Are big with mercy, and shall break
   In blessings on your head.

Judge not the Lord by feeble sense,
   But trust Him for His grace ;
Behind a frowning providence,
   He hides a smiling face.

His purposes will ripen fast,
   Unfolding every hour ;
The bud may have a bitter taste,
   But sweet will be the flower.

Blind unbelief is sure to err,
   And scan His work in vain ;
God is His own interpreter,
   And He will make it plain.

WILLIAM COWPER

Sonnet to Mrs. Unwin

Mary ! I want a lyre with other strings ;
Such aid from Heaven as some have feign'd they drew
An eloquence scarce given to mortals, new,
And undebas'd by praise of meaner things !
That, ere through age or woe I shed my wings,
I may record thy worth, with honour due,
In verse as musical as thou art true,—
Verse, that immortalises whom it sings !
But thou hast little need : there is a book,
By seraphs writ with beams of heavenly light,
On which the eyes of God not rarely look ;
A chronicle of actions just and bright !
   There all thy deeds, my faithful Mary, shine,
   And since thou own'st that praise, I spare thee mine.

To Mary

The twentieth year is well-nigh past,
Since first our sky was overcast ;
Ah would that this might be the last !
         My Mary !

Thy spirits have a fainter flow,
I see thee daily weaker grow—
'Twas my distress that brought thee low,
         My Mary !

Thy needles, once a shining store,
For my sake restless heretofore,
Now rust disus'd, and shine no more,
         My Mary !

For though thou gladly wouldst fulfil
The same kind office for me still,
Thy sight now seconds not thy will,
         My Mary !

But well thou play'd'st the housewife's part,
And all thy threads with magic art
Have wound themselves about this heart,
           My Mary !

Thy indistinct expressions seem
Like language utter'd in a dream ;
Yet me they charm, whate'er the theme,
           My Mary !

Thy silver locks, once auburn bright,
Are still more lovely in my sight
Than golden beams of orient light,
           My Mary !

For could I view nor them nor thee,
What sight worth seeing could I see ?
The sun would rise in vain for me,
           My Mary !

Partakers of thy sad decline,
Thy hands their little force resign ;
Yet, gently prest, press gently mine,
           My Mary !

And then I feel that still I hold
A richer store ten thousandfold
Than misers fancy in their gold,
           My Mary !

Such feebleness of limbs thou prov'st,
That now at every step thou mov'st
Upheld by two ; yet still thou lov'st,
           My Mary !

And still to love, though prest with ill,
In wintry age to feel no chill,
With me is to be lovely still,
           My Mary !

But ah ! by constant heed I know,
How oft the sadness that I show
Transforms thy smiles to looks of woe,
My Mary !

And should my future lot be cast
With much resemblance of the past,
Thy worn-out heart will break at last,
My Mary !

The Poplar-Field

The poplars are fell'd, farewell to the shade
And the whispering sound of the cool colonnade,
The winds play no longer, and sing in the leaves,
Nor Ouse on his bosom their image receives.

Twelve years have elaps'd since I first took a view
Of my favourite field and the bank where they grew,
And now in the grass behold they are laid,
And the tree is my seat that once lent me a shade.

The blackbird has fled to another retreat
Where the hazels afford him a screen from the heat,
And the scene where his melody charm'd me before,
Resounds with his sweet-flowing ditty no more.

My fugitive years are all hasting away,
And I must ere long lie as lowly as they,
With a turf on my breast, and a stone at my head,
Ere another such grove shall arise in its stead.

'Tis a sight to engage me, if anything can,
To muse on the perishing pleasures of man ;
Though his life be a dream, his enjoyments, I see,
Have a being less durable even than he.

On the Loss of the Royal George

Toll for the brave—
The brave ! that are no more :
All sunk beneath the wave,
Fast by their native shore.
Eight hundred of the brave,
Whose courage well was tried,
Had made the vessel heel
And laid her on her side ;
A land-breeze shook the shrouds,
And she was overset ;
Down went the Royal George,
With all her crew complete.

Toll for the brave—
Brave Kempenfelt is gone,
His last sea-fight is fought ;
His work of glory done.
It was not in the battle,
No tempest gave the shock,
She sprang no fatal leak,
She ran upon no rock ;
His sword was in the sheath,
His fingers held the pen,
When Kempenfelt went down
With twice four hundred men.

Weigh the vessel up,
Once dreaded by our foes,
And mingle with your cup
The tears that England owes ;
Her timbers yet are sound,
And she may float again,
Full charg'd with English thunder,
And plough the distant main ;
But Kempenfelt is gone,
His victories are o'er ;
And he and his eight hundred
Must plough the wave no more.

WILLIAM COWPER

Verses supposed to be written by
Alexander Selkirk,
during his solitary abode in the island of Juan Fernandez

I am monarch of all I survey,
  My right there is none to dispute ;
From the centre all round to the sea,
  I am lord of the fowl and the brute.
Oh, solitude ! where are the charms
  That sages have seen in thy face ?
Better dwell in the midst of alarms,
  Than reign in this horrible place.

I am out of humanity's reach,
  I must finish my journey alone,
Never hear the sweet music of speech ;
  I start at the sound of my own.
The beasts, that roam over the plain,
  My form with indifference see ;
They are so unacquainted with man,
  Their tameness is shocking to me.

Society, friendship, and love,
  Divinely bestow'd upon man,
Oh, had I the wings of a dove,
  How soon would I taste you again !
My sorrows I then might assuage
  In the ways of religion and truth,
Might learn from the wisdom of age,
  And be cheer'd by the sallies of youth.

Religion ! what treasure untold
  Resides in that heavenly word !
More precious than silver and gold,
  Or all that this earth can afford.
But the sound of the church-going bell
  These valleys and rocks never heard,
Ne'er sigh'd at the sound of a knell,
  Or smil'd when a Sabbath appear'd.

393

Ye winds, that have made me your sport,
  Convey to this desolate shore
Some cordial endearing report
  Of a land I shall visit no more.
My friends, do they now and then send
  A wish or a thought after me ?
O tell me I yet have a friend,
  Though a friend I am never to see.

How fleet is a glance of the mind !
  Compar'd with the speed of its flight,
The tempest itself lags behind,
  And the swift wing'd arrows of light.
When I think of my own native land,
  In a moment I seem to be there ;
But alas ! recollection at hand
  Soon hurries me back to despair.

But the sea-fowl is gone to her nest,
  The beast is laid down in his lair,
Ev'n here is a season of rest,
  And I to my cabin repair.
There is mercy in every place ;
  And mercy, encouraging thought !
Gives even affliction a grace,
  And reconciles man to his lot.

On observing some names of little note recorded
in the " Biographia Britannica "

Oh, fond attempt to give a deathless lot
To names ignoble, born to be forgot !
In vain, recorded in historic page,
They court the notice of a future age :
Those twinkling tiny lustres of the land
Drop one by one from Fame's neglecting hand :

Lethæan gulfs receive them as they fall,
And dark oblivion soon absorbs them all.
So when a child, as playful children use,
Has burnt to tinder a stale last year's news,
The flame extinct, he views the roving fire—
There goes my lady, and there goes the squire.
There goes the parson, oh ! illustrious spark,
And there, scarce less illustrious, goes the clerk !

The Dog and the Water-Lily

No Fable

The noon was shady, and soft airs
    Swept Ouse's silent tide,
When, 'scap'd from literary cares,
    I wander'd on his side.

My spaniel, prettiest of the race,
    And high in pedigree,
(Two nymphs, adorn'd with every grace,
    That spaniel found for me)

Now wanton'd lost in flags and reeds,
    Now starting into sight
Pursu'd the swallow o'er the meads
    With scarce a slower flight.

It was the time when Ouse display'd
    His lilies newly blown ;
Their beauties I intent survey'd ;
    And one I wish'd my own.

With cane extended far I sought
    To steer it close to land ;
But still the prize, though nearly caught,
    Escap'd my eager hand.

Beau mark'd my unsuccessful pains
   With fix'd consid'rate face,
And puzzling set his puppy brains
   To comprehend the case.

But with a chirrup clear and strong,
   Dispersing all his dream,
I thence withdrew, and follow'd long
   The windings of the stream.

My ramble finish'd, I return'd.
   Beau trotting far before
The floating wreath again discern'd,
   And plunging left the shore.

I saw him with that lily cropp'd
   Impatient swim to meet
My quick approach, and soon he dropp'd
   The treasure at my feet.

Charm'd with the sight, " The world," I cried,
   " Shall hear of this thy deed,
My dog shall mortify the pride
   Of man's superior breed ;

" But, chief, myself I will enjoin,
   Awake at duty's call,
To show a love as prompt as thine
   To Him who gives me all."

Epitaph on a Hare

Here lies, whom hound did ne'er pursue,
   Nor swifter greyhound follow,
Whose foot ne'er tainted morning dew,
   Nor ear heard huntsman's hallo,

Old Tiny, surliest of his kind,
　　Who, nurs'd with tender care,
And to domestic bounds confin'd,
　　Was still a wild Jack-hare.

Though duly from my hand he took
　　His pittance every night,
He did it with a jealous look,
　　And, when he could, would bite.

His diet was of wheaten bread,
　　And milk, and oats, and straw,
Thistles, or lettuces instead,
　　With sand to scour his maw.

On twigs of hawthorn he regal'd,
　　On pippins' russet peel ;
And, when his juicy salads fail'd,
　　Slic'd carrot pleas'd him well.

A Turkey carpet was his lawn,
　　Whereon he lov'd to bound,
To skip and gambol like a fawn,
　　And swing his rump around.

His frisking was at evening hours,
　　For then he lost his fear ;
But most before approaching showers,
　　Or when a storm drew near.

Eight years and five round-rolling moons
　　He saw thus steal away,
Dozing out all his idle noons,
　　And every night at play.

I kept him for his humour' sake,
　　For he would oft beguile
My heart of thoughts that made it ache,
　　And force me to a smile.

But now, beneath this walnut shade
He finds his long, last home,
And waits in snug concealment laid,
Till gentler Puss shall come.

He, still more aged, feels the shocks
From which no care can save,
And, partner once of Tiny's box,
Must soon partake his grave.

The Jackdaw

(*From the Latin of Vincent Bourne*)

There is a bird who, by his coat
And by the hoarseness of his note,
Might be suppos'd a crow ;
A great frequenter of the church,
Where, bishop-like, he finds a perch,
And dormitory too.

Above the steeple shines a plate,
That turns and turns, to indicate
From what point blows the weather.
Look up—your brains begin to swim,
'Tis in the clouds—that pleases him,
He chooses it the rather.

Fond of the speculative height,
Thither he wings his airy flight,
And thence securely sees
The bustle and the raree-show
That occupy mankind below,
Secure and at his ease.

You think, no doubt, he sits and muses
On future broken bones and bruises,
If he should chance to fall.
No ; not a single thought like that
Employs his philosophic pate,
Or troubles it at all.

He sees, that this great roundabout—
The world, with all its motley rout,
    Church, army, physic, law,
Its customs, and its businesses,—
Is no concern at all of his,
    And says—what says he ?—*Caw*.

Thrice happy bird ! I too have seen
Much of the vanities of men ;
    And, sick of having seen 'em,
Would cheerfully these limbs resign
For such a pair of wings as thine,
    And such a head between 'em.

The Castaway

Obscurest night involv'd the sky,
    Th' Atlantic billows roar'd,
When such a destin'd wretch as I,
    Wash'd headlong from on board,
Of friends, of hope, of all bereft,
His floating home for ever left.

No braver chief could Albion boast
    Than he with whom he went,
Nor ever ship left Albion's coast,
    With warmer wishes sent.
He lov'd them both, but both in vain,
Nor him beheld, nor her again.

Not long beneath the whelming brine,
    Expert to swim, he lay ;
Nor soon he felt his strength decline,
    Or courage die away ;
But wag'd with death a lasting strife,
Supported by despair of life.

399

He shouted ; nor his friends had fail'd
   To check the vessel's course,
But so the furious blast prevail'd,
   That, pitiless perforce,
They left their outcast mate behind,
And scudded still before the wind.

Some succour yet they could afford ;
   And, such as storms allow,
The cask, the coop, the floated cord,
   Delay'd not to bestow.
But he (they knew) nor ship, nor shore,
Whate'er they gave, should visit more.

Nor, cruel as it seem'd, could he
   Their haste himself condemn,
Aware that flight, in such a sea,
   Alone could rescue them ;
Yet bitter felt it still to die
Deserted, and his friends so nigh.

He long survives, who lives an hour
   In ocean, self-upheld ;
And so long he, with unspent power,
   His destiny repell'd ;
And ever, as the minutes flew,
Entreated help, or cried—Adieu !

At length, his transient respite past,
   His comrades, who before
Had heard his voice in every blast,
   Could catch the sound no more.
For then, by toil subdu'd, he drank
The stifling wave, and then he sank.

No poet wept him : but the page
   Of narrative sincere,
That tells his name, his worth, his age,
   Is wet with Anson's tear,
And tears by bards or heroes shed
Alike immortalise the dead.

I therefore purpose not, or dream,
    Descanting on his fate,
To give the melancholy theme
    A more enduring date :
But misery still delights to trace
Its semblance in another's case.

No voice divine the storm allay'd,
    No light propitious shone ;
When, snatch'd from all effectual aid,
    We perish'd, each alone :
But I beneath a rougher sea,
And whelm'd in deeper gulfs than he

? CAPTAIN FRANCIS GROSE* (1731 ?-1791)

Epigram

on a lady who squinted

If ancient poets Argus prize,
Who boasted of an hundred eyes,
Sure greater praise to her is due
Who looks an hundred ways with two.

WILLIAM WOTY† (1731 ?-1791)

The Violet

Serene is the morning, the lark leaves his nest,
    And sings a salute to the dawn.
The sun with his splendour illumines the East,
    And brightens the dew on the lawn.
Whilst the sons of debauch to indulgence give way,
    And slumber the prime of their hours,
Let us, my dear Stella, the garden survey,
    And make our remarks on the flowers.

---

* An antiquary of Falstaffian build and character. See Burns's
poems (not in this book) addressed to him.
    † The co-editor, with Francis Fawkes, of the *Poetical Calendar*,
1763.

WILLIAM WOTY

The gay gaudy tulip observe as you walk,
    How flaunting the gloss of its vest !
How proud ! and how stately it stands on its stalk,
    In beauty's diversity dress'd !
From the rose, the carnation, the pink and the clove,
    What odours delightfully spring !
The South wafts a richer perfume to the grove,
    As he brushes the leaves with his wing.

Apart from the rest, in her purple array,
    The violet humbly retreats ;
In modest concealment she peeps on the day,
    Yet none can excel her in sweets :
So humble that, though with unparallel'd grace
    She might e'en a palace adorn,
She oft in the hedge hides her innocent face,
    And grows at the foot of the thorn.

So Beauty, my fair one ! is doubly refin'd,
    When Modesty heightens her charms,
When Meekness, like thine, adds a gem to her mind,
    We long to be lock'd in her arms.
Though Venus herself from her throne should descend,
    And the Graces await at her call,
To thee the gay world would with preference bend,
    And hail thee the *Vi'let* of all.

ROBERT LLOYD* (1733-1764)

Song

Though winter its desolate train
    Of frost and of tempest may bring,
Yet Flora steps forward again,
    And nature rejoices in spring.

* A friend of Cowper's and also of Charles Churchill's.

ROBERT LLOYD

Though the sun in his glories decreas'd
  Of his beams in the evening is shorn,
Yet he rises with joy from the east,
  And repairs them again in the morn.

But what can youth's sunshine recall,
  Or the blossoms of beauty restore ?
When its leaves are beginning to fall,
  It dies, and is heard of no more.

The spring-time of love then employ,
  'Tis a lesson that's easy to learn,
For Cupid's a vagrant, a boy,
  And his seasons will never return.

JAMES BEATTIE, LL.D.* (1735-1803)

Epitaph, *intended for himself*

Escap'd the gloom of mortal life, a soul
  Here leaves its mouldering tenement of clay,
Safe, where no cares their whelming billows roll,
  No doubts bewilder, and no hopes betray.

Like thee, I once have stemm'd the sea of life ;
  Like thee, have languish'd after empty joys ;
Like thee, have labour'd in the stormy strife ;
  Been griev'd for trifles, and amus'd with toys.

Yet, for a while, 'gainst passion's threatful blast
  Let steady reason urge the struggling oar ;
Shot through dreary gloom, the morn at last
  Gives to my longing eye the blissful shore.

Forget my frailties, thou art also frail ;
  Forgive my lapses, for thyself may'st fall ;
Nor read, unmov'd, my artless tender tale,
  I was a friend, O man ! to thee, to all.

* Author of *The Minstrel*.

403

ISAAC BICKERSTAFFE (1735?-1812 *or later*)

Songs from " Love in a Village "

I*

Hope ! thou nurse of young desire,
    Fairy promiser of joy,
Painted vapour, glow-worm fire,
    Temp'rate sweet, that ne'er can cloy.

Hope ! thou earnest of delight,
    Softest soother of the mind,
Balmy cordial, prospect bright,
    Surest friend the wretched find.

Kind deceiver, flatter still,
    Deal out pleasures unpossest,
With thy dreams my fancy fill,
    And in wishes make me blest.

II

There was a jolly miller once,
    Liv'd on the river Dee ;
He work'd and sung, from morn till night,
    No lark more blithe than he.
And this the burthen of his song
    For ever us'd to be,—
" I care for nobody, not I,
    If no one cares for me."

III

How happy were my days, till now !
    I ne'er did sorrow feel,
I rose with joy to milk my cow,
    Or take my spinning-wheel.

* This poem is an alteration and expansion of a song in *The Village Opera* (1729), by Charles Johnson (1679-1748), who should have the credit for the best of these lines.

My heart was lighter than a fly,
　　Like any bird I sung,
Till he pretended love, and I
　　Believ'd his flatt'ring tongue.

Oh ! the fool, the silly, silly fool.
　　Who trusts what man may be ;
I wish I were a maid again,
　　And in my own country.

The Rev. JOHN LANGHORNE, D.D.* (1735-1779)

The Evening Primrose

There are that love the shades of life,
　　And shun the splendid walks of Fame ;
There are that hold it rueful strife
　　To risk Ambition's losing game :

That far from Envy's lurid eye
　　The fairest fruits of Genius rear,
Content to see them bloom and die
　　In Friendship's small but kindly sphere.

Than vainer flowers though sweeter far,
　　The Evening Primrose shuns the day ;
Blooms only to the western star,
　　And loves its solitary ray.

In Eden's vale an aged hind,
　　At the dim twilight's closing hour,
On his time-smoothed staff reclin'd,
　　With wonder view'd the opening flower.

" Ill-fated flower, at eve to blow,"
　　In pity's simple thought he cries,
" Thy bosom must not feel the glow
　　Of splendid suns, or smiling skies.

* Also well known as co-translator (with his brother William)
of Plutarch's *Lives*.

405

" Nor thee the vagrants of the field,
  The hamlet's little train behold ;
Their eyes to sweet oppression yield,
  When thine the falling shades unfold.

" Nor thee the hasty shepherd heeds,
  When love has fill'd his heart with cares,
For flowers he rifles all the meads,
  For waking flowers—but thine forbears.

" Ah ! waste no more that beauteous bloom
  On night's chill shade, that fragrant breath,
Let smiling suns those gems illume !
  Fair flower, to live unseen is death."

Soft as the voice of vernal gales
  That o'er the bending meadow blow,
Or streams that steal through even vales,
  And murmur that they move so slow :

Deep in her unfrequented bower,
  Sweet Philomela pour'd her strain ;
The bird of eve approv'd her flower,
  And answer'd thus the anxious swain.

                              Live unseen !
By moonlight shades, in valleys green,
  Lovely flower we'll live unseen.
Of our pleasures deem not lightly,
Laughing day may look more sprightly,
  But I love the modest mien,
  Still I love the modest mien
Of gentle evening fair, and her star-trained queen.

Didst thou, shepherd, never find,
Pleasure is of pensive kind ?
Has thy cottage never known
That she loves to live alone ?
Dost thou not at evening hour

Feel some soft and secret power,
Gliding o'er thy yielding mind,
Leave sweet serenity behind ;
While all disarm'd, the cares of day
Steal through the falling gloom away ?
Love to think thy lot was laid
In this undistinguish'd shade.
Far from the world's infectious view,
Thy little virtues safely blew.
Go, and in day's more dangerous hour,
Guard thy emblematic flower.

The Wall-Flower

" Why loves my flower, the sweetest flower
    That swells the golden breast of May,
Thrown rudely o'er this ruin'd tower,
    To waste her solitary day ?

" Why, when the mead, the spicy vale,
    The grove and genial garden call,
Will she her fragrant soul exhale,
    Unheeded on the lonely wall ?

" For sure was never beauty born
    To live in death's deserted shade !
Come, lovely flower, my banks adorn,
    My banks for life and beauty made."

Thus Pity wak'd the tender thought,
    And by her sweet persuasion led,
To seize the hermit-flower I sought,
    And bear her from her stony bed.

I sought—but sudden on mine ear
    A voice in hollow murmurs broke,
And smote my heart with holy fear—
    The Genius of the ruin spoke.

" From thee be far th' ungentle deed,
   The honours of the dead to spoil,
Or take the sole remaining meed,
   The flower that crowns their former toil !

" Nor deem that flower the garden's foe,
   Or fond to grace this barren shade ;
'Tis Nature tells her to bestow
   Her honours on the lonely dead.

" For this, obedient Zephyrs bear
   Her light seeds round yon turret's mould,
And undispers'd by tempests there,
   They rise in vegetable gold.

" Nor shall thy wonder wake to see
   Such desert scenes distinction crave ;
Oft have they been, and oft shall be
   Truth's, Honour's, Valour's, Beauty's grave.

" Where longs to fall that rifted spire,
   As weary of th' insulting air ;
The poet's thought, the warrior's fire,
   The lover's sighs are sleeping there.

" When that too shakes the trembling ground,
   Borne down by some tempestuous sky,
And many a slumbering cottage round
   Startles—how still their hearts will lie !

" Of them who, wrapt in earth so cold,
   No more the smiling day shall view,
Should many a tender tale be told,
   For many a tender thought is due.

" Hast thou not seen some lover pale,
   When evening brought the pensive hour,
Step slowly o'er the shadowy vale,
   And stop to pluck the frequent flower ?

" Those flowers he surely meant to strew
   On lost affection's lowly cell ;
Though there, as fond remembrance grew,
   Forgotten, from his hand they fell.

" Has not for thee the fragrant thorn
   Been taught her first rose to resign ?
With vain but pious fondness borne
   To deck thy Nancy's honour'd shrine !

" 'Tis Nature pleading in the breast,
   Fair memory of her works to find ;
And when to Fate she yields the rest,
   She claims the monumental mind.

" Why, else, the o'ergrown paths of Time
   Would thus the letter'd sage explore,
With pain these crumbling ruins climb,
   And on the doubtful sculpture pore ?

" Why seeks he with unwearied toil
   Through Death's dim walks to urge his way,
Reclaim his long-asserted spoil,
   And lead Oblivion into day ?

" 'Tis Nature prompts, by toil or fear
   Unmov'd, to range through Death's domain ;
The tender parent loves to hear
   Her children's story told again.

" Treat not with scorn his thoughtful hours,
   If haply near these haunts he stray ;
Nor take the fair enlivening flowers
   That bloom to cheer his lonely way."

JOHN LANGHORNE

A Farewell Hymn

To the Valley of Irwan

Farewell the fields of Irwan's vale,
  My infant years where Fancy led ;
And sooth'd me with the western gale,
  Her wild dreams waving round my head,
While the blithe blackbird told his tale.
Farewell the fields of Irwan's vale !

The primrose on the valley's side,
  The green thyme on the mountain's head,
The wanton rose, the daisy pied,
  The wilding's blossom blushing red ;
No longer I their sweets inhale.
Farewell the fields of Irwan's vale !

How oft, within yon vacant shade,
  Has evening clos'd my careless eye !
How oft along those banks I've stray'd,
  And watch'd the wave that wander'd by !
Full long shall I their loss bewail.
Farewell the fields of Irwan's vale !

Yet still, within yon vacant grove,
  To mark the close of parting day ;
Along yon flowery banks to rove,
  And watch the wave that winds away ;
Fair Fancy sure shall never fail,
Though far from these, and Irwan's vale.

JOHN LANGHORNE

Translation from Catullus

Lesbia, live to love and pleasure,
    Careless what the grave may say :
When each moment is a treasure,
    Why should lovers lose a day ?

Setting suns shall rise in glory,
    But when little life is o'er,
There's an end to all the story :
    We shall sleep and wake no more.

Give me then a thousand kisses,
    Twice ten thousand more bestow,
Till the sum of boundless blisses,
    Neither we nor envy know.

From Petrarch

Sonnet 238

Wail'd the sweet warbler to the lonely shade ;
    Trembled the green leaf to the summer gale ;
    Fell the fair stream in murmurs down the dale,
Its banks, its flowery banks with verdure spread,
Where, by the charm of pensive Fancy led,
    All as I fram'd the love-lamenting tale,
    Came the dear object whom I still bewail,
Came from the regions of the cheerless dead.

" And why," she cried, " untimely wilt thou die ?
    Ah why, for pity, shall those mournful tears
Start in wild sorrow from that languid eye ?
    Cherish no more those visionary fears,
For me, who range yon light-invested sky !
    For me, who triumph in eternal years ! "

The Rev. JOHN WOLCOT, M.D., " PETER PINDAR "
(1738-1819)

An Anacreontic
To a Kiss

Soft child of Love, thou balmy bliss,
Inform me, O delicious kiss,
Why thou so suddenly art gone ;
Lost in the moment thou art won ?

Yet go, for wherefore should I sigh ?
On Delia's lip with raptur'd eye,
On Delia's blushing lip, I see
A thousand full as sweet as thee.

To Anacreon

Ghost of Anacreon, quit the shades,
　　And with thee bring thy sweet old lyre,
To praise the first of British maids,
　　Whose charms will set thy soul on fire.

But hold ; 'twere better, keep away :
　　Of justice must thy harp despair,
Which suited very well thy day,
　　That saw no damsel half so fair.

Madrigal

Ah ! say not that the bard grows old ;
　　For what to me are passing years ?
I feel not Age's palsied cold :
　　To-day like yesterday appears.

When Beauty beams, the world is gay :
　　What mortal is not then alive ?
Thus kindling at its magic ray,
　　Four-score leaps back to twenty-five.

JOHN WOLCOT

Epigram*

on a learned gentleman, who was, not long since, very forward in censuring Indian delinquents, and threatening them with exemplary punishment, but of late is so greatly changed, as in one instance to become perfectly silent, and in another the avowed defender and protector of the man whom he reprobated and condemned in the strongest terms.

Midas, they say, possess'd the art of old
Of turning whatsoe'er he touch'd to gold ;
This modern statesmen can reverse with ease—
Touch *them* with gold, *they'll turn to what you please.*

The Rev. AUGUSTUS MONTAGUE TOPLADY
(1740-1778)

A Living and Dying Prayer for the Holiest Believer in the World

Rock of Ages, cleft for me,
Let me hide myself in Thee !
Let the Water and the Blood,
From Thy riven side which flow'd,
Be of sin the double cure,
Cleanse me from its guilt and power.

Not the labours of my hands
Can fulfil Thy Law's demands :
Could my zeal no respite know,
Could my tears for ever flow,
All for sin could not atone :
Thou must save, and Thou alone !

* This epigram is attributed to Peter Pindar on the strength of the index of the second volume of the *Asylum for Fugitive Pieces*. But no author's name is given in the text, and the attribution may be due only to faulty indexing.

Nothing in my hand I bring ;
Simply to Thy Cross I cling ;
Naked, come to Thee for dress ;
Helpless, look to Thee for grace,
Foul, I to the fountain fly :
Wash me, Saviour ! or I die.

Whilst I draw this fleeting breath—
When my eye-strings break in death—
When I soar through tracts unknown—
See Thee on Thy Judgment-Throne—
Rock of Ages, cleft for me,
Let me hide myself in Thee !

JOHN COLLINS (1742 ?-1808)

Epitaph

on a poor provincial tragic actor

Here lies a poor old worn-out blade,
  Who, living, toil'd like any Turk ;
Yet never work'd but when he play'd,
  As playing was his only work.

By Playhouse work, till past threescore,
  He liv'd, unheeding Time or Tide ;
And then, shut out from Playhouse door,
  The vet'ran in a Workhouse died.

Thus, though in war he blaz'd, like Mars,
  And shin'd in love, like bright Adonis ;
His exit proves—'twas all a farce.
  Sic transit gloria histrionis.

JOHN COLLINS

Good Old Things

In the days of my youth I've been frequently told,
That the best of good things are despis'd when they're old,
Yet I own, I'm so lost to the modes of this life
As to prize an old friend, and to love an old wife :
And the first of enjoyments, through life, has been mine,
To regale an old friend with a flask of old wine.

In this gay world new fashions spring up every day,
And to make room for them, still the old must give way ;
A new fav'rite at Court will an old one displace,
And too oft an old friend will put on a new face ;
Yet the pride, pomp and splendour of Courts I'd resign,
To regale an old friend with a flask of old wine.

With old England, by some folks, great faults have been
  found,
Though they've since found much greater on New England's
  ground,
And the thief a new region *transportedly* hails,
Quitting old England's coast for a trip to New Wales ;
But such *transporting* trips, pleas'd with home, I'd decline,
To regale an old friend with a flask of old wine.

By the bright golden sun, that gives birth to the day,
Though as old as this globe which he gilds with his ray,
And the moon, which, though new every month, as we're
  told,
Is the same silver lamp near six thousand years old,
Could the lamp of my life last while sun and moon shine,
I'd regale an old friend with a flask of old wine.

JOHN COLLINS

To-Morrow

In the downhill of life when I find I'm declining,
    May my fate no less fortunate be,
Than a snug elbow chair will afford for reclining,
    And a cot that o'erlooks the wide sea ;
With an ambling pad pony to pace o'er the lawn,
    While I carol away idle sorrow,
And, blithe as the lark that each day hails the dawn,
    Look forward with hope for To-morrow.

With a porch at my door, both for shelter and shade, too,
    As the sunshine or rain may prevail ;
And a small spot of ground for the use of the spade, too,
    With a barn for the use of the flail :
A cow for my dairy, a dog for my game,
    And a purse when a friend wants to borrow,
I'll envy no Nabob his riches or fame,
    Or what honours may wait him To-morrow.

From the bleak northern blast may my cot be completely
    Secur'd by a neighbouring hill ;
And at night may repose steal upon me more sweetly,
    By the sound of a murmuring rill :
And while peace and plenty I find at my board,
    With a heart free from sickness and sorrow,
With my friends let me share what To-day may afford,
    And let them spread the table To-morrow.

And when I, at last, must throw off this frail cov'ring,
    Which I've worn for three score years and ten,
On the brink of the grave I'll not seek to keep hov'ring,
    Nor my thread wish to spin o'er again ;
But my face in the glass I'll serenely survey,
    And with smiles count each wrinkle and furrow,
As this old worn out stuff, which is threadbare To-day,
    May become Everlasting To-morrow.

Elegy

Sigh not, ye winds, as passing o'er
  The chambers of the dead you fly ;
Weep not, ye dews, for these no more
  Shall ever weep, shall ever sigh.

Why mourn the throbbing heart at rest ?
How still it lies within the breast !
Why mourn, since Death presents us peace,
And in the grave our sorrows cease ?

The shatter'd bark, from adverse winds,
Rest in this peaceful haven finds ;
And, when the storms of life are past,
Hope drops her anchor here at last.

Sigh not, ye winds, as passing o'er
  The chambers of the dead you fly ;
Weep not, ye dews, for these no more
  Shall ever weep, shall ever sigh.

Song

The season comes when first we met,
  But you return no more ;
Why cannot I the days forget,
  Which time can ne'er restore ?
O days too sweet, too bright to last,
Are you indeed for ever past ?

The fleeting shadows of delight,
  In memory I trace ;
In fancy stop their rapid flight,
  And all the past replace :
But, ah, I wake to endless woes,
And tears the fading visions close !

E E

Song

My mother bids me bind my hair
    With bands of rosy hue ;
Tie up my sleeves with ribbons rare,
    And lace my bodice blue.

" For why," she cries, " sit still and weep,
    While others dance and play ? "
Alas ! I scarce can go, or creep,
    While Lubin is away.

'Tis sad to think the days are gone,
    When those we love were near !
I sit upon this mossy stone,
    And sigh when none can hear.

And while I spin my flaxen thread,
    And sing my simple lay,
The village seems asleep, or dead,
    Now Lubin is away.

Mrs. ANNA LÆTITIA BARBAULD, *née* AIKIN
(1743-1825)

The Mouse's Petition,

found in the trap where he had been confined all night

Oh ! hear a pensive captive's prayer,
    For liberty that sighs ;
And never let thine heart be shut
    Against the prisoner's cries.

For here forlorn and sad I sit,
    Within the wiry grate ;
And tremble at th' approaching morn,
    Which brings impending fate.

Mrs. BARBAULD

If e'er thy breast with freedom glow'd,
    And spurn'd a tyrant's chain,
Let not thy strong oppressive force
    A free-born mouse detain.

Oh ! do not stain with guiltless blood
    Thy hospitable hearth ;
Nor triumph that thy wiles betray'd
    A prize so little worth.

The scatter'd gleanings of a feast
    My scanty meals supply ;
But if thine unrelenting heart
    That slender boon deny,

The cheerful light, the vital air,
    Are blessings widely given ;
Let nature's commoners enjoy
    The common gifts of heaven.

The well taught philosophic mind
    To all compassion gives ;
Casts round the world an equal eye,
    And feels for all that lives.

If mind, as ancient sages taught,
    A never dying flame,
Still shifts through matter's varying forms,
    In every form the same,

Beware, lest in the worm you crush
    A brother's soul you find ;
And tremble lest thy luckless hand
    Dislodge a kindred mind.

Or, if this transient gleam of day
    Be *all* of life we share,
Let pity plead within thy breast
    That little *all* to spare.

419

Mrs. BARBAULD

So may thy hospitable board
  With health and peace be crown'd ;
And every charm of heartfelt ease
  Beneath thy roof be found.

So, when unseen destruction lurks,
  Which mice like men may share,
May some kind angel clear thy path,
  And break the hidden snare.

Sir BROOKE BOOTHBY, Bart. (1743-1824)

Life

What art thou, Life ? The shadow of a dream :
  The past and future dwell in thought alone ;
  The present, ere we note its flight, is gone ;
And all ideal, vain, fantastic, seem.
Whence is thy source ? And whither dost thou tend ?
  So short thy period, and thy form so frail ;
  Poor prisoner ! pent in Death's surrounding vale,
Born but to breathe, to suffer, and to end.

Why, Shadow, bring'st thou on thy raven wing,
  Dark trains of grief, and visions of the night,
  Rather than graces, rob'd in purple light,
Elysian flowers, and love's unclouded spring ;
Since sad, or gay, whatever be thy theme,
Death surely ends at once the dreamer and the dream ?

Song

Discard that frown upon your brow ;
  'Tis you alone I love ;
To witness this eternal vow
  I'll call on mighty Jove !

" O leave the God to soft repose ; "
  The smiling maid replies,
" For Jove but laughs at lovers' oaths
  And lovers' perjuries."

By honour'd Beauty's gentle power,
  By Friendship's holy flame !
" Ah ! what is Beauty, but a flower,
  And Friendship, but a name ? "

By these dear tempting lips, I cried ;
  With arch enchanting look,
" Hold—I'll believe !" the maid replied,
  " But—you've not kiss'd the book ! "

CHARLES DIBDIN (1745-1814)

Poor Tom; or, the Sailor's Epitaph

Here, a sheer hulk, lies poor Tom Bowling,
  The darling of our crew ;
No more he'll hear the tempests howling,
  For Death has broach'd him to.
His form was of the manliest beauty,
  His heart was kind and soft ;
Faithful below he did his duty,
  But now he's gone aloft.

Tom never from his word departed,
    His virtues were so rare ;
His friends were many, and true-hearted,
    His Poll was kind and fair :
And then he'd sing so blithe and jolly,—
    Ah ! many's the time and oft ;
But mirth is turn'd to melancholy,
    For Tom is gone aloft.

Yet shall poor Tom find pleasant weather,
    When He, who all commands,
Shall give, to call life's crew together,
    The word to pipe all hands :
Thus Death, who kings and tars despatches,
    In vain Tom's life has doff'd ;
For, though his body's under hatches,
    His soul is gone aloft.

WILLIAM HAYLEY* (1745-1820)

Song

From glaring show, and giddy noise,
    The pleasures of the vain,
Take me, ye soft, ye silent joys,
    To your retreats again.

Be mine, ye cool, ye peaceful groves,
    Whose shades to love belong ;
Where Echo, as she fondly roves,
    Repeats my Stella's song.

Ah, Stella ! why should I depart
    From solitude and thee,
When in that solitude thou art
    A perfect world to me ?

* Cowper's biographer, and the friend of Blake.

MICHAEL BRUCE (1746-1767)

Daphnis : a Monody

To the memory of a young boy of great parts

I

No more of youthful joys or love's fond dreams,
No more of morning fair or ev'ning mild,
While Daphnis lies among the silent dead
Unsung ; though long ago he trod the path,
The dreary road of death—
Which soon or late each human foot must tread :
He trod the dark uncomfortable wild
By Faith's pure light, by Hope's heav'n-op'ning beams,
By Love whose image gladdens mortal eyes,
And keeps the golden key that opens all the skies.

II

Assist, ye Muses !—and ye will assist ;
For Daphnis, whom I sing, to you was dear :
Ye lov'd the boy, and on his youthful head
Your kindest influence shed.—
So may I match his lays, who to the lyre
Wail'd his lost Lycidas by wood and rill :
So may the Muse my grov'ling mind inspire
To sing a farewell to thy ashes blest ;
To bid fair peace be to thy gentle shade ;
To scatter flow'rets, cropt by Fancy's hand,
In sad assemblage, round thy tomb,
If water'd by the Muse, to latest time to bloom.

III

Oft by the side of Leven's crystal lake,
Trembling beneath the closing lids of light,
With slow short-measur'd steps we took our walk :
Then he would talk
Of argument far, far above his years ;
Then he would reason high,
Till from the east the silver Queen of night
Her journey up Heaven's steep began to make,
And Silence reign'd attentive in the sky.

IV

O happy days ! for ever, ever gone !
When o'er the flow'ry green we ran, we play'd
With blooms bedropt by youthful Summer's hand ;
Or, in the willow shade,
We mimic castles built among the sand,
Soon by the sounding surge to be beat down,
Or sweeping winds ; when, by the sedgy marsh,
We heard the heron, and the wild duck harsh,
And sweeter lark tune his melodious lay,
At highest noon of day.
Among the antic moss-grown stones we'd roam,
With ancient hieroglyphic figures grac'd,
Winged hour-glasses, bones, and skulls, and spades,
And obsolete inscriptions by the hands
Of other ages : ah ! I little thought
That we then play'd o'er his untimely tomb !

V

Where were ye, Muses ! when the leaden hand
Of Death, remorseless, clos'd your Daphnis' eyes ?
For sure ye heard the weeping mother's cries ;
But the dread power of fate who can withstand ?
Young Daphnis smil'd at Death ; the tyrant's darts
As stubble counted. What was his support ?
His conscience, and firm trust in Him whose ways
Are truth ; in Him who sways
His potent sceptre o'er the dark domains
Of Death and Hell ; who holds in straiten'd reins
Their banded legions : " Through the darksome vale
He'll guide my trembling steps with heav'nly ray ;
I see the dawning of immortal day."
He smiling said, and died.

MICHAEL BRUCE

VI

Hail and farewell, blest youth ! soon hast thou left
This evil world ; fair was thy thread of life,
But quickly by the envious Sisters shorn :
Thus have I seen a rose with rising morn
Unfold its glowing bloom, sweet to the smell,
And lovely to the eye ; when a keen wind
Hath tore its blushing leaves, and laid it low,
Stripp'd of its sweets.—Ah ! so,
So Daphnis fell ! long ere his prime he fell !
Nor left he on these plains his peer behind ;
These plains, that mourn their loss, of him bereft,
No more look gay, but desert and forlorn.

VII

Now cease your lamentations, shepherds ! cease :
Though Daphnis died below, he lives above ;
A better life, and in a fairer clime,
He lives : no sorrow enters that blest place,
But ceaseless songs of love and joy resound ;
And fragrance floats around,
By fanning zephyrs from the spicy groves,
And flowers immortal, wafted ; Asphodel
And Amaranth, unfading, deck the ground,
With fairer colours than, ere Adam fell,
In Eden bloom'd : there haply he may hear
This artless song. Ye powers of verse ! improve,
And make it worthy of your darling's ear,
And make it equal to the shepherd's love.

VIII

Thus, in the shadow of a frowning rock,
Beneath a mountain's side, shaggy and hoar,
A homely swain tending his little flock,
Rude, yet a lover of the Muse's lore,
Chanted his Doric strain till close of day,
Then rose, and homeward slowly bent his way.

MICHAEL BRUCE

Ode : to the Cuckoo*

Hail, beauteous stranger of the wood,
    Attendant on the spring !
Now heav'n repairs thy rural seat,
    And woods thy welcome sing.

Soon as the daisy decks the green,
    Thy certain voice we hear :
Hast thou a star to guide thy path,
    Or mark the rolling year ?

Delightful visitant ! with thee
    I hail the time of flowers,
When heav'n is fill'd with music sweet
    Of birds among the bowers.

The schoolboy, wand'ring in the wood
    To pull the flowers so gay,
Starts, thy curious voice to hear,
    And imitates thy lay.

Soon as the pea puts on the bloom,
    Thou fly'st thy vocal vale,
An annual guest, in other lands,
    Another spring to hail.

Sweet bird ! thy bower is ever green,
    Thy sky is ever clear ;
Thou hast no sorrow in thy song,
    No winter in thy year !

O could I fly, I'd fly with thee :
    We'd make, with social wing,
Our annual visit o'er the globe,
    Companions of the spring.

---

* This poem was afterwards claimed by John Logan. The
balance of evidence seems in favour of Bruce as its real author.

MICHAEL BRUCE

Elegy : to Spring

'Tis past : the iron North has spent his rage ;
　Stern winter now resigns the length'ning day ;
The stormy howlings of the winds assuage,
　And warm o'er ether western breezes play.

Of genial heat and cheerful light the source,
　From southern climes, beneath another sky,
The sun, returning, wheels his golden course ;
　Before his beams all noxious vapours fly.

Far to the north grim Winter draws his train
　To his own clime, to Zembla's frozen shore ;
Where, thron'd on ice, he holds eternal reign ;
　Where whirlwinds madden, and where tempests roar.

Loos'd from the bands of frost, the verdant ground
　Again puts on her robe of cheerful green,
Again puts forth her flowers ; and all around,
　Smiling, the cheerful face of Spring is seen.

Behold ! the trees new-deck their wither'd boughs ;
　Their ample leaves the hospitable plane,
The taper elm, and lofty ash disclose ;
　The blooming hawthorn variegates the scene.

The lily of the vale, of flowers the Queen,
　Puts on the robe she neither sew'd nor spun ;
The birds on ground, or on the branches green,
　Hop to and fro, and glitter in the sun.

Soon as o'er eastern hills the morning peers,
　From her low nest the tufted lark upsprings ;
And, cheerful singing, up the air she steers ;
　Still high she mounts, still loud and sweet she sings.

On the green furze, cloth'd o'er with golden blooms
　That fill the air with fragrance all around,
The linnet sits, and tricks his glossy plumes,
　While o'er the wild his broken notes resound.

MICHAEL BRUCE

While the sun journeys down the western sky,
  Along the greensward, mark'd with Roman mound,
Beneath the blithesome shepherd's watchful eye,
  The cheerful lambkins dance and frisk around.

Now is the time for those who wisdom love,
  Who love to walk in Virtue's flowery road,
Along the lovely paths of Spring to rove,
  And follow Nature up to Nature's God.

Thus Zoroastres studied Nature's laws ;
  Thus Socrates, the wisest of mankind ;
Thus heav'n-taught Plato trac'd th' Almighty cause,
  And left the wondering multitude behind.

Thus Ashley gather'd Academic bays ;
  Thus gentle Thomson, as the Seasons roll,
Taught them to sing the great Creator's praise,
  And bear their poet's name from pole to pole.

Thus have I walk'd along the dewy lawn ;
  My frequent foot the blooming wild hath worn ;
Before the lark I've sung the beauteous dawn,
  And gather'd health from all the gales of morn.

And, even when Winter chill'd the aged year,
  I wander'd lonely o'er the hoary plain ;
Though frosty Boreas warn'd me to forbear,
  Boreas, with all his tempests, warn'd in vain.

Then sleep my nights, and quiet bless'd my days ;
  I fear'd no loss, my mind was all my store ;
No anxious wishes e'er disturb'd my ease ;
  Heav'n gave content and health—I ask'd no more.

Now Spring returns : but not to me returns
  The vernal joy my better years have known ;
Dim in my breast life's dying taper burns,
  And all the joys of life with health are flown.

MICHAEL BRUCE

Starting and shiv'ring in th' inconstant wind,
　Meagre and pale, the ghost of what I was,
Beneath some blasted tree I lie reclin'd,
　And count the silent moments as they pass :

The wingèd moments, whose unstaying speed
　No art can stop, or in their course arrest ;
Whose flight shall shortly count me with the dead,
　And lay me down in peace with them that rest.

Oft morning dreams presage approaching fate ;
　And morning dreams, as poets tell, are true,
Led by pale ghosts, I enter Death's dark gate,
　And bid the realms of Light and Life adieu.

I hear the helpless wail, the shriek of woe ;
　I see the muddy wave, the dreary shore,
The sluggish streams that slowly creep below,
　Which mortals visit, and return no more.

Farewell, ye blooming fields ! ye cheerful plains !
　Enough for me the church-yard's lonely mound,
Where Melancholy with still Silence reigns,
　And the rank grass waves o'er the cheerless ground.

There let me wander at the shut of eve,
　When sleep sits dewy on the labourer's eyes,
The world and all its busy follies leave,
　And talk with Wisdom where my Daphnis lies.

There let me sleep forgotten in the clay,
　When death shall shut these weary aching eyes,
Rest in the hopes of an eternal day,
　Till the long night is gone, and the last morn arise.

RICHARD FENTON (1746-1821)

Song

Tell me, what can mean this riot
  In my pulse, when Damon's nigh ;
That my breast is never quiet,
  Ever heaving with a sigh ?
If such tokens don't discover
What it is to be a lover,
  Then, O tell me ! what am I ?

But, alas ! poor thoughtless creature !
  By each pulse betray'd, and sigh,
There's a tongue in every feature,
  And a thousand in the eye,
Which to Damon will discover
What it is to be a lover,
  And to tell him what am I.

Song

When forc'd from thee, my soul's delight,
  What cares distract my throbbing breast !
My anxious day, my anxious night,
  Strangers alike to rest :
For though I know thee still sincere,
Yet love is full of doubt and fear.

How vain the joys that tempt the eye,
  And music melting on the ear !
Indifferent to each sight am I,
  And every sound I hear :
A body's only left with me,
For still my soul attends on thee.

430

As, when the sun withdraws his ray,
    Clos'd is the snowdrop's lilied cup ;
So shuts my heart, when thou'rt away,
    And locks thy image up.
How long shall then this night remain,
Till thou unlock my heart again ?

Sir WILLIAM JONES, Knight (1746-1794)

From the Persian

On parent knees, a naked, new-born child,
Weeping thou sat'st, while all around thee smil'd :—
So live, that sinking in thy last long sleep,
Calm thou mayst smile while all around thee weep.

Written in Berkeley's " Siris "

Before thy mystic altar, heav'nly Truth,
I kneel in manhood, as I knelt in youth :
Thus let me kneel, till this dull form decay,
And life's last shade be brighten'd by thy ray :
Then shall my soul, now lost in clouds below,
Soar without bound, without consuming glow.

Au Firmament

" Would I were yon blue field above,"
    Said Plato, warbling am'rous lays,
" That with ten thousand eyes of love,
    On thee for ever I might gaze."

My purer love the wish disclaims,
    For were I, like Tiresias, blind,
Still should I glow with heavenly flames,
    And gaze with rapture on thy mind.

431

The Rev. JOHN LOGAN (1748-1788)

Song

The day is departed, and round from the cloud
    The moon in her beauty appears ;
The voice of the nightingale warbles aloud
    The music of love in our ears :
Maria, appear ! now the season so sweet
    With the beat of the heart is in tune ;
The time is so tender for lovers to meet
    Alone by the light of the moon.

I cannot, when present, unfold what I feel,
    I sigh—can a lover do more ?
Her name to the shepherds I never reveal,
    Yet I think of her all the day o'er.
Maria, my love ! Do you long for the grove ?
    Do you sigh for an interview soon ?
Does e'er a kind thought run on me as you rove
    Alone by the light of the moon ?

Your name from the shepherds whenever I hear,
    My bosom is all in a glow ;
Your voice when it vibrates so sweet through mine ear,
    My heart thrills—my eyes overflow.
Ye powers of the sky, will your bounty divine
    Indulge a fond lover his boon ?
Shall heart spring to heart, and Maria be mine,
    Alone by the light of the moon ?

The Rev. GEORGE HUDDESFORD (1749-1809)

A Case of Conscience ;

submitted to a late Dignitary of the Church on his narcotic
exposition of the following text :
" Watch and pray, lest ye enter into temptation."

By our Pastor perplext,
    How shall we determine ?—
" Watch and Pray," says the Text,
    " Go to sleep," says the Sermon.

Mrs. CHARLOTTE SMITH, *née* TURNER (1749-1806)

To Spring

Again the wood, and long withdrawing vale,
  In many a tint of tender green are dress'd,
Where the young leaves unfolding scarce conceal
  Beneath their early shade the half-form'd nest
Of finch or wood-lark ; and the primrose pale,
  And lavish cowslip, wildly scatter'd round,
Give their sweet spirits to the sighing gale.
  Ah ! season of delight ! could aught be found
To soothe awhile the tortur'd bosom's pain,
  Of sorrow's rankling shaft to cure the wound,
  And bring life's first delusions once again,
'Twere surely met in thee !—Thy prospect fair,
Thy sounds of harmony, thy balmy air,
Have power to cure all sadness—but despair.

Sonnet

Should the lone wanderer, fainting on his way,
  Rest for a moment of the sultry hours,
And though his path through thorns and roughness lay,
  Pluck the wild rose, or woodbine's gadding flowers ;
Weaving gay wreaths beneath some sheltering tree,
  The sense of sorrow he awhile may lose ;
So have I sought thy flowers, fair Poesy !
  So charm'd my way, with friendship and the Muse.
But darker now grows life's unhappy day,
  Dark, with new clouds of evil yet to come ;
Her pencil sickening Fancy throws away ;
  And weary Hope reclines upon the tomb,
And points my wishes to that tranquil shore,
Where the pale spectre, Care, pursues no more.

CHARLOTTE SMITH

To Fancy

Thee, queen of shadows! shall I still invoke,
    Still love the scenes thy sportive pencil drew,
When on mine eyes the early radiance broke
    Which show'd the beauteous, rather than the true!
Alas! long since those glowing tints are dead,
    And now 'tis thine in darkest hues to dress
The spot where pale Experience hangs her head
    O'er the sad grave of murder'd Happiness!
Through thy false medium then no longer view'd,
    May fancied pain and fancied pleasure fly,
        And I, as from me all thy dreams depart,
Be to my wayward destiny subdu'd;
    Nor seek perfection with a poet's eye,
        Nor suffer anguish with a poet's heart!

The Gossamer

O'er faded heath-flowers spun, or thorny furze,
    The filmy gossamer is lightly spread;
Waving in every sighing air that stirs,
    As fairy fingers had entwin'd the thread:
A thousand trembling orbs of lucid dew
    Spangle the texture of the fairy loom,
As if soft Sylphs, lamenting as they flew,
    Had wept departed summer's transient bloom:
But the wind rises, and the turf receives
    The glittering web: so, evanescent, fade
Bright views that youth with sanguine heart believes;
    So vanish schemes of bliss, by Fancy made;
Which, fragile as the fleeting dreams of morn,
Leave but the wither'd heath and barren thorn.

The Rt. Hon. RICHARD BRINSLEY SHERIDAN, M.P.
(1751-1816)

Songs from " The Duenna "

I

I ne'er could any lustre see
In eyes that would not look on me ;
I ne'er saw nectar on a lip,
But where my own did hope to sip.
Has the maid who seeks my heart
Cheeks of rose, untouch'd by art ?
I will own the colour true,
When yielding blushes add their hue.

Is her hand so soft and pure ?
I must press it, to be sure ;
Nor can I be certain then,
Till it, grateful, press again.
Must I, with attentive eye,
Watch her heaving bosom sigh ?
I will do so, when I see
That heaving bosom sigh for me.

II

Had I a heart for falsehood fram'd,
   I ne'er could injure you ;
For though your tongue no promise claim'd,
   Your charms would make me true.

To you no soul shall bear deceit,
   No stranger offer wrong ;
Bur friends in all the ag'd you'll meet,
   And lovers in the young.

But when they learn that you have blest
   Another with your heart,
They'll bid aspiring passion rest ;
   And act a brother's part.

Then, Lady ! dread not here deceit,
   Nor fear to suffer wrong ;
For friends in all the ag'd you'll meet,
   And brothers in the young.

RICHARD BRINSLEY SHERIDAN

Song from " The School for Scandal "

Here's to the maiden of bashful fifteen !
   Here's to the widow of fifty !
Here's to the flaunting extravagant quean ;
   And here's to the housewife that's thrifty !

       Let the toast pass,
       Drink to the lass !
   I'll warrant she'll prove an excuse for the glass !

Here's to the charmer, whose dimples we prize !
   Now to the maid who has none, sir !
Here's to the girl with a pair of blue eyes ;
   And here's to the nymph with but one, sir !

       Let the toast pass,
       Drink to the lass !
   I'll warrant she'll prove an excuse for the glass !

Here's to the maid with a bosom of snow !
   Now to her that's as brown as a berry !
Here's to the wife with a face full of woe ;
   And now to the girl that is merry !

       Let the toast pass,
       Drink to the lass !
   I'll warrant she'll prove an excuse for the glass !

For let them be clumsy, or let them be slim,
   Young or ancient, I care not a feather !
So fill a pint bumper, quite up to the brim ;
   And let us e'en toast them together !

       Let the toast pass,
       Drink to the lass !
   I'll warrant she'll prove an excuse for the glass !

THOMAS CHATTERTON (1752-1770)

Songe to Ælla,

Lorde of the Castel of Brystowe ynne daies of yore

Oh thou, orr what remaynes of thee,
Ælla, the darlynge of futurity,
Lett thys mie songe bolde as thie courage be,
  As everlastynge to posteritye.
Whanne Dacya's sonnes, whose hayres of bloude-redde hue
Lyche kynge-cuppes brastynge wythe the morning due,
  Arraung'd ynne dreare arraie,
  Upponne the lethale daie,
Spredde farre and wyde onne Watchets shore ;
  Than dyddst thou furiouse stande,
  And bie thie valyante hande
Beesprengedd all the mees wythe gore.

Drawne bie thyne anlace felle,
Downe to the depthe of helle
Thousandes of Dacyanns went ;
Brystowannes, menne of myghte,
Ydar'd the bloudie fyghte,
And actedd deeds full quent.

Oh thou, whereer (thie bones att reste)
  Thye Spryte to haunte delyghteth beste,
Whetherr upponne the bloude-embrewedd pleyne,
  Orr whare thou kennst fromm farre
  The dysmal crye of warre,
Orr seest somme mountayne made of corse of sleyne ;
  Orr seest the hatchedd stede,
  Yprraunceynge o'er the mede,
And neighe to be amenged the poynctedd speeres ;
  Or ynne blacke armoure staulke arounde
  Embattel'd Brystowe, once thie grounde,
And glowe ardurous onn the Castle steeres ;

Orr fierye round the mynsterr glare ;
　Lette Brystowe stylle be made thie care ;
Guarde ytt fromme foemenne and consumynge fyre ;
　Lyche Avones streme ensyrke ytte rounde,
　Ne lette a flame enharme the grounde,
Tylle ynne one flame all the whole world expyre.

Mynstrelles Songe

(*From Ælla*)

O ! synge untoe mie roundelaie,
O ! droppe the brynie teare wythe mee,
Daunce ne moe atte hallie daie,
Lycke a reynynge ryver bee ;
　Mie love ys dedde,
　Gon to hys death-bedde,
　Al under the wyllowe tree.

Blacke hys cryne as the wyntere nyghte,
Whyte hys rode* as the sommer snowe,
Rodde hys face as the mornynge lyghte,
Cale he lyes ynne the grave belowe ;
　Mie love ys dedde,
　Gon to hys deathe-bedde,
　Al under the wyllowe tree.

Swote hys tyngue as the throstles note,
Quycke ynn daunce as thoughte canne bee,
Defte hys tabour, codgelle stote,
O ! hee lyes bie the wyllowe tree :
　Mie love ys dedde,
　Gonne to hys deathe-bedde,
　Alle underre the wyllowe tree.

* Complexion.

Harke ! the ravenne flappes hys wynge,
In the briered delle belowe ;
Harke ! the dethe-owle loude dothe synge,
To the nyghte-mares as heie goe ;
   Mie love ys dedde,
    Gonne to hys deathe-bedde,
    Al under the wyllowe tree.

See ! the whyte moone sheenes onne hie ;
Whyterre ys mie true loves shroude ;
Whyterre yanne the mornynge skie,
Whyterre yanne the evenynge cloude ;
   Mie love ys dedde,
    Gon to hys deathe-bedde,
    Al under the wyllowe tree.

Heere, uponne mie true loves grave,
Schalle the baren fleurs be layde,
Nee one hallie Seyncte to save
Al the celness of a mayde.
   Mie love ys dedde,
    Gonne to hys deathe-bedde,
    Alle under the wyllowe tree.

Wythe mie hondes I'lle dente the brieres
Rounde his hallie corse to gre,
Ouphante fairie, lyghte youre fyres,
Heere mie boddie stylle schalle bee.
   Mie love ys dedde,
    Gon to hys death-bedde,
    Al under the wyllowe tree.

Comme, wythe acorne-coppe and thorne,
Drayne mie hartys blodde awaie ;
Lyfe and all yttes goode I scorne,
Daunce bie nete, or feaste by daie.
   Mie love ys dedde,
    Gon to hys death-bedde,
    Al under the wyllowe tree.

Waterre wytches, crownede wythe reytes,*
Bere mee to yer leathalle tyde.
I die ; I comme ; mie true love waytes.
Thos the damselle spake, and dyed.

SUSANNA HARRISON (1752-1784)

Thou God Seest Me

Thou God of Justice and of Grace,
 Who would not fear Thy Name ?
Thy Omnipresence fills all space,
 Thine Eyes through nature flame.

No secret thought can ever shun
 The notice of Thine Eye ;
From Thee conceal'd no act be done,
 For Thou art ever nigh.

Thine Eye surveys the ground I tread,
 Whene'er I rove abroad ;
Within the curtains of my bed
 I lie in sight of God.

O be this solemn truth inscrib'd
 For ever on my heart,
Lest vile deceit should be imbib'd,
 And I from truth depart.

Give me, O Lord, this holy fear,
 For 'tis a gift divine :
The soul, that views Thee ever near,
 No evil can design.

* Water-flags.

JOHN CODRINGTON BAMPFYLDE (1754-1796)

Sonnet

Written in a country retirement

Around my porch and lonely casement spread,
The myrtle never sere, and gadding vine,
With fragrant sweet-briar love to intertwine ;
And in my garden's box-encircled bed
The pansy pied, and musk-rose white and red ;
The pink, the lily chaste, and sweet woodbine,
Fling odours round ; thick-woven eglantine
Decks my trim fence ; in which, by silence led,
The wren hath wisely built her mossy cell,
Shelter'd from storms, in courtly land so rife,
And nestles o'er her young, and warbles well.
'Tis here with innocence in peaceful glen
I pass my blameless moments far from men,
Nor wishing death too soon, nor asking life.

Song

To Chloe kind and Chloe fair,
With sparkling eye and flowing hair,
Tune the harp, and raise the song ;
Such as to Beauty doth belong !

Let the strain be sweet and clear ;
Such as through the listening ear,
In well-according harmony,
May with the tranced soul agree.

She is Pleasure's blooming Queen :
In the morn more fresh her mien,
When awaken'd from repose,
Than the summer's dewy rose :
In the evening brighter far
Than the ocean-bathed star.

And when night, the friend of love,
Bids the silent hour improve,
To the ravish'd senses she
Gives joy, and bliss, and ecstasy.

The Rev. GEORGE CRABBE (1754-1832)

(Poems before 1800 *only)*

Mira

My Mira, shepherds, is as fair
    As sylvan Nymphs who haunt the vale,
As Sylphs who dwell in purest air,
    As Fays who skim the dusky dale,
As Venus was when Venus fled
From watery Triton's oozy bed.

My Mira, shepherds, has a voice
    As soft as Syrinx in her grove,
As sweet as Echo makes her choice,
    As mild as whispering virgin-love ;
As gentle as the winding stream,
Of Fancy's song when poets dream.

The Comparison

Friendship is like gold refin'd,
    And all may weigh its worth ;
Love like the ore, brought undesign'd
    In virgin beauty forth.

Friendship may pass from age to age,
    And yet remain the same ;
Love must in many a toil engage,
    And melt in lambent flame.

The Resurrection

The wintry winds have ceas'd to blow,
    And trembling leaves appear ;
And fairest flowers succeed the snow,
    And hail the infant year.

So, when the world and all its woes
    Are vanish'd far away,
Fair scenes and wonderful repose
    Shall bless the new-born day,—

When, from the confines of the grave
    The body too shall rise ;
No more precarious passion's slave,
    Nor error's sacrifice.

'Tis but a sleep—and Sion's King
    Will call the many dead :
'Tis but a sleep—and then we sing,
    O'er dreams of sorrow fled.

Yes ! wintry winds have ceas'd to blow,
    And trembling leaves appear,
And Nature has her types to show
    Throughout the varying year.

My Birthday

Aldborough, Dec. 24, 1778

Through a dull tract of woe, of dread,
The toiling year has pass'd and fled :
And, lo ! in sad and pensive strain,
I sing my birthday date again.

Trembling and poor, I saw the light,
New waking from unconscious night :
Trembling and poor I still remain
To meet unconscious night again.

Time in my pathway strews few flowers
To cheer and cheat the weary hours ;
And those few strangers, dear indeed,
Are chok'd, are check'd, by many a weed

Life

Think ye the joys that fill our early day,
   Are the poor prelude to some full repast ?
Think you they *promise ?*—ah ! believe they *pay ;*
   The purest ever, they are oft the last.
The jovial swain that yokes the morning team,
   And all the verdure of the field enjoys,
See him, how languid ! when the noontide beam
   Plays on his brow, and all his force destroys.
So 'tis with us, when, love and pleasure fled,
   We at the summit of our hill arrive :
Lo ! the gay lights of Youth are past—are dead,
   But what still deepening clouds of Care survive !

Night

The sober stillness of the night
   That fills the silent air,
And all that breathes along the shore
   Invite to solemn prayer.

Vouchsafe to me that spirit, Lord !
   Which points the sacred way,
And let Thy creatures here below
   Instruct me how to pray.

A Farewell

The hour arriv'd ! I sigh'd and said,
How soon the happiest hours are fled !
On wings of down they lately flew,
But then their moments pass'd with you ;
And still with you could I but be,
On downy wings they'd always flee.

Say, did you not, the way you went,
Feel the soft balm of gay content ?
Say, did you not all pleasures find,
Of which you left so few behind ?
I think you did : for well I know
My parting prayer would make it so !

GEORGE CRABBE

May she, I said, life's choicest goods partake ;
Those, late in life, for nobler still forsake—
The bliss of one, th' esteem'd of many live,
With all that Friendship would, and all that Love can give!

Sir JOHN HENRY MOORE, Bart. (1756-1780)

Song

Indeed, my Cælia, 'tis in vain ;
   Away with this coquettish art,
These froward looks, this forc'd disdain,—
   Believe me, you mistake your part :
   'Tis kindness now alone can move,
   Can guide the wandering shaft of Love,
And fix it in the youthful heart.

Time was, indeed, a scornful beauty
   ('Twas then the mode, or history lies)
Was courted with obsequious duty,
   Was won with prayers, and tears, and sighs :
   Love now by other maxims rules ;
   The god who made our fathers fools
But serves to make their offspring wise.

Yet though you've lost the power of teasing,
   Let no regrets perplex your mind ;
You still retain the gift of pleasing,
   And that's a better art, you'll find :
   Suppose then that I said and swore
   Whate'er each puppy vow'd before,
And own at once you will be kind.

Nor talk of constancy and truth,
   Eternal flames, and such droll fancies ;
'Tis like perpetual health and youth,
   And only met with in romances :
   While pleasure courts us, let's be gay,
   Nor think about a future day,
Care of itself too fast advances.

445

As the world changes, we must change,
  'Tis all a farce, 'tis all a jest ;
Then if 'tis now the mode to range,
    Why should the thought disturb our rest ?
    Heroic love has flown away,
    Fine sentiments have had their day ;
Who knows but all is for the best ?

WILLIAM BLAKE (1757-1827)

Song

How sweet I roam'd from field to field
And tasted all the summer's pride,
Till I the prince of love beheld
Who in the sunny beams did glide !

He shew'd me lilies for my hair,
And blushing roses for my brow ;
He led me through his gardens fair
Where all his golden pleasures grow.

With sweet May dews my wings were wet,
And Phœbus fir'd my vocal rage ;
He caught me in his silken net,
And shut me in his golden cage.

He loves to sit and hear me sing,
Then, laughing, sports and plays with me ;
Then stretches out my golden wing,
And mocks my loss of liberty.

Song

My silks and fine array,
  My smiles and languish'd air,
By Love are driven away ;
  And mournful lean Despair
Brings me yew to deck my grave :
Such end true lovers have.

His face is fair as heaven
  When springing buds unfold :
O why to him was't given,
  Whose heart is wintry cold ?
His breast is Love's all-worshipp'd tomb,
Where all Love's pilgrims come.

Bring me an axe and spade,
  Bring me a winding-sheet ;
When I my grave have made,
  Let winds and tempests beat :
Then down I'll lie, as cold as clay :
True love doth pass away !

Song

Memory, hither come,
And tune your merry notes :
And, while upon the wind
Your music floats,
I'll pore upon the stream
Where sighing lovers dream,
And fish for fancies as they pass
Within the watery glass.

I'll drink of the clear stream,
And hear the linnet's song ;
And there I'll lie and dream
The day along :
And when night comes, I'll go
To places fit for woe,
Walking along the darken'd valley
With silent Melancholy.

To The Muses

Whether on Ida's shady brow,
Or in the chambers of the East,
The chambers of the sun, that now
From ancient melody have ceas'd ;

Whether in Heav'n ye wander fair,
Or the green corners of the earth,
Or the blue regions of the air
Where the melodious winds have birth ;

Whether on chrystal rocks ye rove,
Beneath the bosom of the sea
Wand'ring in many a coral grove,
Fair Nine, forsaking Poetry !

How have you left the ancient love
That bards of old enjoy'd in you !
The languid strings do scarcely move !
The sound is forc'd, the notes are few !

Introduction to the Songs of Innocence

Piping down the valleys wild,
    Piping songs of pleasant glee,
On a cloud I saw a child,
    And he laughing said to me :

" Pipe a song about a Lamb ! "
    So I pip'd with merry cheer.
" Piper, pipe that song again " ;
    So I pip'd : he wept to hear.

" Drop thy pipe, thy happy pipe ;
    Sing thy songs of happy cheer ! "
So I sang the same again,
    While he wept with joy to hear.

" Piper, sit thee down and write
    In a book that all may read."
So he vanish'd from my sight ;
    And I pluck'd a hollow reed,

And I made a rural pen,
    And I stain'd the water clear,
And I wrote my happy songs
    Every child may joy to hear.

WILLIAM BLAKE

The Shepherd

How sweet is the Shepherd's sweet lot !
From the morn to the evening he strays ;
He shall follow his sheep all the day,
And his tongue shall be filled with praise.

For he hears the lamb's innocent call,
And he hears the ewe's tender reply ;
He is watchful while they are in peace,
For they know that their Shepherd is nigh.

The Tiger

Tiger, tiger, burning bright,
In the forests of the night,
What immortal hand or eye
Could frame thy fearful symmetry ?

In what distant deeps or skies
Burnt the fire of thine eyes ?
On what wings dare he aspire ?
What the hand dare seize the fire ?

And what shoulder and what art
Could twist the sinews of thy heart ?
And, when thy heart began to beat,
What dread hand and what dread feet ?

What the hammer ? What the chain ?
In what furnace was thy brain ?
What the anvil ? What dread grasp
Dare its deadly terrors clasp ?

When the stars threw down their spears,
And water'd heaven with their tears,
Did He smile His work to see ?
Did He who made the lamb make thee ?

Tiger, tiger, burning bright
In the forests of the night,
What immortal hand or eye
Dare frame thy fearful symmetry ?

Infant Sorrow

My mother groan'd, my father wept,
Into the dangerous world I leapt ;
Helpless, naked, piping loud,
Like a fiend hid in a cloud.

Struggling in my father's hands,
Striving against my swaddling bands,
Bound and weary, I thought best
To sulk upon my mother's breast.

JOHN ST. LEDGER (——17—)

Extempore *

*to a lady of Tory principles, appearing at the Theatre Royal,
Dublin, with an orange lily in her breast, on King William's
Birth-night.*

Thou little Tory, why the jest
Of wearing orange in thy breast ;
When that same breast, betraying, shows
The whiteness of the rebel rose ?

* From *An Asylum for Fugitive Pieces*, where the author is called
" the late." I know nothing more of him.

JOHN PHILIP KEMBLE (1757-1823)

An Expostulation *

When late I attempted your pity to move,
  Why seem'd you so deaf to my prayers ?
Perhaps it was right to dissemble your love,
  But—why did you kick me down stairs ?

ROBERT BURNS (1759-1796)

(*Poems in English only*)

To Mary in Heaven

Thou lingering star, with lessening ray,
  That lov'st to greet the early morn,
Again thou usherest in the day
  My Mary from my soul was torn.
O Mary ! dear departed shade !
  Where is thy place of blissful rest ?
Seest thou thy lover lowly laid ?
  Hear'st thou the groans that rend his breast ?

That sacred hour can I forget ?
  Can I forget the hallow'd grove,
Where by the winding Ayr we met,
  To live one day of parting love ?
Eternity will not efface
  Those records dear of transports past ;
Thy image at our last embrace—
  Ah ! little thought we 'twas our last !

---

* Text from the *Asylum for Fugitive Pieces* (1785). This epigram
appears in a slightly less good form in Kemble's play, *The Panel*
(acted 1788, printed 1789), an alteration of Bickerstaffe's *'Tis well
it's no Worse* (1770). The verses do not occur in Bickerstaffe's version. Possibly, however, Kemble did not write them, and they
should be attributed, in such an event, to that most prolific poet
Anon.

Ayr gurgling kiss'd his pebbled shore,
　O'erhung with wild woods, thickening green ;
The fragrant birch, and hawthorn hoar,
　Twin'd amorous round the raptur'd scene.
The flowers sprang wanton to be prest,
　The birds sang love on every spray,
Till too too soon, the glowing west
　Proclaim'd the speed of winged day.

Still o'er these scenes my memory wakes,
　And fondly broods with miser care !
Time but the impression deeper makes,
　As streams their channels deeper wear.
My Mary, dear departed shade !
　Where is thy blissful place of rest ?
Seest thou thy lover lowly laid ?
　Hear'st thou the groans that rend his breast ?

My Heart's in the Highlands

My heart's in the Highlands, my heart is not here ;
My heart's in the Highlands a-chasing the deer ;
Chasing the wild deer, and following the roe,
My heart's in the Highlands, wherever I go.
Farewell to the Highlands, farewell to the North,
The birth-place of valour, the country of worth ;
Wherever I wander, wherever I rove,
The hills of the Highlands for ever I love.

Farewell to the mountains, high cover'd with snow ;
Farewell to the straths and green valleys below ;
Farewell to the forests and wild-hanging woods ;
Farewell to the torrents and loud-pouring floods.
My heart's in the Highlands, my heart is not here ;
My heart's in the Highlands a-chasing the deer ;
Chasing the wild deer, and following the roe,
My heart's in the Highlands, wherever I go.

ROBERT BURNS

The Charming Month of May

It was the charming month of May,
When all the flowers were fresh and gay,
One morning, by the break of day,
 The youthful, charming Chloe ;

From peaceful slumber she arose,
Girt on her mantle and her hose,
And o'er the flowery mead she goes,
 The youthful, charming Chloe.

 Lovely was she by the dawn,
  Youthful Chloe, charming Chloe,
 Tripping o'er the pearly lawn,
  The youthful, charming Chloe.

The feather'd people you might see
Perch'd all around on every tree ;
In notes of sweetest melody
 They hail the charming Chloe ;

Till, painting gay the eastern skies,
The glorious sun began to rise,
Out-rival'd by the radiant eyes
 Of youthful, charming Chloe.

The Rev. WILLIAM LISLE BOWLES (1762-1850)

At Dover Cliffs
July 20, 1787

On these white cliffs, that calm above the flood
 Uplift their shadowing heads, and, at their feet,
 Scarce hear the surge that has for ages beat,
Sure many a lonely wanderer has stood ;
And, whilst the lifted murmur met his ear,
 And o'er the distant billows the still Eve
 Sail'd slow, has thought of all his heart must leave
To-morrow ; of the friends he lov'd most dear ;
Of social scenes, from which he wept to part :

But if, like me, he knew how fruitless all
  The thoughts that would full fain the past recall,
Soon would he quell the risings of his heart,
And brave the wild winds and unhearing tide,
The World his country, and his God his guide.

At Ostend

July 22, 1787

How sweet the tuneful bells' responsive peal!
  As when, at opening morn, the fragrant breeze
  Breathes on the trembling sense of wan disease,
So piercing to my heart their force I feel!
And hark! with lessening cadence now they fall,
  And now, along the white and level tide,
  They fling their melancholy music wide;
Bidding me many a tender thought recall
Of summer days, and those delightful years
  When by my native streams, in life's fair prime,
  The mournful magic of their mingling chime
First wak'd my wond'ring childhood into tears
But seeming now, when all those days are o'er,
The sounds of joy once heard, and heard no more.

Time

O Time! who know'st a lenient hand to lay
  Softest on sorrow's wound, and slowly thence
  (Lulling to sad repose the weary sense)
The faint pang stealest unperceiv'd away;
  On thee I rest my only hope at last,
And think, when thou hast dried the bitter tear
That flows in vain o'er all my soul holds dear,
  I may look back on every sorrow past,
And meet life's peaceful evening with a smile—
  As some lone bird, at day's departing hour,
  Sings in the sunbeam, of the transient shower
Forgetful, though its wings are wet the while:—
Yet ah! how much must that poor heart endure,
Which hopes from thee, and thee alone, a cure!

Sir SAMUEL EGERTON BRYDGES* (1762-1837)

To a Lady in Illness

February 15, 1783

New to the world, when all was fairy ground,
    And shapes romantic swam before my sight,
      Thy beauty caught my soul, and tints, as bright
And fair as Fancy's dream, in thee I found :
In cold experience when my hopes were drown'd,
    And life's dark clouds o'er-veil'd in mists of night
      The forms, that wont to fill me with delight ;
Thy view again dispell'd the darkness round.

Shall I forget thee, when the pallid cheek,
    The sighing voice, wan look, and plaintive air,
No more the roseate hue of health bespeak ?
    Shall I neglect thee as no longer fair ?
No, lovely maid ! If in my heart I seek,
    Thy beauty deeply is engraven there.

THOMAS RUSSELL (1762-1788)

Sonnet,

supposed to be written at Lemnos

On this lone isle, whose rugged rocks affright
    The cautious pilot, ten revolving years
      Great Pæan's son, unwonted erst to tears,
Wept o'er his wound : alike each rolling light
Of heaven he watch'd, and blam'd its lingering flight ;
    By day the sea-mew screaming round his cave
      Drove slumber from his eyes ; the chiding wave
And savage howlings chas'd his dreams by night.

Hope still was his : in each low breeze, that sigh'd
    Through his rude grot, he heard a coming oar,
In each white cloud a coming sail he spied ;
    Nor seldom listen'd to the fancied roar
Of Œta's torrents, or the hoarser tide
    That parts fam'd Trachis from th' Euboic shore.

---

* A distinguished editor of Elizabethan literature. As a poet he
was more voluminous than interesting.

THOMAS RUSSELL

Sonnet 10

Could then the babes from yon unshelter'd cot
   Implore thy passing charity in vain ?
Too thoughtless youth ! what though thy happier lot
   Insult their life of poverty and pain !
What though their Maker doom'd them thus forlorn
   To brook the mockery of the taunting throng,
Beneath th' oppressor's iron scourge to mourn,
   To mourn, but not to murmur at his wrong !

Yet when their last late evening shall decline,
   Their evening cheerful, though their day distrest,
A hope perhaps more heavenly-bright than thine,
   A grace by thee unsought and unpossest,
A faith more fix'd, a rapture more divine,
   Shall gild their passage to Eternal Rest.

Sonnet to Valclusa

What though, Valclusa, the fond bard be fled,
   That woo'd his fair in thy sequester'd bowers,
Long lov'd her living, long bemoan'd her dead,
   And hung her visionary shrine with flowers !
What though no more he teach thy shades to mourn
   The hapless chances that to love belong,
As erst, when drooping o'er her turf forlorn,
   He charm'd wild Echo with his plaintive song !

Yet still, enamour'd of the tender tale,
   Pale Passion haunts thy grove's romantic gloom,
Yet still soft music breathes in every gale,
   Still undecay'd the fairy-garlands bloom,
Still heavenly incense fills the fragrant vale,
   Still Petrarch's Genius weeps o'er Laura's tomb.

HELEN MARIA WILLIAMS (1762-1827)

Sonnet to Hope

O ever skill'd to wear the form we love,
  To bid the shapes of fear and grief depart ;
Come, gentle Hope ! with one gay smile remove
  The lasting sadness of an aching heart.
Thy voice, benign Enchantress ! let me hear ;
  Say that for me some pleasures yet shall bloom,
That Fancy's radiance, Friendship's precious tear,
  Shall soften, or shall chase, misfortune's gloom.
But come not glowing in the dazzling ray,
  Which once with dear illusions charm'd my eye,
O ! strew no more, sweet flatterer ! on my way
  The flowers I fondly thought too bright to die ;
Visions less fair will soothe my pensive breast,
That asks not happiness, but longs for rest !

The Rev. JAMES HURDIS, D.D. (1763-1801)

Canzonet

In my bosom contentment shall reign,
  And despair shall torment me no more,
I have seen my lov'd fair one again,
  And she came with a smile to my door.

I have seen her, though transient her stay,
  Though time would not loiter and wait,
And the shower has not yet wash'd away
  The small print of her foot at my gate.

Rapid day, the strong reason explain
  Why thy steeds were so quick to be gone,
To remove my sweet angel again,
  And to leave me to linger alone.

JAMES HURDIS

Come again, and, to merit my praise,
  Travel slow through the regions above,
And I'll give thee the gratefullest lays,
  Which can flow from the bosom of love.

O, return, and, to win my good will,
  When I see her approach from afar,
Turn thy steeds with their heads to a hill,
  And lock fast every wheel of thy car.

SAMUEL ROGERS (1763-1855)

An Italian Song

Dear is my little native vale,
The ring-dove builds and murmurs there ;
Close by my cot she tells her tale
To every passing villager.
The squirrel leaps from tree to tree,
And shells his nuts at liberty.

In orange-groves and myrtle-bowers,
That breathe a gale of fragrance round,
I charm the fairy-footed hours
With my lov'd lute's romantic sound ;
Or crowns of living laurel weave,
For those that win the race at eve.

The shepherd's horn at break of day,
The ballet danc'd in twilight glade,
The canzonet and roundelay
Sung in the silent green-wood shade ;
These simple joys, that never fail,
Shall bind me to my native vale.

SAMUEL ROGERS

A Wish

Mine be a cot beside the hill,
A bee-hive's hum shall soothe my ear ;
A willowy brook, that turns a mill,
With many a fall shall linger near.

The swallow, oft, beneath my thatch,
Shall twitter from her clay-built nest ;
Oft shall the pilgrim lift the latch,
And share my meal, a welcome guest.

Around my ivied porch shall spring
Each fragrant flower that drinks the dew ;
And Lucy, at her wheel, shall sing,
In russet gown and apron blue.

The village church, among the trees,
Where first our marriage vows were giv'n,
With merry peals shall swell the breeze,
And point with taper spire to Heav'n.

The Alps, at Daybreak

The sun-beams streak the azure skies,
And line with light the mountain's brow :
With hounds and horns the hunters rise,
And chase the roebuck through the snow.

From rock to rock, with giant-bound,
High on their iron poles they pass ;
Mute, lest the air, convuls'd by sound,
Rend from above a frozen mass.

The goats wind slow their wonted way,
Up craggy steeps and ridges rude ;
Mark'd by the wild wolf for his prey,
From desert cave or hanging wood.

And while the torrent thunders loud,
And as the echoing cliffs reply,
The huts peep o'er the morning-cloud,
Perch'd, like an eagle's nest, on high.

On a Girl Asleep*

Sleep on, and dream of Heav'n awhile.
Though shut so close thy laughing eyes,
Thy rosy lips still seem to smile,
And move, and breathe delicious sighs !—

Ah, now soft blushes tinge her cheeks,
And mantle o'er her neck of snow.
Ah, now she murmurs, now she speaks
What most I wish—and fear to know.

She starts, she trembles, and she weeps !
Her fair hands folded on her breast.
—And now, how like a saint she sleeps !
A seraph in the realms of rest !

Sleep on secure ! Above control,
Thy thoughts belong to Heav'n and thee !
And may the secret of thy soul
Repose within its sanctuary !

* This poem was, I think, written in the early years of the nineteenth century. It is so beautiful, however, that I cannot forbear from printing it here.

HENRY HEADLEY (1765-1788)

Rosalind's Dying Complaint

to her sleeping child

Alas ! my dearest baby,
   I grieve to see thee smile ;
I think upon thy rueful lot,
   And cold's my heart the while.

'Gainst wind and tide of worldly woe
   I cannot make my way ;
To lull thee in my bosom warm,
   I feel I must not stay.

My mother will not hear me speak,
   My father knits his brow :
Sweet Heavens ! were they never young,
   That thus they treat me [now] ?

Ye souls unkind, a fate like mine
   O never may ye prove !
Nor live to find how bitter 'tis
   To miss the man ye love.

My friends they all forsake me,
   Nor comfort will afford ;
They laugh while I am thinking .
   " My true love broke his word."

May God amend their cruel hearts,
   For surely they're to blame ;
They little know what 'tis to feel
   The heaviness of shame.

Th' ungentle hand of rude mischance
   Has reft my heart of rest ;
And frighted hope, of cheerless eye,
   Lies strangled in my breast.

'Twas yester-eve at midnight hour,
  I waked but to weep ;
I kiss'd my baby's pretty hand,
  And watch'd it while asleep ;

Its cruel far-off father
  My tender thoughts embrac'd,
And in my darling's infant look
  His lovely likeness trac'd ;

With smileless look a spectre form
  Advancing seem'd to appear,
While Fancy toll'd the death-bell slow
  Across my startled ear :

Full well I knew its fearful sound,
  That sternly seem'd to say—
" Go, speed thee to the grass-green turf,
  For thou must die to-day ! "

WILLIAM KENDALL (1768-1832)

To Maria

On a favourite red-blossomed thorn

Though purest tints at opening morn
  O'er Heaven's pale azure beam ;
With purer lustre, lovely thorn,
  Thy rosy flowerets gleam.

Yet vainly strives that fleeting bloom
  With Mary's blush to vie :
Her blushes cheer the wintry gloom
  When all thy blossoms die !

WILLIAM KENDALL

Song

Sleepless eyelids dim with tears,
　　Languid accents, breathing woe,
Sighs of sorrow, throbbing fears—
　　Lovers, only lovers, know !

What though ALL in life's short day
　　Feel awhile the storm of grief ;
Hope affords a transient ray,
　　Fleeting pleasures yield relief.

Fame at length rewards the brave ;
　　Time can envy's self destroy :
But o'er love's neglected slave
　　Ages pass, nor waft a joy.

INDEX OF FIRST LINES

INDEX OF FIRST LINES

INDEX OF FIRST LINES

INDEX OF FIRST LINES

INDEX OF FIRST LINES

469

INDEX OF FIRST LINES

INDEX OF FIRST LINES

INDEX OF FIRST LINES

INDEX OF FIRST LINES

473

INDEX OF FIRST LINES

INDEX OF FIRST LINES

INDEX OF FIRST LINES

INDEX OF FIRST LINES

INDEX OF FIRST LINES

Printed in England at
The Westminster Press, Harrow Road
London, W.9